Sigmund Freud's
The Interpretation of Dr

MANCHESTER
UNIVERSITY PRESS

TEXTS · IN · CULTURE

SERIES EDITORS

Stephen Copley and Jeff Wallace

ADVISORY EDITORS

David Aers, University of East Anglia
Lynda Nead, Birkbeck College, London
Gillian Beer, Girton College, Cambridge
Roy Porter, Wellcome Institute for the History of Medicine
Anne Janowitz, University of Warwick
Bernard Sharratt, University of Kent

This series offers a set of specially commissioned, cross-disciplinary essays on a text of seminal importance to Western culture. Each text has had an impact on the way we think, write and live beyond the confines of its original discipline and it is only through an understanding of its multiple meanings that we can fully appreciate its importance.

ALREADY PUBLISHED

Charles Darwin's *The Origin of Species*
David Amigoni, Jeff Wallace (eds)

Adam Smith's *The Wealth of Nations*
Stephen Copley, Kathryn Sutherland (eds)

Niccolò Machiavelli's *The Prince*
Martin Coyle (ed.)

Simone de Beauvoir's *The Second Sex*
Ruth Evans (ed.)

TEXTS · IN · CULTURE

Sigmund Freud's

THE INTERPRETATION OF DREAMS

New interdisciplinary essays

LAURA MARCUS

editor

Manchester University Press
Manchester and New York

distributed exclusively in the USA by St. Martin's Press

Published by Manchester University Press
Oxford Road, Manchester M13 9NR, UK
and Room 400, 175 Fifth Avenue, New York, NY 10010, USA
http://www.man.ac.uk/mup

Distributed exclusively in the USA by
St. Martin's Press, Inc., 175 Fifth Avenue, New York,
NY 10010, USA

Distributed exclusively in Canada by
UBC Press, University of British Columbia, 6344 Memorial Road,
Vancouver, BC, Canada V6T 1Z2

British Library Cataloguing-in-Publication Data
A catalogue record for this book is available from the British Library

Library of Congress Cataloging-in-Publication Data applied for

ISBN 0 7190 3973 8 *hardback*
      0 7190 3974 6 *paperback*

First published 1999

05 04 03 02 01 00 99   10 9 8 7 6 5 4 3 2 1

Typeset in Palatino with Ellington Light
by Best-set Typesetter Ltd., Hong Kong
Printed in Great Britain
by Bell & Bain Ltd, Glasgow

Contents

Series introduction   *page*   vi
Abbreviations   viii
Chronology   ix

LAURA MARCUS
1   Introduction: histories, representations,
autobiographics in *The Interpretation of Dreams*   1

TREVOR PATEMAN
2   How to do things in dreams   66

JOHN FORRESTER
3   Dream readers   83

JAMES HOPKINS
4   Patterns of interpretation: speech, action and dream   123

RACHEL BOWLBY
5   The other day: the interpretation of day-dreams   160

STEPHEN FROSH
6   Freud's dreams, Dora's dreams   183

ROBERT J. C. YOUNG
7   Freud's secret: *The Interpretation of Dreams* was a
Gothic novel   206

Notes on contributors   232
Select bibliography   233
Index   238

Series introduction

Texts are produced in particular cultures and in particular historical circumstances. In turn, they shape and are shaped by those cultures as they are read and re-read in changing circumstances by different groups with different commitments, engagements and interests. Such readings are themselves then re-absorbed into the ideological frameworks within which the cultures develop. The seminal works drawn on by cultures thus have multiple existences within them, exerting their influence in distinct and perhaps contradictory ways. As these texts have been 'claimed' by particular academic disciplines, however, their larger cultural significance has often been obscured.

Recent work in cultural history and textual theory has stimulated critical awareness of the complex relations between texts and cultures, highlighting the limits of current academic formations and opening the possibility of new approaches to interdisciplinarity. At the same time, however, the difficulties of interdisciplinary work have become increasingly apparent at all levels of research and teaching. On the one hand the abandonment of disciplinary specialisms may lead to amorphousness rather than challenging interdisciplinarity; on the other, interdisciplinary approaches may in the end simply create new specialisms or subspecialisms, with their own well guarded boundaries. In these circumstances, yesterday's ground-breaking interdisciplinary study may become today's autonomous (and so potentially circumscribed) discipline, as has happened, it might be argued, in the case of some forms of History of Ideas.

The volumes in this series highlight the advantages of interdisciplinary work while at the same time encouraging a critical reflexiveness about its limits and possibilities; they seek to stimulate consideration both of the distinctiveness and integrity of individual disciplines, and of the transgressive potential of interdisciplinarity. Each volume offers a collection of new essays on a text of seminal intellectual and cultural importance, displaying the insights to be gained from the juxtaposition of disciplinary perspectives and from the negotiation of disciplinary boundaries. Our editorial stance is avowedly 'cultural', and in this sense the volumes represent a challenge to the conception of authorship which locates the significance of the text in the individual act of creation; but we assume that no issues (including those of interdisciplinarity and authorship) are foreclosed, and that individual volumes, drawing contributions from a broad range of disciplinary standpoints, will raise questions about the texts they examine more by the perceived disparities of approach that they encompass than by any interpretative consensus that they demonstrate.

All essays are specially commissioned for the series and are designed to be approachable to non-specialist as well as specialist readers: substantial editorial introductions provide a framework for the debates conducted in each volume, and highlight the issues involved.

Stephen Copley, University of York
Jeff Wallace, University of Glamorgan
General Editors

Abbreviations

The version of *The Interpretation of Dreams* referred to throughout this volume is the James Strachey authorized translation. The essays refer to the text in the *Standard Edition of the Complete Psychological Works* (London: The Hogarth Press and the Institute of Psychoanalysis, 1958) and/or to the same translation in the *Penguin Freud Library* (Harmondsworth: Penguin, 1976).

The introduction refers extensively to the letters written by Freud to Wilhelm Fliess, collected in *The Complete Letters of Sigmund Freud to Wilhelm Fliess 1887–1904*, ed. and trans. Jeffrey Moussaieff Masson (Cambridge, Mass.: Harvard University Press, 1985).

SE   *Standard Edition* (SE IV = volume 4, etc.)

PFL   *Penguin Freud Library* (PFL 4 = volume 4, etc.)

F/F   *Sigmund Freud to Wilhelm Fliess*

Chronology

Major biographical, political and cultural events surrounding *The Interpretation of Dreams* and other works by Freud

1856　Birth of Sigmund Freud in Freiberg, Moravia, to Jakob Freud and Amalie Nathanson Freud

1860　Freud family settles in Vienna

1864　Founding of liberal newspaper, the *Neue Freie Presse*; literary editor is Theodor Herzl, founder of modern Zionism

1865　Opening of Ringstrasse in Vienna (the boulevards and new civic buildings replacing the medieval city walls, gates and ghetto areas) and industrial/commercial growth

1867–78　Constitutional changes in Austria, including liberal constitution of December 1867. In *The Interpretation of Dreams* Freud recalls 'the cheerful hopes of the days of the *Bürger* ministry' (SE IV 193).

1869　Publication of Eduard von Hartmann's *Philosophy of the Unconscious*

1873　Sigmund Freud enters medical department at University of Vienna

　　　Stock market crashes, initiating depression and exacerbating anti-liberalism and anti-Semitism

1874　Publication of Franz Brentano's *Psychology from the Empirical Standpoint*, exploring the subjective basis of a relation to the world and the constitutive power of the self

1876–82　Research student in Ernst Brücke's (Helmholtzian) Institute of Physiology, studying nerve cells; meets Josef Breuer in late 1870s; receives medical degree in 1881

1876　Heinrich Schliemann discovers Mycenaean tombs; archaeology, and Ancient Greek and Egyptian civilizations, to become crucial to Freud's models of unconscious life

1879　Wilhelm Wundt, professor of philosophy in Leipzig, founds world's first psychological laboratory; Francis Galton publishes accounts of his 'word association test', an important influence on Freud's technique of 'free association', developed in the 1890s

1882　Meets Martha Bernays; enters Vienna General Hospital, where he works first in the department of psychiatry and subsequently in the department of nervous diseases

　　　Formation of Austrian Reform Association, the main organ of Viennese anti-Semitism, and of the German National Association, led by Georg von Schönerer, standing on the 'brutal fact of race'

1883   G. Stanley Hall founds psychological laboratory at Johns Hopkins University, USA; Emil Kraepelin produces first classification of mental disorders; publication of Francis Galton's *Inquiry into Human Faculty and its Development*

1885   Travels to Paris to study Jean-Martin Charcot's work on the nervous system and with hysterical patients at the Salpetrière; accepted as translator of Charcot's work into German

Publication of Ernst Mach's 'The analysis of sensations'

1886   Opens private practice in Vienna; marriage to Martha Bernays; presents paper, 'On male hysteria', to the Imperial Society of Physicians of Vienna

Publication of Richard Krafft-Ebing's *Psychopathia Sexualis*

Publication of Friedrich Nietzsche's *Beyond Good and Evil*

1887   Meets Wilhelm Fliess, a Berlin physician, and correspondence between the two men commences

Schonerer introduces bill into Parliament seeking to undo Jews' emancipation and reinstate legal restrictions on Jewish life

1889   First International Congress of Psychology held in Paris

Founding of Social Democratic Party of Austria, following Marxist programme

1890   First workers' march in Vienna, organized by party led by Viktor Adler, a former fellow-student of Freud's at the University of Vienna and the future Social Democrat leader

Publication of William James's *The Principles of Psychology* and Sir James Frazer's *The Golden Bough*

1891   Publication of monograph, 'On aphasia', in which Freud explores relationship between psychological and physiological mechanisms; moves with Martha and children to Berggasse 19, former home of Viktor Alder, and Freud's home until his departure to England in 1938

1893   Publication of Freud and Breuer's 'On the psychical mechanism of hysterical phenomena: preliminary communication'

Christian Socials, led by Karl Lueger, formally enter Viennese politics

1895   Publication of Freud and Breuer's *Studies on Hysteria*; Freud undertakes first full analysis of one of his dreams, 'the dream of Irma's injection'; writes 'Project for a scientific psychology'

Victory of Lueger in Viennese municipal elections and increasing exclusion of Liberal Party from political power

1896   Delivers lecture on 'The aetiology of hysteria', in which he explores the foundations of hysteria in the sexual seduction of children by adults; first uses term 'psychoanalysis'; death of Jakob Freud in October

Dr Morton Prince founds *The Journal of Abnormal Psychology* in Boston, introducing term 'psychoanalysis' to America in first volume

Herzl (who comes to figure in Freud's dreams of assimilation and exile) publishes *The Jewish State*, attacked by most assimilated Jews

1897   Begins self-analysis; gradual relinquishing of his 'seduction theory', and emergence of theory of childhood sexuality and the power of unconscious wishes; reports memory of 'Oedipal' desires in his childhood self, and universal nature of the 'compulsion', in a letter to Fliess of 15 October

Lueger becomes mayor of Vienna: Freud writes of 'the increasing importance of the effects of the anti-Semitic movement upon our emotional life'

1898–99 Writes *The Interpretation of Dreams*, which is published in November 1899

1899   Otto Bauer (brother of Ida Bauer ('Dora')) formulates Austromarxism

1900   In last quarter, Freud analyses 'Dora' (Ida Bauer)

Emergence of science of genetics, following redisovery of Mendelism

1901   Writes 'Dora's' case-history in January – first titled 'Dreams and hysteria', subsequently 'Fragment of an analysis of a case of hysteria' – making dream-interpretation central; first visit to Rome, the city of his dreams; publishes *On Dreams*; increasing estrangement from Fliess

Publication of Thomas Mann's *Buddenbrooks*

1902   Appointed professor extraordinarius (a post which did not confer the rights of faculty members) at the university after a series of failed applications on his behalf; in a number of Freud's dreams, the delay in his promotion is linked to anti-Semitism within the university system, Viennese society, and the Empire more generally

Founds 'Psychological Wednesday Society' (later the 'Vienna Psycho-Analytical Society'); Wilhelm Stekel and Alfred Adler are founder members

1903   Final break with Fliess

Publication of Otto Weininger's *Sex and Character*

Premiere of Hugo von Hofmannsthal's *Elektra* in Berlin

1904   Publishes *Psychopathology of Everyday Life*

1905   Publishes *Jokes and their Relation to the Unconscious, Three Essays on the Theory of Sexuality* and 'Fragment of a case of analysis' ('Dora')

Viennese feminist Rosa Mayreder publishes 'Critique of femininity'

1906   Jung begins correspondence with Freud

Publication of Iwan Bloch's *Das Sexualleben unserer Zeit (The Sexual Life of Our Time)*

1907   Publication of *Delusions and Dreams in Jensen's 'Gradiva'*

1908   Publication of 'Creative writers and day-dreaming'; first International Psycho-Analytical Congress held in Salzburg; first meeting with Ernest Jones, a key figure in the dissemination of psychoanalysis in Britain, and subsequently Freud's biographer

Publication of Arthur Schnitzler's novel *Der Weg ins Freie* (*The Road to Freedom*), exploring Jewish and masculine crises of identity

1909   Second German edition of *The Interpretation of Dreams* (enlarged and revised); visits USA, lecturing at Clark University, Worcester, Massachussets, at invitation of G. Stanley Hall, and travelling with Jung and Sandor Ferenczi

1910   Nuremberg Congress of Psycho-Analysis; founding of International Psycho-Analytic Association and of *Zentralblatt für Psychoanalyse*, jointly edited by Alfred Adler and Wilhelm Stekel; 'The Wolf-Man' comes to Freud for analysis; publishes *Leonardo*, his most significant work of biography

1911   Third German edition of *The Interpretation of Dreams* (enlarged and revised); publication of 'Psycho-analytic notes on an autobiographical account of a case of paranoia (dementia paranoides)' (Schreber); Weimar Congress of Psycho-Analysis in September; break with Adler, who sets up Society for Free Psychoanalytic Research

Publication of Wilhelm Stekel's *Die Sprache des Traumes* (*The Language of Dreams*) and Havelock Ellis's *The World of Dreams*

1912   Founding of journal *Imago* by Hanns Sachs, to be edited by Freud and Otto Rank, and intended to take psychoanalysis into broader cultural spheres

Publication of Ernest Jones's *Papers on Psychoanalysis*

1913   Publishes *Totem and Taboo*, conjoining psychoanalysis and anthropology; break with Jung; publication of first English translation (by A. A. Brill) of *The Interpretation of Dreams*

Fourth International Psycho-Analytic Congress held in Munich in September; Jones founds the London Psychoanalytic Society, after papers on Freud's theories of dreams and of the unconscious are read at annual British Medical Association meeting

1914   Fourth German edition of *The Interpretation of Dreams* (enlarged and revised); publication of *On the History of the Psychoanalytic Movement* and 'On narcissism: an introduction'; A. A. Brill's translation of *The Psychopathology of Everyday Life* published in Britain

Outbreak of World War One, July–August

1915   Writes essays on war and death, and begins work on papers on *Metapsychology*; second English edition of *The Interpretation of Dreams* (reprint of first)

1916–17 Publishes *Introductory Lectures on Psychoanalysis*, which includes work on dreams

1918   Budapest Congress of Psycho-Analysis, September

Armistice, 11 November

1919   Fifth German edition of *The Interpretation of Dreams* (enlarged and revised)

Jones re-forms London Psychoanalytic Society as British Psychoanalytic Society

1920   Death of Freud's daughter Sophie; publishes *Beyond the Pleasure Principle*, taking on the question of traumatic dreams (more particularly those of shell-shock victims), the 'compulsion to repeat' and 'mastery through repetition'; addresses international congress at The Hague on 'Supplements to the theory of dreams', qualifying wish-fulfilment theory and noting significance of punishment and traumatic dreams; made a full professor of the university, but no seat on the board of the faculty.

International Journal of Psycho-Analysis founded

1921   Sixth German edition of *The Interpretation of Dreams* (reprint of fifth edition, with new preface and revised bibliography); publication of *Group Psychology and the Analysis of the Ego*

1922   Seventh German edition of *The Interpretation of Dreams* (reprint of sixth edition)

1923   Publication of *The Ego and the Id*, shortly after George Groddeck's *The Book of the It* (Es); diagnosis of cancer and first of more than thirty operations; death of grandson Heinz

Otto Rank publishes *The Trauma of Birth*, subsequently repudiated by Freud

1925   *The Interpretation of Dreams* published in *Gesammelte Schriften*, 2 and part of 3 (enlarged and revised); publication of *An Autobiographical Study*; Marie Bonaparte arrives in Vienna for analysis

1926   Publication of *Inhibitions, Symptoms and Anxiety*

1927   Publication of *The Future of an Illusion*

1930   Eighth German edition of *The Interpretation of Dreams* (enlarged and revised); Freud awarded Goethe Prize for Literature

1931   Publication of 'Female sexuality'

1932   Publication of *New Introductory Lectures on Psychoanalysis*, containing a number of lectures on dreams and dream theory. 'Why war' written with Einstein; third English edition of *The Interpretation of Dreams*, revised and retranslated

1933   Hitler becomes Chancellor of Germany; works by Freud, along with those of Einstein and Thomas Mann, burned in Berlin; foreigners (including Jews) banned from sitting on central executive of medical societies, a ban extended to psychoanalytic organizations; Jung becomes president of the International General Medical Society for Psychotherapy, and editor of the Nazi-controlled *Zentralblatt für Psychotherapie*

1934   In Austria, Chancellor Dolfuss quells Socialist uprising in February

1937   Discovery of Freud's letters to Fliess, and purchase by Marie Bonaparte; partial publication of letters in 1954: full publication in 1985

1938   Hitler enters Austria on 12 March; President Roosevelt intervenes to persuade authorities to grant Freud an exit visa to leave Vienna; with help of Marie Bonaparte and Ernest Jones, Freud and immediate family travel to Paris and then London; incomplete English-language edition of *The Interpretation of Dreams* in *The Basic Writings of Sigmund Freud*

1939   Publication of *Moses and Monotheism*; death of Freud on 23 September 1939
Second World War declared in September

1940   Publication of *An Outline of Psycho-Analysis*

1942   *The Interpretation of Dreams* printed in *Gesammelte Werke*, double volume 2/3 (reprint of eighth edition)

1953   English translation (by James Strachey) of *The Interpretation of Dreams*, *Standard Edition of the Complete Psychological Works* IV and part of V.

1954   Publication of *The Origins of Psychoanalysis*, incorporating a selection of Freud's letters to Fliess and 'A Project for a Scientific Psychology'

1976   Publication of English translation of *The Interpretation of Dreams* in *Penguin Freud Library* 4

1985   Publication of *The Complete Letters of Sigmund Freud to Wilhelm Fliess 1887–1904*

1

Introduction: histories, representations, autobiographics in *The Interpretation of Dreams*

LAURA MARCUS

the dream [book] is suddenly taking shape, without any special motivation, but this time I am sure of it . . . No other work of mine has been so completely my own, my own dung heap, my seedling and a *nova species mihi* on top of it. (28 May 1899, F/F, 353)

Histories

The role of dreams in psychoanalysis

The interpretation of dreams is the royal road to a knowledge of the unconscious activities of the mind. (PFL 4, 769: SE V, 608)

The Interpretation of Dreams is one of the founding texts of the twentieth century. Published in November 1899, its publication date was given on the title page of the first edition as 1900, nudging it over into the new century. Its impact was initially muted; it sold only 351 copies in its first six years and did not go into a second edition until 1909.[1] Yet it has had an incalculable influence on modern consciousness, changing the way in which individuals in the twentieth century have thought about their waking as well as their sleeping lives.

Its intellectual ramifications have been equally far-reaching, as disciplines sometimes remote from each other have intersected to read and interpret its interpretations: linguistics and semiotics, literary studies, film theory, psychology, philosophy and hermeneutics, history of ideas, history of science. It is undoubtedly a key text for understanding the nature of interdisciplinary knowl-edge.[2] It is also the most important and influential text of psycho-analysis itself. The British analyst Ella Freeman Sharpe, in her study *Dream Analysis* (1937), described it as 'the first text-book for psycho-analysts',[3] and the function and significance of dreams and dream-interpretation (in analytic training, practice and theory) continue to preoccupy psychoanalysis to the present day.[4]

In *The Interpretation of Dreams* Freud provided the most com-prehensive account of the psychoanalytic conception of the mind. The leading metaphor of the text is that of the journey, with Freud guiding the reader through the landscape of mental life. The text is divided into seven chapters which explore: (I) the existing literature on dreams; (II) the 'associative' method of dream-interpetation, in which Freud analysed one of his own dreams as a 'specimen' dream; (III) the overarching thesis that 'a dream is the fulfilment of a wish'; (IV) the role of distortion in dreams; (V) the material and sources of dreams, including typical dreams; (VI) the 'dream-work', the means by which the 'latent' (unconscious) dream thoughts are disguised and transformed into the 'manifest' dream content; (VII) the metapsychology of the dream-processes, including the workings of 'regression', 'wish-fulfilment' and 'repression'.

While Chapters II to VI primarily explore the workings of both dreams and dream-interpretation, Chapter VII investigates the nature of the mental apparatus which not only produces dreams but seems to require them for its effective functioning. Freud's theories postulated two central theses: first, that dreams have a meaning accessible to interpretation; and second, that they have a function. Dreams are 'compromise formations', expres-sions of wishes and of defenses against those wishes.[5] In Freud's model of the dream and its immediate history, the motive behind the dream is a repressed (unconscious) wish, which comes into contact with a thought or train of thoughts during the course of the day. The thought, or an association to it, is revived in the dream as, in Richard Wollheim's phrase, 'the proxy of the wish'.[6] The wish thus finds an outlet, but is also defended against, or censored by, the distortions of the dream work.

A substantial part of *The Interpretation of Dreams* is given over to the revelation of the wishes underlying apparently painful or unsatisfactory dreams. The distinction between the 'latent' dream thoughts and the 'manifest' dream content enabled Freud to maintain the wish-fulfilment thesis against the seeming evidence of the dream. Wishes are represented as fulfilled in the latent rather than the manifest dream, and it is the latent content of the dream which is continuous with mental life and with which analysis is concerned. Moreover, the conflictual model of psychic life which underlay all Freud's thinking became increasingly apparent in the later editions of the text, as Freud emphasized the splitting between the dreamer and his or her dream-wishes. A footnote added in 1919 analogizes this through the fairy-tale of the sparring man and wife, whose greedy, punitive wishes cancel each other out: 'a dreamer's relation to his wishes is a quite peculiar one. He repudiates them and censors them – he has no liking for them, in short' (PFL 4, 737: SE V, 580–1). One of the stories *The Interpretation of Dreams* tells is that of the development from the simple wishes of childhood and their hallucinatory dream-fulfilments to the complex, ambivalent dream productions of adult life.[7]

As Ernest Jones notes, Freud's interest in dreams was of long standing. Freud kept a 'private notebook on dreams'[8] and in the act of recording his own dreams lies the embryo of *The Interpretation of Dreams*, based so substantially on Freud's own dream-life and arising out of his self-analysis in the 1890s. In 1882, Freud wrote to Martha Bernays, to whom he had just become engaged: 'I have such unruly dreams. I never dream about matters that have occupied me during the day, only of such themes as were touched on once in the course of the day and then broken off.'[9] This observation was to become one of the central tenets of Freud's dream theory, elaborated in his account of the significance of the 'day's residues' and of the 'dream day', the day preceding the dream. Freud's focus on the diurnal, and the relationship between day-dreams and night-dreams, is taken up by Rachel Bowlby in her chapter in this book.

The book that we know as *The Interpretation of Dreams* is in fact a palimpsestic text, an accretion and accumulation of eight editions, incorporating the history of Freud's modifications, addenda and, at points, exclusions.[10] Freud also published a short work entitled *On Dreams* (*Über den Traum*) in 1901, in order to present a

more accessible version of his dream theories to a broader public.[11] *The Interpretation of Dreams* is undoubtedly a denser and
more complex text than its popularizing version, but Freud's very
project in his study of dreams was to give a certain credence to the
'popular' understanding of dreams. (As he wrote in his essay
'Psychoanalysis and telepathy' (1921): 'Not for the first time
would [psychoanalysis] be offering its help to the obscure but
indestructible surmises of the common people against the obscu-
rantism of educated opinion.'[12]) While Freud insisted on the scientific basis of his dream analyses, he also disparaged medical and
scientific approaches which, emphasizing the purely somatic and
physiological motivations for dreams, were unable to find them
meaningful. One of Freud's tasks was to transform the popular
and/or archaic understanding of the dream's 'meaning' as a relation to the future, as prophecy, to an understanding of its relation
to the dreamer's past, recent and remote.

As Didier Anzieu notes, the significance of dreams for Freud
was that they allowed him to explore the crucial question of the
relationship between general psychology (the study of the 'normal' mind) and psychopathology (the study of the 'abnormal'
mind). The dream presented itself as a psychical phenomenon
which was half way between the two fields: '[It] is at once a
normal phenomenon (everyone has at least one dream every
night) and a pathological phenomenon (the dream is a brief hallucination).'[13] Whereas Freud's work in the late 1890s on dreams on
the one hand and clinical questions of neuroses on the other had
seemed to be separate issues, he began to recognize that they were
closely linked and that what explained dreams also explained
neurotic symptoms. As he wrote in his *Introductory Lectures on
Psychoanalysis*: 'the study of dreams is not only the best preparation for the study of the neuroses, but dreams are themselves
a neurotic symptom, which, moreover, offers us the priceless
advantage of occurring in all healthy people' (PFL 1, 111: SE XV,
83).

Dream analysis played little or no part in Freud's work with
patients in the 1890s; hypnosis was the central technique at this
time, as he and Breuer demonstrated in *Studies in Hysteria* (1895).
The interpretation of dreams was, by contrast, at the heart of
Freud's analysis of 'Dora' (Ida Bauer), undertaken at the end of

1900, and written up in the January of 1901, though not published until 1905. Between the female patients of *Studies in Hysteria* and the Dora of Freud's case-history is Irma, the composite figure of Freud's specimen dream in *The Interpretation of Dreams* (discussed more fully below), and the focus of feminist readings of Freud's dream book. 'Fragment of an analysis of a case of hysteria' ['Dora'] (whose initial title was 'Dreams and hysteria') is structured around dream analysis; the case-history was indeed intended to show, Freud writes:

> how dream-interpretation is woven into the history of a treatment and how it can become the means of filling in amnesias and elucidating symptoms. It was not without good reasons that in the year 1900 I gave precedence to a laborious and exhaustive study of dreams (*The Interpretation of Dreams*) over the publications upon the psychology of the neuroses which I had in view. (PFL 8, 39: SE 7, 10)

As Freud described the case-history to Wilhelm Fliess: 'the interpretations are grouped round two dreams, so it is really a continuation of the dream book' (25 January 1901, F/F, 433). The 'continuation' is in the direction of the sexual aetiology of the neuroses, and towards a synthesis of dream theory and theories of sexuality. Dora has become the most widely-discussed of Freud's case-histories, with Freud's treatment of Dora coming to represent the relationship of psychoanalysis to women, femininity and female sexuality. The relationship between Freud's dreams and Dora's dreams, *The Interpretation of Dreams* and 'Fragment of an analysis of a case of hysteria', is explored by Stephen Frosh in his chapter in this book.[14]

Laying the foundations

The Interpretation of Dreams was preceded by the 'Project for a scientific psychology' (unpublished in Freud's lifetime), a 'psychology for neurologists', as Freud described it.[15] This work, as James Strachey notes in his editorial introduction to the *The Interpretation of Dreams*, contains sections constituting a first approach to a coherent theory of dreams (PFL 4, 39: SE IV, xv). These anticipate the most important discovery of the dream book – the distinction between primary and secondary processes. In this sense, Freud could rightly claim that *The Interpretation of Dreams* 'was finished in all essentials at the beginning of 1896',[16] although, as Strachey comments, three points of theoretical importance were established later: the existence of the Oedipus complex and the emphasis on the *infantile* roots of the unconscious wishes underlying dreams; the omnipresence in dreams of the wish to sleep; the part played by 'secondary revision', an aspect of the crucial distinction between the 'latent' dream thoughts which motivate the dream, and the 'manifest' dream content (PFL 4, 42: SE IV, xviii–xix).

In the 'Project for a scientific psychology' Freud developed an account of the functioning of neurones (the 'material particles' out of which the mental apparatus is constructed) and of the distribution of energy or quantity throughout the mental apparatus. He sought to understand the relationship between stimulation received from inside as well as outside the organism, and the co-existence of two seemingly exclusive processes: the laying down of 'memory-traces', and the modifications to the system thereby entailed, and the perpetual openness of the system to new perceptions. His answer was to postulate the existence of neurones of two types – one of which is turned towards the world and receives perceptual stimuli without retaining any trace of them and a second which is stimulated from the interior of the body (by, for example, instincts and needs) and in which momentary excitations are transformed into permanent traces or memories. He subsequently added a third type of neurone, as a way of introducing 'consciousness' into his account. The existence of internal as well as external stimuli and of energy arising endogenously means that a complex model of stimulation-discharge is required; one that moves beyond a 'reflex arc model' (in which a quantity of stimulation is discharged as a quantity of energy) to a model in which energy is accumulated and tension is balanced rather than merely eliminated.

The difference between the classes of neurones, as Richard Wollheim notes in his study of Freud, is located in the protoplasm that lies between them and through which the paths of conduction – the 'contact barriers' or (in a subsequent appellation) 'synapses' – run.[17] The passage of quantity or energy breaks down the contact barriers and establishes permanent pathways or 'facilitations' through the system. These facilitations, and their differential relationships, give to the mental apparatus a form of memory, enabling it to follow paths of conduction previously followed in the pursuit of a satisfaction of a need or 'wish'. The system is governed by the 'pleasure–unpleasure' series: the experience of satisfaction leaves behind a 'wish' or 'wishful' state; the experience of pain an 'apprehension'.

There is, however, a major flaw in the functioning of the system. In a wishful state, the mental apparatus follows the path of conduction previously followed on the occasion of the original experience of satisfaction from which the wishful state derives. In the event of an excessive flow of quantity:

> what will arise is not simply a memory image of the wished-for object but an image invested with all the strength of a perception. If that happens, idea will be mistaken for reality, the wished-for object for an object actually present, and discharge will actually occur. Since, however, the object is not present, is not real, but is imaginary, there will be an absence of satisfaction.[18]

Freud called this phenomenon 'hallucinatory wish-fulfilment'. It is a part of 'primary process' thinking, which does not distinguish between satisfaction acquired in the outer world and in the inner world of phantasy. What is required, Freud postulated, in the mental development of the species and of the individual, is the introduction of the 'reality principle' (or 'secondary process' thinking), in which pleasure can be deferred, attendant upon an indication of reality, free-flowing energy 'bound', and ideas and images inserted into trains of thought. The primary processes survive, however, in those areas of mental (and linguistic) life which so fascinated Freud: dreams, slips of the tongue, symptoms and jokes.

The model of the mental apparatus explored in the 'Project' (which some of his critics have characterized as a biologism happily superseded) in fact found later outlets in some of Freud's key metapsychological writings, including those, such as 'A note upon the mystic writing-pad' and *Beyond the Pleasure Principle*, which have absorbed his most radical commentators.[19] Its impact on *The Interpretation of Dreams*, in some senses its twin text, was also profound. We might note, for example, the insistence on the 'wish', the wishful state and wish-fulfilment; on memory and memory-traces; on hallucinatory states and the dream as an hallucination; on the repetition of impressions and their routes of association by means of trains of thought to repressed, infantile wishes; on the relationship between thought and perception; on the 'binding' of energies and the distinction between primary and secondary processes; on dreams as 'compromise formations', binding unconscious 'thoughts' while allowing them to emerge in disguised form and 'condensing' diverse materials (thoughts, ideas, memories) into composite images.

The paths traversed on the conceptual and theoretical 'journey' of *The Interpretation of Dreams* which, in the sections of the text on the dream-work and dream-interpretation, are the paths, chains or trains of mental and mnemic association, can also be understood as the pathways or 'facilitations' of the mental apparatus, the tracks or traces laid down by the movement of energy (driven by external excitations and by impulse, instinct, wish, appetite, need, desire) through the system. 'What we describe as our "character" is based on the memory-traces of our impressions', Freud writes (PFL 4, 688: SE V, 539).[20]

In the section on 'Regression' in Chapter VII of *The Interpretation of Dreams*, Freud reproduces the model of a psychical apparatus which can accommodate both the laying down of memory-traces and an openness to perceptual stimuli. In the 'Project', Freud sought for an understanding of the relationship, and potential confusion, between ideas (which might include a visual component) and perceptions (purely visual): in *The Interpretation of Dreams* he explores the phenomenon whereby dream thoughts are transformed into visual images and, to a lesser extent, speech. Freud suggests that in 'hallucinatory' dreams (exampled by the dream of the burning child, with which he opens Chapter VII) excitation is transmitted in a retrogressive direction, 'starting from thoughts, to the pitch of complete sensory vividness . . . *In regression the fabric of the dream-thoughts is resolved into its raw material*' (PFL 4, 693: SE V, 543). Visual and sensory representations, Freud suggests, characterize infantile mentation:

> we cannot dismiss the probability that in dreams too the transformation of thoughts into visual images may be in part the result of the *attraction* which memories couched in visual form and eager for revival bring to bear upon thoughts cut off from consciousness and

> struggling to find expression. On this view a dream might be described as *a substitute for an infantile scene modified by being transferred onto a recent experience.* The infantile scene is unable to bring about its own revival and has to be content with returning as a dream. (PFL 4, 696–7: SE V, 546)

Leaving aside for the moment Freud's haunting representation of the 'infantile scene' as a kind of *revenant*, 'returning as a dream', what is striking about this discussion is Freud's equation of infantile and archaic thought. The dream, he suggests, is regressive, returning us to our earliest wishes and impulses: 'Dreaming is a piece of infantile life that has been superseded' (PFL 4, 721: SE V, 567). Drawing upon the link made by numerous nineteenth-century commentators between ontogeny and phylogeny, the history of the individual and that of the race or species, Freud further suggests that dreams return us to the forms of mentation of 'primitive' humanity:

> Behind this childhood of the individual we are promised a picture of a phylogenetic childhood – a picture of the development of the human race, of which the individual's development is in fact an abbreviated recapitulation influenced by the chance circumstances of life . . . Dreams and neuroses seem to have preserved more mental antiquities than we could have imagined possible; so that psychoanalysis may claim a high place among the sciences which are concerned with the reconstruction of the earliest and most obscure periods of the beginnings of the human race. (PFL 4, 700: SE V, 548–9)

In Freud's thought, anthropology is invariably allied to theories of language. The transformation of latent dream-thoughts into sensory images and visual scenes, he wrote in his 'Revision of dream-theory' (*New Introductory Lectures on Psychoanalysis* (1933 [1932])), entails the dropping away of 'the conjunctions and prepositions, the changes in declension and conjugation . . . just as in a primitive language without any grammar, only the raw material of thought is expressed and abstract terms are taken back to the concrete ones that are at their basis' (PFL 2, 48–9: SE XXII, 20). Increasingly, Freud linked 'primitive' mentation with the use of 'symbols': 'The copious employment of symbols, which have become alien to conscious thinking, for representing certain objects and processes is in harmony alike with the archaic regression in the mental apparatus and with the demands of the censorship' (PFL 2, 49: SE XXII, 20). I discuss the significance of 'symbolism' for Freudian dream theory below.

The Freud–Fliess correspondence

A significant source for our knowledge of the 'origins' of psychoanalysis is Freud's correspondence with Wilhelm Fliess, a Berlin doctor and biologist with whom Freud maintained an intense personal and intellectual friendship for some fifteen years – one which constituted, a number of commentators have claimed, an unacknowledged transference on Freud's part. Freud's career was marked by a succession of interlocutors and disciples to whom he entrusted his ideas and aspirations. Fliess replaced Josef Breuer, with whom Freud had worked on his theories of hysteria, as the trusted fellow worker in the psychological field, and between 1887 and the early 1900s Freud, in his letters to Fliess, explored his scientific researches and theoretical speculations and gave support to Fliess's biological theories.[21]

Freud outlined substantial portions of the 'Project for a scientific psychology'. He recounted his 'discovery' of the origins of neurosis and his subsequent turn from the 'real event' (of the sexual seduction of children) to the fantasy aspects of memory and the active nature of childhood sexuality.[22] He also recorded the progress of his 'self-analysis', undertaken during the middle years of the 1890s and itself inseparable from the 'dream book' and from the founding concepts of psychoanalysis. *The Interpretation of Dreams*, as I discuss later in this introduction, is a work of autobiography, deriving in large part, in Melvin Lansky's words, 'from Freud's exhaustive associations among the elements of written texts of his own dreams'.[23]

On 23 September 1895, Freud wrote to Fliess: 'A dream the day before yesterday yielded the funniest confirmation of the conception that dreams are motivated by wish-fulfilments' (F/F, 140). At the end of October 1896, he reported the news of his father's death to Fliess and, a week later, that 'in [my] inner self the whole past has been reawakened by this event' (F/F, 201–2). He accompanies the account of the impact of his father's death with an interpretation of one of his dreams, a dream which made its way into *The Interpretation of Dreams*. The death of his father and the reawakening of the past attendant upon it thus become closely linked to the investigation of dreams and their meaning.

The first reference to the 'dream book' comes in a letter written on 16 May 1987: 'I have been looking into the literature and feel like the Celtic imp: "Oh, how glad I am that no one, no one knows . . ." No one even suspects that the dream is not nonsense but wish-fulfilment' (F/F, 243). The 'dream', he wrote in September 1897, stands secure despite the collapse of his theory of the neuroses, a theory earlier represented in Freud's dreams in the 'wish to catch a *Pater* as the originator of neuroses' (31 May 1897, F/F, 249).

Freud's letters in the autumn of 1987 recount the progress of his self-analysis as a process which cuts across the borders between waking and sleeping:

> For the last four days my self-analysis . . . has continued in my dreams and has presented me with the most valuable elucidations and clues. At certain points I have the feeling of being at the end, and so far I have always known where the next dream-night would continue. (3 October 1897, F/F, 268).

As J.-B. Pontalis writes: 'for a certain time [Freud] literally made appointments with his dreams and, even more astonishingly, his dreams kept the appointments'.[24]

His dreams, Freud suggests, continue and collude with his self-analysis, while he finds in them the crucial 'scenes' and influences of his childhood: his nurse, who was 'my teacher in sexual matters'; his mother, towards whom 'libido . . . was awakened' when, at the age of two, he journeyed with her from Leipzig to Vienna, 'during which we must have spent the night together and there must have been an opportunity of seeing her *nudam*' (3 October 1897, F/F, 268). From this he extrapolated 'a single idea of general value':

> I have found, in my own case too, [the phenomenon of] being in love with my mother and jealous of my father, and I now consider it a universal event in early childhood . . . If this is so, we can understand the gripping power of *Oedipus Rex* . . . the Greek legend seizes upon a compulsion which everyone recognizes because he senses its

existence within himself. Everyone in the audience was once a bud-
ding Oedipus in fantasy and each recoils in horror from the dream
fulfilment here transplanted into reality, with the full quantity of
repression which separates his infantile state from his present one.
(15 October 1897, F/F, 272)

The 'inner work', as Freud described his self-analysis, thus reveals to him the 'universal' condition on which psychoanalysis
founds its central theories of sexuality and social organization –
the Oedipus complex. In his early formulations of Oedipal desire
(for that of the parent of the opposite sex) and hostile rivalry (for
that of the parent of the same sex), Freud did not differentiate
between the cases of the male and female child, but developed his
theory on the model of the little boy. In this sense, the male
becomes the 'universal' subject of *The Interpretation of Dreams*.

The 'Project for a scientific psychology', Freud's self-analysis,
the dream book, the death of his father, the repudiation of the
'seduction theory' in favour of the power of fantasy and infantile
sexuality, the 'discovery' of the Oedipal self within, and the force
of repression, which starts, Freud wrote to Fliess, 'from the feminine aspect' (F/F, 246), form a complex web of interconnections,
in part forged in the letters to Fliess. The links are the emphases
on phantasies and wishes and on the ways in which structures in
the present – including dreams and neurotic or hysterical symptoms – catch up infantile, 'archaic' wishes into their narrative
organization as they are simultaneously pulled back, by memory
and desire, to the mother, herself linked for Freud with the realms
of myth, the archaic and pre-history.

'No one, no one knows . . .'

As Freud himself suggests throughout *The Interpretation of
Dreams*, and despite his claim to Fliess that 'no one knows', other
commentators on dreams anticipated or shared a number of his
findings on the structure and function of dreaming. Henri
Ellenberger, in his important study of psychiatry, psychology and
psychoanalysis *The Discovery of the Unconscious*, records the wide-
spread nature of research into dreams in the latter half of the
nineteenth century.[25] Romanticism, Ellenberger notes, with its
fascination with dreams and dreaming, was followed by an era
of positivism which 'brought the notion that dreams were a

meaningless by-product of automatic and uncoordinated brain activity occurring during sleep'.[26] The mid-nineteenth century, however, also saw the appearance of the work of three great pioneers of dream investigation – that of Scherner, Maury, and Hervey de Saint-Denis, work that was to have an important influence on Freud's dream theories.

These theorists, and several of their near contemporaries, including the British psychologist James Sully,[27] explored a number of the themes that were to preoccupy Freud: representation in dreams as a language of symbols and, in particular, the importance of the house as a symbol for the human body (Scherner); the role of memory in the production of dreams and of chains of associations between old and recent memories (Maury, Hervey); the importance of the 'dream-work' (*Traumarbeit*) (Robert, Maury, Hervey), including those processes now so substantially associated with Freudian theory – 'the fusion of representations into one image and . . . the attribution of a neutral act to another subject (in modern terms, condensation and displacement)'.[28] Ellenberger also points to the work of Delage, who propounded a concept of dynamic energy, 'implying that the representations loaded with psychic energy repress or inhibit each other, or can fuse together, that there are in dreams chains of association that can sometimes be partially reconstructed, and that old memories can be called forth from dream through association with recent images'.[29]

In Ellenberger's account (and in the work of other analysts of 'the unconscious before Freud'), Freudian dream theory therefore owed much to the vast dream literature of the nineteenth century, despite Freud's complaints to Fliess about its futility. Freud's originality, Ellenberger suggests, resides in four innovations: (1) the model of the dream with its distinction of manifest and latent content and its specific pattern of being lived simultaneously in the present and the remote past; (2) Freud's contention that the manifest content is a distortion of the latent content, resulting from repression by the censor; (3) the application of free association as a method for the analysis of dreams; (4) the introduction of systematic dream interpretation as a tool of psychotherapy.[30]

Distinctions between what was borrowed and what was new are of course crucial. Ellenberger and others to a large extent pass

over, however, the specific, discursive ways in which Freud represents the work of his predecessors and contemporaries in the
field. Nor do they address the complex and compelling narrative
Freud developed in *The Interpretation of Dreams*, which gathers up
prior knowledges as it unfolds.

Freud devotes the first chapter of *The Interpretation of Dreams*
to the work of other dream theorists. He discusses in some detail
those views with which his own theories will accord, including:
'the fact that dreams have at their command memories which are
inaccessible in waking life' (PFL 4, 71: SE IV, 12–13); childhood
experience as one of the sources from which dreams derive material for reproduction (PFL 4, 74: SE IV, 15); the derivation of
dream elements from the very last days before they were
dreamed (PFL 4, 76: SE IV, 17); the centrality of visual images to
dreams (PFL 4, 95: SE IV, 33); the importance of laws of association for dreams (PFL 4, 124: SE IV, 58); the view (the crux of
Freudian dream theory) 'that ideas in dreams and psychoses have
in common the characteristic of being *fulfilments of wishes*' (PFL 4,
163: SE IV, 91). As Freud presents the situation, other commentators have failed less in specific insights than in pursuing these
insufficiently far:

> Hildebrandt (1875) is unquestionably right in asserting that we
> should be able to explain the genesis of every dream-image if we
> devoted enough time and trouble to tracing its origin. He speaks of
> this as 'an increasingly laborious and thankless task. For as a rule it
> ends in hunting out every kind of utterly worthless psychical event
> from the remotest corners of the chambers of one's memory, and in
> dragging to light once again every kind of indifferent moment of
> the past from the oblivion in which it was buried in the very hour,
> perhaps, after it occurred.' I can only regret that this keen-sighted
> author allowed himself to be deterred from following the path
> which had this inauspicious beginning; if he had followed it, it
> would have led him to the very heart of dreams. (PFL 4, 79: SE IV,
> 19–20)

The 'path . . . to the very heart of dreams' is, by implication, the
one that Freud, and *The Interpretation of Dreams*, will follow. Later
in the same chapter, Freud refers to Delage's identification of
dream material 'as consisting of fragments and residues of the

preceding days and of earlier times' (PFL 4, 151: SE IV, 81) and his finding that 'Psychical material that has been suppressed comes to light in dreams' (PFL 4, 152: SE IV, 82). Yet 'At this point, unluckily, Delage interrupts his train of thought'. Instead of pursuing the psychical material to its source in the unconscious, Delage opts for 'the ruling theory of the partial awakening of the brain' (PFL 4, 152: SE IV, 82). 'Path' or 'train of thought' – no other dream theorist, Freud suggests, has been willing to pursue them as far as he intends to. And where other theorists have held either to the view that dreams draw on past experience and memory or to the (seemingly contradictory) belief that dreams are inspired by recent impressions, Freud will show that both accounts are true.

The dream theories existing at the time of Freud's writing (of the earlier, rather than later editions of the text) are thus subjected to a number of criticisms. Freud is most critical of prevailing medical and scientific views that the stimuli for dreams are somatic in kind; that is, that dreams are triggered by organic sensation and bodily needs:

> Anyone who is inclined to take a low view of psychical functioning in dreams will naturally prefer to assign their source to somatic stimulation; whereas those who believe that the dreaming mind retains the greater part of its waking capacities have of course no reason for denying that the stimulus to dreaming can arise within the dreaming mind itself. (PFL 4, 130–1: SE IV, 64)

Even those writers for whom there are determinants other than somatic ones tend to 'take a low view' of the meaningfulness of dreams, Freud suggests. Throughout *The Interpretation of Dreams*, Freud refers to the ways in which the inability to interpret or 'read' dream-contents results in the claim that they are 'nonsensical and worthless'. The question of the 'value' of dreams is a central one. It is the focus for dream interpetation in classical antiquity: 'The distinction was drawn between truthful and valuable dreams, sent to the sleeper to warn him or foretell the future, and vain, deceitful and worthless dreams, whose purpose it was to mislead or destroy him' (PFL 4, 59: SE IV, 3). The question of 'value' persists despite the demise of belief in the prophetic nature of dreams. Freud quotes a number of his contemporaries for whom the distinctive aspect of dreaming is its focus on the insignificant, its lack of 'value':

> Hildebrandt (1875, 11): 'For the remarkable thing is that dreams derive their elements not from major and stirring events nor the powerful and compelling interests of the preceding day, but from incidental details, from the worthless fragments, one might say, of what has been recently experienced or of the remoter past. A family bereavement, which has moved us deeply and under whose immediate shadow we have fallen asleep late at night, is blotted out of our memory till with our first waking moment it returns to it again with disturbing violence. On the other hand, a wart on the forehead of a stranger whom we met in the street and to whom we gave no second thought after passing him *has* a part to play in our dream. (PFL 4, 78: SE IV, 18)

The superficiality of dream theory, as Freud presents it, its failure to pursue the dream to its heart, results in the view that dreams are themselves superficial productions. Much of Freud's analysis in *The Interpretation of Dreams* will be given over to explanation of precisely the effects that a commentator such as Hildebrandt describes (as in the passage above), primarily through concepts of the transference or 'displacement' of 'value'. The dream, whose primary function is to protect sleep, works to 'bind' anxiety; it 'displaces' 'essential elements, charged as they are, with intense interest', treating them 'as though they were of small value' (PFL 4, 415: SE IV, 306). The dream-work (which transforms the latent dream-thoughts into manifest dream-content) effects 'a complete "transvaluation of all psychical values"' (PFL 4, 443: SE IV, 330).[31] Such disguises have blinded commentators to the fact that '[d]reams are never concerned with trivialities; we do not allow our sleep to be disturbed by trifles' (PFL 4, 270: SE IV, 182). No fragment is 'worthless', for it is the means by which the foundations of the dream can be traced.

It is striking that the language used by the dream theorists quoted by Freud is also that so often used by late nineteenth- and early twentieth-century commentators to describe the experience of 'modernity': kaleidoscopic, fleeting, impressionistic, anonymous. Freud quotes Strumpell on the ways in which dreams pick up 'passing glimpses of people or things, or odd fragments of what one has read, and so on' (PFL 4, 78: SE IV, 19). In the passage from Hildebrandt, quoted above, it is as if the stuff of nineteenth-century fiction (the family bereavement) is pushed aside by the imagery of metropolitan modernity, here given a grotesque aspect in the 'wart on the forehead of a stranger whom we met in the street and to whom we gave no second thought after passing him'. Dreams, in these accounts, become a form of urban phantasmagoria.

The Interpretation of Dreams deploys the language of optics, as I discuss more fully below, but it is noticeable that Freud does not take up the 'kaleidoscope' analogies of the dream theorists he quotes. He shifts the optical analogy from an instrument that represents, for these nineteenth-century commentators, a disordered and chaotic visual regime, to the apparatus of scientific endeavour – the microscope and, in particular, the composite photography used by Francis Galton in his *Inquiries into Human Faculty*, which becomes an analogue for the process of 'condensation' in the dream-work.[32] Freud does not overtly 'revalue' the fleeting, mutable aspects of dream-life and modernity, but the complex interplay, and at times tension, between models of receptive and retentive surfaces, dailiness and timelessness, (contingent) associations and (universal) symbolism, disallows any simple distinction between surface and depth, trivia and significance, in dreams and their interpretations.

The royal road to the unconscious

Those who go forward only very slowly can progress much further if they always keep to the right path, than those who run and wander off it. (Descartes, *Discourse on Method*)[33]

The whole thing is planned on the model of an imaginary walk. At the beginning, the dark forest of authors (who do not see the trees), hopelessly lost on wrong tracks. Then a concealed path through which I lead the reader – my specimen dream with its peculiarities, details, indiscretions, bad jokes – and then suddenly the high ground and the view and the question: which way do you want to go now? (6 August 1899, F/F, 365)

Freudian theory, as has often been claimed, overturned Cartesianism and its self-certainties, effecting an epistemological revolution in Western thought. *The Interpretation of Dreams* is, like Descartes's *Discourse on Method*, an 'autobiography' which becomes a 'method', and one in which the author makes the transition from the singular, autobiographical 'I' to a universal selfhood. Freud, like Descartes, finds universal truth in his own experience, mentation and dreams. Whereas Descartes's universal 'I', however, is the reasoning *Cogito*, in Freud's account the subject is driven by impulses and desires of which 'it' is not conscious, and the 'I' is dispersed into multiple identities and identifications.

The term 'method' derives from the Greek *hodos*, road or way. Descartes makes much of the metaphor of the 'path' or 'road' of the individual life, writing, for example: 'I consider myself very fortunate to have found myself, from my early youth, on certain paths which led me to considerations and maxims out of which I have constructed a method'.[34] Freud, too, places the metaphor of the journey at the centre of *The Interpretation of Dreams* while making the terrain a very different one from Descartes's. Dreams may indeed be 'the royal road to the unconscious' and dream theory the only secure ground under Freud's feet, but the paths that *The Interpretation of Dreams* follows are, more often than not, far from straight. Not only is there a multiplicity of starting points ('Having followed one path to its end, we may now retrace our steps and choose another starting-point for our rambles through the problems of dream-life' (PFL 4, 247: SE IV, 163)): the interpretative path often ends in a tangle of roots.

The attention Freud calls to the structure of the text, the route of the journey, attests not only to the book's organizational complexity (as his letters to Fliess show, he was unsure of where to place the chapter on existing dream theories, writing it last and ultimately placing it first) but to the organizational complexity of dreams: 'The dream-thoughts to which we are led by interpretation cannot, from the nature of things, have any definite endings; they are bound to branch out in every direction into the intricate network of our world of thought. It is at some point where this meshwork is particularly close that the dream-wish grows up, like a mushroom out of its mycelium' (PFL 4, 672: SE V, 525). Psychic life, as Freud presents it, seems to erupt through the surfaces of his text. As he wrote in the preface to the first edition: 'The broken threads which so frequently interrupt my presentation are nothing less than the many points of contact between the problem of the formation of dreams and the more comprehensive problems of psychopathology' (PFL 4, 44: SE IV, xxiii).

The final section of *The Interpretation of Dreams*, 'The psychology of the dream-processes', is at one level a move beyond interpretation: 'It is only after we have disposed of everything that has to do with the work of interpretation that we can begin to realize the incompleteness of our psychology of dreams' (PFL 4, 654: SE V, 510–11). Opening with 'The dream of the burning child', 'which raises no problem of representation' and yet 'call[s] for explanation', Freud takes up the metaphor of the journey:

> before starting off along this new path, it will be well to pause and look around, to see whether in the course of our journey up to this point we have overlooked anything of importance. For it must be clearly understood that the easy and agreeable portion of our journey lies behind us. Hitherto, unless I am greatly mistaken, all the paths along which we have travelled have led us towards the light – towards elucidation and fuller understanding. But as soon as we endeavour to penetrate more deeply into the mental process involved in dreaming, every path will end in darkness. (PFL 4, 654: SE V, 511)

In Freud's version of the *Pilgrim's Progress* or *Aeneid* (the source of the legend on the title page of *The Interpretation of Dreams* – '*Flectere si nequeo superos, Acheronta movebo*' ('If I cannot bend the higher powers I will move the infernal regions'))[35] the traveller is led into darkness, the 'underworld', in the final stages of the journey rather than, as in traditional epic structure, emerging from darkness into light.

The play of light and darkness in Freud's conceptual schema is also a movement between revelation and disguise, manifest and latent contents, progression and regression, interpretation and obfuscation. Chapter VI, 'The dream-work', uses an interpretative methodology to explore and expose the various disguises and concealments entailed in the transformation from dream-wish to dream-scene, interpreting or undisguising dreams along associative paths. Chapter VII, 'The psychology of the dream-processes', leads us into the 'dark continent' of mental processes: 'we have been obliged to build our way out into the dark. If we are not wholly in error, other lines of approach are bound to lead us into much the same region and the time may then come when we shall find ourselves more at home in it' (PFL 4, 700: SE V, 549). We are seeking, it would seem, to accustom ourselves to the darkness.

It is striking that Freud uses the darkest, or starkest, dream recounted in the text, 'The dream of the burning child', to open and to punctuate the final section of the text. The dream's very transparency, Freud suggests, its absence of disguise, opens the door into the most secret reaches of psychic life. The dream was recounted to him, Freud states, by a woman patient who had heard it in a lecture on dreams: 'its actual source is still unknown to me' (PFL 4, 652: SE V, 509). The woman patient proceeded to 're-dream' the dream, 'taking it over' rather as Freud takes it over for his own text. This 'model dream', whose 'source' is unknown, leads the dream interpreter into the darkness.

Throughout the text, Freud has alluded to realms of obscurity inaccessible to interpretative strategies, as in his image of the dream's navel: 'There is at least one spot in every dream at which it is unplumbable – a navel, as it were, that is its point of contact with the unknown' (PFL 4, 186 n. 2: SE IV, 111 n. 1). The Gothic elements of *The Interpretation of Dreams* (discussed by Robert Young in his chapter in this volume), its emphases on death-dreams, on figures in dreams as *revenants* and ghosts, on the uncanny and unknown, are at one with the darkness in which (most) dreams are dreamed. 'The dream of the burning child' is also the point at which psychoanalytic and occultist dream discourses become most closely linked. With its ghostly representation of a dead child who 'speaks' from beyond the grave and its suggestion of telepathic communication, the dream, and Freud's account of it, becomes an allusion to the unfathomable, 'haunted' realms of psychical life, in which the power of the 'wish' might be such as to breach the boundaries between selves and to cross distances in space and time.[36]

Representations

Dream interpretation and symbolism
The dream of the burning child, Freud suggests, leads us beyond the work of interpretation and into 'the structure of the apparatus

of the mind' (PFL 4, 654: SE V, 511). In this introduction I have leapt over the question of interpretation in order to explore the relationship between Freud's model of the psychic apparatus and *The Interpretation of Dreams*, and now need to retrace my steps. I will not discuss the more fundamental philosophical issues relating to Freudian dream interpretation, which are explored in James Hopkins's chapter in this volume.[37]

At its most basic (and I draw here on the account of dream-interpretation Freud gave in his *Introductory Lectures on Psychoanalysis* as well as on *The Interpretation of Dreams* itself), interpreting, for Freud, 'means finding a hidden sense in something' (PFL 1, 115: SE XV, 87). It is the dreamer himself, Freud asserts, who should tell us what his dreams mean. The 'manifest content' of the dream is a disguised, distorted or 'displaced' version of the 'latent dream thoughts', and therefore the meaning of the dream will not be readily accessible to its dreamer:

> We do not require him to tell us straight away the sense of his dream, but he will be able to find its origin, the circle of thoughts and interests from which it sprang . . . We shall once more ask the dreamer how he arrived at the dream, and once more his first remark is to be looked on as an explanation . . . we should divide the dream into its elements and start a separate inquiry into each element. (PFL 1, 134–5: SE XV, 104–5)

The method is that of 'free association'. The associative method is not, however, arbitrary in Freud's account, but determined by and dependent 'on groups of strongly emotional thoughts and interests, "complexes", whose participation is not known at the moment – that is to say, is unconscious' (PFL 1, 136–8: SE XV, 109). The associations 'to the dream-element will be determined both by the dream-element and also by the unconscious genuine thing behind it' (PFL 1, 142: SE XV, 112). Interpretation proceeds by tracing the path or 'chain' of associations from the dream-element (the substitute for the dream-thought) back to 'the genuine thing which is being held back' (PFL 1, 142: SE XV, 112). Meaning is not constituted, as in traditional hermeneutics, by the interrelationship between part and whole ('we can only form a proper judgement of the rebus if we put aside criticisms . . . of the whole composition and its part', Freud writes of dream structure (PFL 4,

382: SE IV, 278)) but by the 'translation' from one system to another, element by element.

The work of interpretation is an undoing of the dream-work which transformed the latent dream into the manifest one. Proceeding in the reverse direction, interpretation seeks to arrive at the latent dream (or dream-thoughts) from the manifest one, although, as Freud notes, 'we need not suppose that every association that occurs during the work of interpretation had a place in the dream-work during the night':

> It is true that in carrying out the interpretation in the waking state we follow a path which leads back from the elements of the dream to the dream-thoughts and that the dream-work followed one in the contrary direction. But it is highly improbable that these paths are passable both ways. It appears, rather, that in the daytime we drive shafts which follow along fresh trains of thoughts and that these shafts make contact with the intermediate thoughts and the dream-thoughts now at one point and now at another. (PFL 4, 680: SE V, 532)

The degree of ease or difficulty of the interpretative task will depend very largely on the degree of distortion between latent thoughts and manifest dream content, and this in turn is substantially determined by the workings both of dream-'censorship' and 'resistance' to interpretation. The 'censorship' is a 'permanent [psychic] institution which has as its aim the maintenance of the distortion' (PFL 1, 174: SE XV, 141); the resistance to interpretation is 'only a putting into effect of the dream-censorship', which continues to exert its hold beyond dreaming life. While the 'fundamental technical rule of analysis' in general, and dream-interpretation in particular, is that no idea should be held back (a 'rule' Freud admits to breaching a number of times in his analysis of his own dreams), 'resistance' is itself one of the most important clues in the search for the unconscious motivating material of the dream: 'It amounts, in fact, to a special distinguishing mark.' The degree of the 'resistance' and of the distortion of unconscious material is greater in proportion to the significance of that material.

Distortion in dreams might be signalled by gaps in the dream itself (Freud gives an example of a dream in which the forbidden elements emerge as mumbled, indecipherable speech). More generally, dream-distortion works by means of a 'displacement of accent' (PFL 1, 172: SE XV, 140), which often entails, as discussed above, the 'transvaluation' of unconscious material so that 'the psychical accent is shifted from an important element on to another which is unimportant, so that the dream appears differently centred and strange' (PFL 1, 208: SE XV, 174). 'Displacement' is also an aspect of the dream-work (discussed below), whereby 'a latent element is replaced not by a component part of itself but by something more remote – that is, by an allusion' (PFL 1, 208: SE XV, 174).

The third type of 'displacement' is fundamental to dream mentation in its entirety. As we have seen, Freud's theory of dreams centres upon the transformation of unconscious thoughts, and a 'wish' in particular, into a 'hallucinatory experience' in which the wish can be represented as fulfilled: '*Dreams are things which get rid of (psychical) stimuli disturbing to sleep, by the method of hallucinatory satisfaction*' (PFL 1, 168: SE XV, 136). They entail the transformation of thoughts into experiences, and it is this alteration that must first be undone in the process of interpreting a dream. The visual, concrete images and representations of the manifest dream have to be 'translated' back into the dream-thoughts:

> Here we have a new type of relation between the manifest and latent dream-elements. The former is not so much a distortion of the latter as a representation of it, a plastic, concrete, portrayal of it, taking its start from the wording. But precisely on that account it is once more a distortion, for we have long since forgotten from what concrete image the word originated and therefore fail to recognize it when it is replaced by the image. (PFL 1, 152: SE XV, 121)

In this account, the dream-image returns us to the forms of 'primitive', visual thinking out of which language systems have evolved. The process would thus be from the ('primitive') concrete image to the word which has replaced it (the substance of the latent dream-thought) and then (back) to the concrete image as represented in the dream. The associations between latent and manifest elements, dream-thoughts and dream-images, are thus 'determined' not only by the specific paths of the dreamer's associations but by the 'course of linguistic evolution' (PFL 4, 532: SE V, 407).

In this model of dream-interpretation, 'universal' meanings enter quietly alongside individual associations as determinants. Yet this is one of the most contentious aspects of Freud's account of dreams and dream-interpretation. Whereas Freud at times asserts the interpretative necessity of the dreamer's individual associations to the dream-thoughts, pitting his methods against the 'symbolic' method of dream-interpretation which uses a fixed set of keys or a 'cryptography' for deciphering dreams, other sections of the text open up a space for 'universal' symbols and 'typical dreams', whose meanings can be deciphered in the absence of the dreamer's particular associations. Freud indeed argued that the dream interpreter becomes aware of the existence of a (universal) symbol when the dreamer is unable to provide associations for a particular dream element: in this sense symbols appear in dreams as 'mute' elements (PFL 1, 183: SE XV, 150).

The greater number of additions in the various editions of *The Interpretation of Dreams* are those concerned with symbolism in dreams. In the second (1909) and third (1911) editions, Freud added substantial new material on sexual symbolism to the end of the section on 'Typical dreams' in Chapter V. The fourth edition (1914) saw a more major structural change, with a new section on symbolism introduced into Chapter VI; in subsequent editions Freud continued to add to this material. While Freud recognized 'the presence of symbolism in dreams from the very beginning', he claims, 'it was only by degrees and as my experience increased that I arrived at a full appreciation of its extent and significance' (PFL 4, 466: SE V, 350). The history of Freud's developing interest in 'symbolism' is inseparable from that of his relationships with other figures in the psychoanalytic movement, including Wilhelm Stekel, Herbert Silberer and, perhaps most significantly, Carl Gustav Jung. As John Forrester has shown in *Language and the Origins of Psychoanalysis*, the concept of symbolism and the theory of the symbol underlay virtually all the areas of interaction and (later) dissension between Freud and Jung: 'In the final analysis, Jung and Freud's differences lay in their perception of the relationship between language, symbol and reality.'[38]

The sections on 'symbolism' in *The Interpretation of Dreams* and in the *Introductory Lectures on Psychoanalysis* contain the material that came to be most closely associated with

Freudianism – the location of 'Freudian symbols'. Freud asserts that 'Symbols are stable translations', that '[t]he range of things which are given symbolic representation in dreams is not wide: the human body as a whole, parents, children, brothers and sisters, birth, death, nakedness' (PFL 1, 186: SE XV, 153), and that '[t]he very great majority of symbols in dreams are sexual symbols' (PFL 1, 188: SE XV, 153). Such symbolism is not peculiar to dreams but 'is characteristic of unconscious ideation, in particular among the people, and it is to be found in folklore, and in popular myths, legends, linguistic idioms, proverbial wisdom and current jokes, to a more complete extent than in dreams' (PFL 4, 467–8: SE V, 351 (added 1909)).

Freud thus marshals a form of cultural anthropology against those critics who might accuse him of arbitrary associationism. He argues that the symbolism on which dreams draw is unconscious to the dreamer, belonging to his unconscious mental life, and that symbolic relations go back to the very origins of human organization and of language: 'the symbolic relation would be the residue of an ancient verbal identity'. He contrasts the symbolic relation given by 'conceptual and linguistic identity' in prehistoric times (PFL 4, 468: SE V, 352) with the 'arbitrary judgement of the dream interpreter' in ancient times and the 'reckless interpretations' of his contemporary Wilhelm Stekel.[39] The 'symbolic' aspect of Freudian dream theory also relates to Freud's desire to insert psychoanalysis into broader cultural spheres, and to make 'links with mythology and philology, with folklore, with social psychology and the theory of religion', in which psychoanalysis would provide 'the technical method and the points of view whose application in these other fields should prove fruitful' (PFL 1, 202: SE XV, 167–8).

Freud insisted that interpretation based on a knowledge of symbols was not a technique which could replace or compete with the associative one, but that it formed a 'supplement' to the latter (PFL 1, 184: SE XV, 151). In *The Interpretation of Dreams*, he refers to the adoption of a combined technique, 'which on the one hand rests on the dreamer's associations and on the other hand fills the gaps from the interpreter's knowledge of symbols'. Dream-symbols (like all dream-elements) frequently have more than one or even several meanings and 'as with Chinese script,

the correct interpretation can only be arrived at on each occasion from the context' (PFL 4, 470: SE V, 353).

Subsequent commentators on Freudian dream theory and, in particular, on his models of interpretation have been less happy with Freud's attempts to combine the two distinct methods. Richard Wollheim gives the question of symbolism scant attention: 'in the massive application of symbolism to dream interpretation it would seem that Freud was heavily influenced by a pupil later to go astray, Wilhelm Stekel'.[40] Nicholas Rand and Maria Torok argue that the 'symbolic' and 'associative' techniques are 'diametrically opposed orientations' which 'cannot help but collide ... The enquiry into the personal psychic sense of dreams cannot be compatible with reliance on a catalog of invariable and universally valid meanings'.[41] Their arguments are representative of a late twentieth-century culture which values 'each and every one's distinctive signification'[42] over 'universal' meanings, freedom over determination, poetics over anthropology. Yet, as Freud's arguments suggest, the associative and the symbolic methods of interpretation are intertwined; linguistic identity, the foundation of Freudian dream-interpretation, cannot be purely 'personal', but must always be bound into a collective history of linguistic usage.

The language of dreams

In his exploration of the 'regressive' transmutation of ideas into visual pictures in the dream (PFL 2, 47: SE XXII, 19), Freud, as Patricia Kitcher argues, drew upon concepts central to nineteenth-century comparative philology, including the idea of linguistic evolution as the move from concreteness to abstraction and belief in the existence of universal symbols.[43] Kitcher sees Freud's linguistic approaches to the dream as a mark of his entrapment by nineteenth-century philological paradigms, an aspect of the problematic reliance of his 'interdisciplinary' project on knowledges in the process of supersession.

Freud's text should, instead, be situated at the historical and cultural intersection of comparative philology and the new 'science' of linguistics emergent at the beginning of the twentieth century. It is Freud's linguistic (rather than philological) preoccupations in *The Interpretation of Dreams* that have made the text so important to twentieth-century commentators. His account of the 'dream-work', in particular, allowed crucial links to be forged between psychoanalytic theory and semiotic and structuralist thought. As Malcolm Bowie writes: 'Where philology took Freud into a whimsical no-man's-land, linguistics, as manipulated by Lacan, could return psychoanalysis to the tasks Freud was best at: the working out and the coherent articulation of psychical structure.'[44]

The lengthiest and, arguably, the most important section of *The Interpretation of Dreams*, 'The dream-work', explores the processes of 'translation' from 'dream-thoughts' into 'dream-content'. The proto-linguistic processes by which 'dream-thoughts' are translated into 'dream-content' Freud terms 'the dream-work', whose key devices are 'condensation', 'displacement', 'symbolization' (as an aspect of 'considerations of representability') and 'secondary revision'. The 'dream-work' and its devices are discussed by Trevor Pateman in his chapter in this volume.

The links Freud makes between dream and linguistic mechanisms are central to the history of the alliances between psychoanalysis and literature. Although structural linguistics most substantially took up Freud's account of the mechanisms of the dream-work to explore the workings of literature and language, such preoccupations also emerged in earlier psychoanalytic writings. Ella Freeman Sharpe's work of the 1930s is of interest here. It has important links with the writings of the critic and theorist William Empson on 'ambiguity' in literary language.[45] It also anticipates the work of structural linguistics in its 'approach [to] the subject of dream mechanisms through the avenue of the accepted characteristics of poetic diction':[46] The laws of poetic diction, evolved by the critics from great poetry and the laws of dream formation as discovered by Freud, spring from the same unconscious sources and have many mechanisms in common.[47] Exploring the workings of simile and metaphor, metonymy and synecdoche (which she allies to Freud's category of 'displacement') onomatopoeia, punning, parallelism and antithesis, Sharpe shifts much of the focus away from 'unconscious [universal] symbolism' and towards the history of the individual as the history of his or her first encounters with language:

> One may assume because of one's knowledge of symbols that *a pier* in a dream will signify the phallus. But I find that one often gets into touch with human experience more quickly if one remembers that 'pier' and 'peer' sound alike, that 'peer' means 'look' and that 'piers' are to be found at the seaside where opportunities of looking and seeing are many.[48]

Words, in Sharpe's account, take their connotations from the first contexts in which we encounter them, that is, phonetically: 'We need to remember that the sound of a word and its first significance will be implicit in another word (or phrases) of the same sound but of different meaning.'[49] Sharpe points to 'the help to be obtained in elucidating dreams from the simple fact that the bridges of thought are crossed and re-crossed by names, that the basis of language is implied metaphor and that we all learned our mother tongue phonetically'.[50]

Of the mechanisms of the 'dream-work' described by Freud, the first two processes, condensation and displacement, have proved particularly central to Freudian and post-Freudian analysts and to literary theorists, who have seen them as the primary axes of figurative language. The linguist Roman Jakobson, in his study of aphasia, classified both 'displacement' and 'condensation' as belonging to the metonymic pole of language (following the principle of contiguity), while 'identification' and 'symbolism' (following the principle of similarity) belong to the metaphoric pole.[51] The analyst and theorist Jacques Lacan, in his radical 'return to Freud', simplified this structure and allied 'condensation' with metaphor and 'displacement' with metonymy.[52] Lacan's endeavour, as Bowie argues, was to locate a 'symbolic order' intrinsic to both language and the unconscious: 'The unconscious, in so far as it becomes visible and audible in speech, symptoms, dreams and involuntary acts of omission or commission, is governed by the same rules as all other systems.'[53] Freud 'refers to the play of the signifier' in *The Interpretation of Dreams*, Lacan claimed, and he based his account of the unconscious and its linguistic structuration substantially upon Freud's exposition of the 'dream-work'.

The linguistic dimensions of Freud's text have a related aspect in the focus on the 'tense' of the meaningfulness of dreams. Freud argues that the dream transforms the 'optative' (the tense of a wish) into the present (the wish (hallucinatorily) fulfilling itself). The final paragraph of *The Interpretation of Dreams* powerfully presents the shift in tense and temporality his dream theories have produced:

> And the value of the dreams for giving us knowledge of the future? There is of course no question of that. It would be truer to say instead that they give us knowledge of the past. For dreams are derived from the past in every sense. Nevertheless the ancient belief that dreams foretell the future is not wholly devoid of truth. By picturing our wishes as fulfilled, dreams are after all leading us into the future. But this future which the dreamer pictures as the present, has been moulded by his indestructible wish into a perfect likeness of the past. (PFL 4, 783: SE V, 621)

The temporalities of dreams, memories and phantasies were central to Freud's thought. This preoccupation emerges, for example, in 'Creative writers and day-dreaming' (1907), in which Freud sets out to show that creative writing can be understood as an extension of childhood 'play' and that it shares the mechanism of the day-dream. The theoretical model underlying this thesis is the one developed in *The Interpretation of Dreams*: 'A strong experience in the present awakens in the creative writer a memory of an earlier experience (usually belonging to his childhood) from which there now proceeds a wish which finds its fulfilment in the creative work. The work itself exhibits elements of the recent provoking occasion as well as of the old memory' (PFL 14, 139: SE IX, 151). 'The connections that exist between the life of the writer and his works' are to be understood in the context of a thesis 'concerning the relation between phantasy and the three periods of time' – past, present and future – 'which are strung together, as it were, on the thread of the wish that runs through them' (PFL 14, 135: SE IX, 148). In this way Freud transmutes the stasis of recurrent fantasy into biographical time and duration (that relationship to past, present and future that the hermeneutic philosopher and historian Wilhelm Dilthey, for example, saw as essential both to historical consciousness and hermeneutic understanding[54]), but translates the life-course (and its intimate relationship to development, ambition, progress) into 'the thread of the wish'. This weaves, in the case of the male artist and day-dreamer, the most self-gratifying of yarns.

Inscriptions

Freud opens 'The dream-work' chapter by drawing an analogy between the dream and the 'rebus', or picture puzzle, composed of a mixture of pictographic, phonetic and ideogrammatic elements and thus requiring a different process of translation for each part. Freud's picture puzzle is largely modelled on the hieroglyphics (Egyptian in particular) which fascinated nineteenth-century philologists and contributed to the dream of recapturing an originary language and universal language. It also suggests, however, a modernist and even surrealist collage, 'form[ing] a poetical phrase of the greatest beauty and significance' (PFL 4, 382: SE IV, 278).

The theorist and historian of psychoanalyis Jean Laplanche has challenged Lacan's formulation 'the unconscious is structured like a language', arguing, in his *New Foundations for Psychanalysis*, that 'we adopt an explicitly anti-Freudian stance' in identifying the unconscious with verbal language.[55] Laplanche quotes a passage from Freud's essay 'The claims of psychoanalysis to scientific interest' in support of his claim. Freud wrote:

> I shall no doubt be overstepping common linguistic usage in postulating an interest in psychoanalysis on the part of philologists, that is of experts in *speech* [those who are concerned with the *logos*, with discourse JL]. For in what follows, 'speech' must be understood not merely to mean the expression of thought in words but to include the speech of gesture and every other method, such, for instance, as writing, by which mental activity can be expressed. (SE XIII, 176)

This passage suggests that Freud saw 'language' as inclusive of both the verbal and the non-verbal. Laplanche argues that verbal language was indeed secondary for Freud at a number of levels (historical, topographical, 'economic'), and points to the primacy of perception in Freud's model.

Laplanche finds the most productive aspect of Lacan's 'linguistic' model in his distinction between 'a signifier *of* (the signified)' and 'a signifier *to*'. The distinction, and Laplanche's account of the second category, the signifier *to*, as 'that aspect of the signifier which signifies to someone, which interpellates someone, in the sense that we can speak of an official signifying a court decision, or issuing a distraint order or prefectoral decree . . .

without its addressee necessarily knowing *what* it signifies'[56] recalls the language philosopher J. L. Austin's distinction between
'constative' and 'performative' utterances, between using language to describe states of affairs and *doing* things with words.[57]
Mapping the concept of 'the signifier *to*' on to the performative
utterance, Laplanche lends support to the idea of the 'perfor-
mativity' of dreams themselves. Such a concept illuminates a
number of Freud's dreams, as recorded and analysed in *The Interpretation of Dreams*, in which the dream comes to embody the
'wish' which is itself the fulfilment of the 'wish-fulfilment' theory
of dreams. It also maps on to recent theorisations of dreams and
their role in analysis, in which the significance of the dream lies
less in its latent meaning than in the event or fact of its having
been dreamed and of its recounting in the analytic session, in
which it becomes a form of signifier *to* the analyst.

Laplanche also gives credence to Lacan's 'image of hiero-
glyphs in the desert, or of cuneiform characters carved on a tablet
of stone . . . they are intended to signify something to us, but we
do not necessarily have a signified which we can ascribe to
them'.[58] Laplanche nominates an 'enigmatic signifier', which we
could read back into Freud's model of the 'rebus' and into his
account of the dream's navel, that point beyond which interpretation cannot go. Such a reading would imply the radical
untranslatability of dream language (or of certain of its elements),
its 'existence which is phenomenologically different',[59] without
suggesting that it is meaningless.

This could lead us back to a model of dream language as
ancient or 'archaic' inscription, thus describing the route of
Freud's philological inquiries. Alternatively, the focus on a hiero-
glyphic consciousness might bring us to a version of modernity as
the empire of signs. In a recent study, *The Lure of Dreams: Sigmund
Freud and the Construction of Modernity*, Harvie Ferguson argues
that Freud's is a theory of representations rather than of language.
He addresses the ways in which Freud's models of 'inscription'
upon the surfaces of the psychic apparatus provide an analogue
to the experience of modernity:

> The historically significant metaphors of mirror and writing pad, of
> reflection and inscription, are here combined into a single contra-

dictory mechanism. Both outer (objective) and inner (subjective) reality became fused to a single depthless surface upon which dimensionless associations are fleetingly brought to life . . . It is only as representations upon the same interactive surface that we become aware of anything, and it is only in terms of these that we can attempt to suggest the unconscious as the necessary deduction of a permanent process supporting the illumination of transitory signs.[60]

The more familiar account of Freudian theory as a 'depth psychology' is thus superseded by a focus on surfaces and surface inscriptions. This focus can also be found in an important essay on dreams from 1950, Erik Erikson's essay on the specimen dream, the dream of Irma's injection, in which Eriksen argues for 'an aesthetic receptivity to the surface of the dream, the product of the dreaming ego'.[61] This approach marked a shift from 'depth' to 'surface' in dream analysis, and an emphasis on the dream-function and its 'performative' status.

Harvie Ferguson and others, reading Freud as a theorist of modernity, also draw upon those aspects of his work which resonate most closely with the ideas of modernist thinkers such as Georg Simmel and Walter Benjamin. The links drawn between Freud and these thinkers relate primarily to their concepts of the 'shock' experience of modern life and to the image of modern consciousness as a receiving apparatus whose survival depends on its armouring against the shock of the new. That Freud's conception of the mental apparatus is also an account of modernity is not made fully explicit in his writings until *Beyond the Pleasure Principle* (1922), in which he describes the psychological effects of modern warfare, but his model of the surface of the mind, receiving but not retaining 'impressions', has striking echoes in Simmel's highly influential essay, 'The metropolis and mental life'.[62]

From the 'Project' (1895) to *Beyond the Pleasure Principle* (1922) and beyond, Freud sought to describe the mental apparatus through its dual, contradictory abilities to receive new impressions and to retain earlier ones, and he turned to the apparatus or technologies of writing and/or of vision as analogues for such processes. Thus, in his essay 'A note upon the mystic writing-pad', he uses 'a small contrivance' for writing, manufactured and sold under the name of the 'mystic writing-pad', to image the relationship between the system Pcpt.-Cs. ('which receives perceptions but retains no permanent trace of them, so that it can react like a clean sheet to every new perception') and the unconscious, which preserves 'permanent traces of the excitations which have been received' (PFL 11, 430: SE XIX, 228). The top sheets of the writing-pad (a celluloid sheet which acts like the 'protective shield' on the surface of the mental apparatus and a sheet of waxed paper beneath it which receives the writing/ stimuli) only hold the marks of writing as long as they are in contact with the waxen slab underneath it; once separated, all graphic traces are erased from the paper. It is the underlying slab which retains these traces permanently.

The modern device is also 'a return to the ancient method of writing on tablets of clay or wax'. While the wax slab retains permanent traces, the 'appearance and disappearance of the writing [can be compared] with the flickering-up and passing-away of consciousness in the process of perception' (PFL 11, 433: SE XIX, 231). The double temporalities here suggest the layering of past and present; they also articulate the paradox of modernity itself which, in Charles Baudelaire's striking formulation, is 'the ephemeral, the fugitive, the contingent, the half of art whose other half is the eternal and the immutable'.[63]

The optical unconscious

the interpretation of dreams is like a window through which we can get a glimpse of the interior of [the mental] apparatus. (PFL 4, 312: SE IV, 219)

In making the distinction between the receptive and the retentive parts of the mental apparatus, Freud alludes to Breuer's assertion in *Studies in Hysteria* that 'The mirror of a reflecting telescope cannot at the same time be a photographic plate' (PFL 4, 687 n. 1: SE V, 538 n. 1).[64] The analogy is linked to a network of optical images running throughout *The Interpretation of Dreams*, indicating the importance of instruments of vision in the nineteenth and early twentieth centuries as analogues for the workings of consciousness. In Chapter VII, in the section on 'Regression', for example, Freud writes:

we should picture the instrument which carries out our mental functions as resembling a compound microscrope or a photographic apparatus, or something of the kind. On that basis, physical locality will correspond to a point inside the apparatus at which one of the preliminary stages of an image comes into being. In the microscope and telescope, as we know, these occur in part at ideal points, regions in which no tangible component of the apparatus is situated. (PFL 4, 685: SE V, 536)

The purpose of the optical analogy here is to move away from a biologistic model of mental life, in which psychical events are held to take place in specific areas of the brain, and to substitute an account of psychical (or, indeed, 'virtual') locality. 'Everything that can be an object of our internal perception is *virtual*, like the image produced in a telescope by the passage of light-rays', Freud asserts (PFL 4, 771: SE V, 611). The microscope and telescope as analogues not only suggest a scientific precision, as I argued earlier, but produce another of the dream-book's 'non-lieux' – '*ein anderer Schauplatz*' (another scene).

The visual medium or 'apparatus' with which dreaming has the most striking affinities is film. Psychoanalysis and cinema emerged in tandem at the end of the nineteenth century – twin sciences or technologies of fantasy, dream, virtual reality and screen memory. For the surrealists, film both simulated dreams and brought dream-life into waking life. In 1930 Antonin Artaud wrote (linking cinema with dream-interpretation rather than with dreams themselves): 'If the cinema is not made to interpret dreams or what pertains to the realm of dreams in conscious life, it does not exist.'[65] As J.-B. Pontalis writes: 'the flux of images and their emotive charge combined with the state of the dreamer, enraptured by the "interior show" of a "*cinema parfait*", unite to fill, unrestrainedly and of their own accord, the living-dreaming subject's expectancies'.[66] Pontalis goes on to argue that the surrealist approach to dreams was largely at odds with that of Freud, who defended himself against 'the oneiric eloquence of the romantic tradition' (of which surrealism could be said to be a product) in his emphases on distortion, 'work', and interpretation.[67]

Freud expressed as little interest in cinema as in surrealism[68] but the relationship between dreams and films, dream and cinema, is nonetheless a profound and complex one. It has been explored most substantially by film theorists, although psycho-analytic theory has also produced its own accounts of the relationship between dreams (and mental life more generally) and cinema. The plethora of psychoanalytic and psychological studies of dream-life in the 1920s and 1930s was linked, as I argue elsewhere, to the development of film aesthetics, while writings on dreams and dream-life in the early twentieth century found new forms of assocation and analogy in film.[69] The intense debates over visual/verbal representations in the transition from silent to sound film in the 1920s had highly significant counterparts in the discussions over the visual or verbal dimensions, and the alphabetical or pictorial scripts, of dream-language.

Freud's account of the 'apparatus' of the mind had a crucial influence on later filmic 'apparatus theories', most notably the work of film theorists such as Jean-Louis Baudry and Christian Metz, who, in the 1970s, made a theoretical return to the machinery and apparatus of the cinema, constructing, as Stephen Heath has noted, a conceptual synthesis of the technological and metapsychological.[70] Constance Penley, in her feminist critique of apparatus theory (or, in the term she borrows, the 'bachelor machine') summarises it in these terms:

> Broadly speaking, the cinematic apparatus achieves its specific effects (the impression of reality, the creation of a fantasmatically unified spectator-subject, the production of the desire to return to the cinema) because of its success in re-enacting or mimicking the scene of the unconscious – the psychical apparatus – and duplicating its mechanisms by way of illusion.[71]

Metz took up the concept of cinema as an extension or prosthesis of the psyche, thus extending the implications of Freud's assertion in his 'A note upon the mystic writing-pad' that 'all the forms of auxiliary apparatus which we have invented for the improvement or intensification of our sensory functions are built on the same model as the sense organs themselves or portions of them: for instance, spectacles, photographic cameras, trumpets' (PFL 11, 430: SE XIX, 228). Baudry's work, as Penley notes, more radically 'identifies the psychical apparatus and topography with that of the cinematic apparatus. For Baudry, 'the cinema is . . . a faultless technological simulacrum of the systems Ucs and Pcs-Cs and their interrelations.'[72]

Baudry's essay 'The apparatus', drawing on Freud's 'Project for a scientific psychology' and on his discussion in Chapter VII of *The Interpretation of Dreams*, emphasizes the significance of 'regression'. 'Cinema', Baudry writes, 'offers a simulation of regressive movement which is characteristic of dream – the transformation of thoughts by means of figuration . . . It is evident that cinema is not dream: but it reproduces an impression of reality, it unlocks, releases a cinema effect which is comparable to the impression of reality caused by dream.'[73] The human subject, Baudry suggests, is driven 'to produce machines which would not only complement or supplement the workings of the secondary process [the 'prosthetic' apparatus], but which could represent his own overall functioning to him: he is led to produce mechanisms mimicking, simulating the apparatus which is no other than himself'.[74] In this account, the cinema ceases to be merely an analogy for the mental apparatus, and becomes a machine which replicates the very workings of the unconscious.

Film theory's fascination with psychoanalysis has its counterpart in psychoanalytic writings, in which a number of analysts and theorists have taken up the cinematic dimensions of such concepts as 'projection', 'scene' and 'screen[ing]'. Thus Sharpe, for example, wrote, in an account of 'dramatization' as a dream mechanism, that 'a film of moving pictures is projected on the screen of our private inner cinema'. She also explored in some detail an anxiety dream in which:

> A man is acting for the screen. He is to recite certain lines of the play. The photographers and voice recorders are there. At the critical moment the actor forgets his lines. Time and again he makes the attempt with no result. Rolls of film must have been spoilt.[75]

In Sharpe's analysis of the dream, the associations reveal an infantile situation in which 'the dreamer was once the onlooker when his parents were "operating" together. The baby was the original photographer and recorder and he stopped the parents in the "act" by noise. The baby did not forget his lines!'

> The 'return of the repressed' is given in the dream by the element 'rolls of film must have been wasted' telling us by the device of

metonymy, of a huge amount of faecal matter the baby was able to pass at that moment.

Illustrated in this dream are some of the profoundest activities of the psyche. We have the recording of sight and sound by the infant and the incorporation by the senses of sight and hearing of the primal scene. We have evidence of this incorporated scene by its projection into the dream dramatization. The modern invention of the screen of the cinema is pressed into service as the appropriate symbol, the screen being the modern external device corresponding to the internal dream picture mechanism.[76]

Sharpe's analysis strongly recalls (while also making explicit the film/dream analogy) Freud's account of one of the most famous dreams of psychoanalysis, his patient 'the Wolf-Man's' childhood dream of observing, through a window, a number of white wolves sitting on a tree and looking at him. 'He had woken up and seen something', Freud comments. 'The attentive looking, which in the dream was ascribed to the wolves, should rather be shifted on to him. At a decisive point, therefore, a transposition has taken place' (PFL 9, 265: SE XVII, 34–5). Behind the content of the dream, Freud suggests, lies the 'primal scene', the *Urszene*, in which the very young child observed the parents' sexual intercourse.

In *The Image and the Past*, the psychoanalyst Bertram Lewin comments on such scenes more generally in the context of the 'constructions' made by the analyst, which fill the analysand's 'memory gap with a properly ordered picture or story about something now forgotten':[77]

The extent to which the visual is stressed in constructions is impressive. Most constructed memories and most recovered, sometimes attested, memories are of scenes, notably of course of the primal scene and of the difference between the sexes. Notable too is the frequent immobility of the processed mental picture, whether screen memory, dream element, or fantasy. They are 'stills', whereas the events from which they stem are often full of motion. They are as if immobilized for better viewing.[78]

In the mid-1940s, Lewin published an influential paper, 'Sleep, the mouth and the dream screen', outlining his concept of the 'dream screen'.[79] Whereas commentators on Freud's model of dream-language as inscription have noted that inscriptions require a writing surface (hence the importance of the 'mystic writing-pad' as an analogy for the mental apparatus), Lewin explored the idea that projections require a screen:

> The dream screen, as I define it, is the surface on which a dream appears to be projected. It is the blank background, present in the dream though not necessarily seen, and the visually perceived action in ordinary manifest dream contents takes place on it or before it.[80]

In Lewin's account, the dream screen is the hallucinatory representation of the mother's breast, a repetition of the infant's experience of breast-feeding, which once acted as a prelude to sleep. The forgetting of dreams, Lewin argues, is often imaged as a rolling up or away of the dream screen, repeating the experience of the withdrawal of the breast:

> When one falls asleep, the breast is taken into one's perceptual world: it flattens out or approaches flatness, and when one wakes up it disappears, reversing the events of its entrance. A dream appears to be projected on this flattened breast – the dream screen – provided, that is, that the dream is visual; for if there is no visual content the dream screen would be blank, and the manifest content would consist solely of impressions from other fields of perception.[81]

The distinction between the screen and the dream-images projected onto it also allows for a distinction to be drawn between sleep, (the blank screen) and dream (the play and projection of visual images). This distinction was left largely untheorized in *The Interpretation of Dreams*, although Freud also claims that the wish to sleep motivates all dreaming, the function of dreams being to protect sleep. Lewin extends this in the claim that 'the dream screen is sleep itself', not only the breast, but also 'that content of sleep or the dream which fulfils the wish to sleep ... The blank dream screen is the copy of primary infantile sleep'.[82] (Lewin qualified this in a later essay, 'Reconsideration of the dream screen', arguing that the dream screen is not a real but a 'hallucinatory fulfilment of a wish to sleep'.[83]) Despite the centrality of the cinematic metaphor, Lewin is in fact less concerned with the visual contents of the dream (which 'fulfil wishes other than the wish to sleep'[84]), focusing primarily on the phenomenon of the blank screen. In 'Reconsideration of the dream screen',

Lewin notes that the Wolf-Man was looking at a closed window at the beginning of his famous dream, 'that is, at a glass dream screen'.[85]

In 'Inferences from the dream screen', Lewin raises the question of remembering and forgetting dreams as an issue of the preservation or destruction of a record:

> a dreamer may distinguish the dream text from that on which it is recorded, so that paper, film, or phonograph record, all representatives of the dream screen, may be preserved, while the content is subjected to further distortion and more or less effaced. The dreamer who mars or effaces the record has two motives: he wishes to destroy or censor the dream content, he wishes to preserve the dream screen.[86]

Lewin pursues the issues of representation and transcription so central to Freud's understanding of the dream. The distinction between dream content and dream screen in the quotation above also recalls (while changing the relations, so that the 'screen' becomes imbued with affect, is medium and memory, rather than a purely receptive surface) the division into the receptive and retentive parts of the mental apparatus which characterizes Freud's models of perception, consciousness and the unconscious.

As Jacques Derrida noted, in 'Freud and the scene of writing', 'the necessity of accounting simultaneously . . . for the permanence of the trace and for the virginity of the receiving substance, for the engraving of furrows and for the perennially intact bareness of the perceptive surface', motivated all Freud's analogical imaginings.[87] Yet whereas Derrida argues for a conceptual progression from the optical metaphors of *The Interpretation of Dreams* to the scriptural model of the writing machine in 'A note upon the mystic writing-pad', finding only the latter instrument capable of representing the complex dualities of Freud's model of mind and memory, the theoretical work discussed in this section suggests the possibility of holding the optical (understood, crucially, as screen as well as projector) and the scriptural in tandem and, indeed, of showing their interconnectedness.

'The dream screen', Lewin wrote in his earliest essay on the topic, 'may partake of cutaneous qualities; the original fusion of breast and the sleeper's skin in babyhood may enable the skin to register itself on the dream screen.'[88] Lewin's equation of 'skin' and 'screen' has been taken up by, among others, the psychoanalytic theorist Didier Anzieu, who has worked extensively on *The Interpretation of Dreams* as a work of self-analysis and whose more recent work explores questions of ego boundaries, primarily through the imagery of skin and envelope.[89]

Anzieu's work, like that of some of the other theorists discussed above, extends Freud's claim in 'The metapsychology of dreams' (1917) that 'A dream is . . . among other things, a *projection*: an externalization of an internal process' (PFL 11, 231: SE XIV, 223) and, in 'The ego and the id' (1923), that 'The ego is first and foremost a bodily ego: it is not merely a surface entity, but is itself the projection of a surface' (PFL 11, 364: SE XIX, 26). Freud's emphases in this essay on the ego as a bodily 'projection,' and on the body, and its surface, as 'a place from which both external and internal perceptions may spring' (PFL 11, 364: SE XIX, 25), allows us to bring together the concepts of 'projection' as 'prosthesis' (the body extended or projected into the world) and as a 'screening', whereby not only the subject's body but his/her relationship to the 'skin', the screen/surface, of the other (the mother) is projected or imaged. We can thus understand the (gendered) accounts of perception discussed in this section as accounts of the functioning of a corporeal ego which conjoins the body and the external world, and the ego as, in Elizabeth Grosz's words, 'something like an internal screen onto which the illuminated and projected images of the body's outer surfaces are directed'.[90] In reading these emphases back into *The Interpretation of Dreams*, we are also reminded how substantially the 'body' is figured in Freud's dream-book, despite his unease over the 'somatic element' in dreams, and of the extent to which mind/body and inner perception/outer world dichotomies are crossed and transgressed.

In 'The film of the dream', a chapter of *The Skin Ego*, Anzieu pursues the concept of the dream as an impressionable 'pellicule', whose dual meaning encompasses both the fine membrane protecting and enveloping parts of natural organisms and the film used in photography, 'the thin layer serving as a base for the sensitive coating that is to receive the impression'. Whereas 'the skin ego' separates inside and outside, the dream is a 'pellicule' which puts external stimuli and internal instinctual pressures on the same plane, flattening out their differences':

> it is a fragile membrane, quick to break and be dissipated (hence anxious awakening), an ephemeral membrane (it lasts only as long as the dream lasts . . .)
>
> Moreover, the dream is an impressionable 'pellicule'. It registers mental images which are usually visual in nature, though they do occasionally have subtitles or a sound track; sometimes the images are stills, as in photography, but most often they are strung together in an animated sequence as in cinematography or, to use the most up-to-date comparison, a video film. What is activated here is one of the functions of the skin ego, that of a sensitive surface, capable of registering traces and inscriptions. Otherwise the skin ego, or at least the dematerialized and flattened image of the body, provides the screen against which the figures in the dream which symbolize or personify the psychological forces and agencies in conflict appear. The film may be defective, the reel may get stuck or let in light, and the dream is erased. If everything goes well, we can on waking develop the film, view it, re-edit it or even project it in the form of a narrative told to another person.[91]

In Anzieu's striking account, one of the dream's functions is to repair the skin ego, 'daily reconstructing the psychical envelope' which has been damaged, 'riddled with holes', by the encroachments of daily experience: 'The holes in the skin ego . . . are transposed by the work of representation to locations where the scenarios of the dream may then unfold . . . The nocturnal dream . . . re-weaves by night those parts of the skin ego that have become unravelled by day under the impact of exogenous and endogenous stimuli'.[92] Anzieu thus draws extensively on the concept of 'trauma' as a wound to, or breach in, the 'protective shield' on the surface of (or, rather, surrounding and enveloping) the psychical apparatus, while emphasizing that the dream has a healing or reparative function. Like many post-Freudian analysts and theorists, Anzieu is thus less concerned with the dream's meaning and its interpretation than with the function of the 'good dream', and indeed the importance of the very capacity for dreaming, for the damaged psyche. Such accounts echo the words of a mid-nineteenth-century scientist, Johannes Purkinje, quoted by Freud: 'Many of the spirit's wounds which are being constantly re-opened during the day are healed by sleep, which covers them and shields them from fresh injury' (PFL 4, 154: SE IV, 83).

Lewin, Anzieu and others, in their cinematographic analogies, have shifted the emphasis from the psychical/optical 'apparatus' as machine to 'film' itself (the recording medium), bringing together, as I have suggested, the optical and the scriptural through an emphasis on inscription and on the play of sign upon surface. A further context for this discussion is the psychoanalytic concept of 'transitional space', theorized most substantially by the analyst Donald Winnicott. As Sara Flanders writes, in her introduction to *The Dream Discourse Today*: 'All cultural phenomena take place in transitional space, all creativity, either in a formally defined space, the boundaries of the page, the canvas, the stage, or, internally, through the capacity to stage an inner play.'[93] The importance of the dream-space is also emphasized by Pontalis – 'every dream presupposes a space where the presentation can take place' – and linked to the primacy of the visible in dreams, which, Pontalis argues, has not been dwelt upon enough: 'the dream is what makes things visible, what gives its visible place to *déjà vu*, which had become invisible'.[94]

A critical question arises at this point, however: where is the dreamer located in the dream-space? Is he or she a spectator or an actor in the theatre of the dream? The philosopher and psychoanalytic theorist Mikkel Borch-Jacobsen has argued, in his work on fantasy and representation, that we need to 'subject to a thoroughgoing reinterpretation metaphors on which Freud and his successors depended heavily: metaphors of "scene", "stage", and "staging" – in other words, all the "representative theatricality" that persistently subtends the psychoanalytic theory of desire'.[95] This is not only because such metaphors seem too closely tied to the theatricalities of Freud's (pre-psychoanalytic) contemporaries – as in Charcot's theatres of hysteria – but because they are insufficiently attuned to the cleavage between the subject who plays a part in the spectacle and the subject who is a spectator – that is, between:

> the stage where one is playing – the 'other stage', 'the other place', Freud writes, doubtless meaning that it is unlocalizable, unplaceable, irreducible to any spatiality and to any visibility – and

the stage that one sees, the stage on which one speaks. The former will always be invincibly inaccessible to the latter ... I am *in* the fantasy, there where I am the other 'before' seeing him, there where I am the mimetic model even 'before' he arises in front of me, there where I am acting out before any distancing, any drawing back: a nonspecular identification (blind mimesis) in which consists (if he/it consists) the entire 'subject' of the fantasy. That is to say, unquestionably, the 'subject', no more and no less.[96]

For Borch-Jacobsen, 'mimesis' (as a form of identification) precedes desire: desire (and the 'wish' which fuells the dream) is itself mimetic, in that desire is always the desire to be (in the place of) another. The dream-work, in this account, is 'exclusively preoccupied with the relation of likeness': 'the otherness called "unconscious" no longer designates, rigorously speaking, that part of myself about which I wish to remain ignorant; rather it designates my identity or my very sameness *as that of another* – the *starke Gemeinsannkeit* [strong affinity] that connects me with an other that I am "myself" '.[97] The question of identity as identification is taken up in the following section.

Autobiographics

Self-analysis: 'I always find it uncanny when I can't understand someone in terms of myself'[98]

It has long been recognized that psychoanalysis was, in crucial ways, dependent on autobiographical acts. Derrida posed what he called a 'simplified' question about the relationship between Freud's 'autobiography' and psychoanalytic theory: 'How can an autobiographical writing, in the abyss of an unterminated self-analysis, give to a world-wide institution *its* birth'.[99] Shoshana Felman writes that, from her own analysis, she 'learned how dreams are indeed, concretely and materially, the royal road to the unconscious, how they were susceptible of telling us *about our own autobiography another story* than the one we knew or had believed to be our own'. This 'drove me to look closely at the way in which Freud's theory implies, in fact, a *revolution* in the very *theory of autobiography,* and at the way in which, in writing down his new theory of dreams *Freud was in effect writing his own autobiography'.*[100]

The Interpretation of Dreams, rather than *An Autobiographical Study*, defined by Michel Neyraut as 'periautobiography', an account of the origins and development of a professional or intellectual career,[101] has come to be seen as Freud's 'true' autobiography. It is seen to embody 'the person' of Freud as the 'impersonality' of *An Autobiographical Study* does not. It is indeed striking that the later, 'official' autobiography does not mention the self-analysis, as if to drive a wedge between the self-analysis which made 'autobiography' possible, and the text which was, generically and institutionally, designated as Freud's autobiography.

Freud's self-analysis of the 1890s and the autobiographical act of *The Interpretation of Dreams*, although inextricably linked, are not identical with each other. *The Interpretation of Dreams* is a textual artefact, whereas it is less certain where and in what forms Freud's 'self-analysis' exists. Marthe Robert suggests that there is reason to believe that it continued beyond 1902, the year in which Freud's letters to Fliess informing him about its progress ceased, and 'that Freud had to resume it at certain intervals over a long period of time. He never claimed that it was completely successful.'[102] The 'self-analysis', however systematically undertaken, was worked through in multiple ways: in self-observation, in dreams which feed into the themes with which the waking Freud was concerned, in letters, notebooks, theoretical writings, autobiographical fragments, and in *The Interpetation of Dreams* itself. In psychoanalytic terms, the 'self-analysis' is indeed definitionally impossible. 'My self-analysis is still interrupted', Freud wrote to Fliess. 'I can only analyse myself with objectively acquired knowledge (as if I were a stranger); self-analysis is really impossible, otherwise there would be no [neurotic] illness' (14 November 1897, F/F, 281). This contradiction, as John Forrester suggests in his essay in this volume, is in part resolved by Freud and his commentators' emphases on his 'transferential' relationships with interlocutors. The relationship with Fliess, and the letters to him, written at one point on an almost daily basis, enabled the positions of analyst and analysand to become occupied in more mobile ways than the term 'self-analysis' would suggest.

Freud's biographers have also, however, represented the self-analysis as an isolated act – both singular and lonely – and as unique, founding and final. Ernest Jones described it in the terms of a heroic, epic journey, on the model of Carl Jung's mid-life 'descent into the underworld':[103] 'In the summer of 1897 . . . Freud undertook his most heroic feat – a psycho-analysis of his own unconscious. It is hard for us nowadays to imagine how momentous this achievement was, that difficulty being the fate of most pioneering exploits. Yet the uniqueness of the feat remains. Once done it is done forever. For no one again can be the first to explore those depths.'[104]

In this account, Freud's unconscious is universalized to stand for everyone's unconscious. This is also an essential strategy for Freud himself, in his generation of, in Derrida's terms, a universal theory from his self-analysis. Freud's extrapolations from self to other and from other to self are circular. He finds Oedipus in himself, universalizes the 'complex', and then returns it to the self as a question of empathy and identification. His letter to Fliess is worth quoting again: 'I have found love of the mother and jealousy of the father in my own case too, and now believe it to be a general phenomenon of early childhood . . . the Greek myth seizes on a compulsion which everyone recognizes because he has felt traces of it in himself' (15 October 1897, F/F, 272)

John Forrester's essay analyses such devices and strategies in detail, showing how Freud's complex identification of and with his putative readers creates 'the reader' of the Freudian text. The success of Freud's specificiation of the reader-function is revealed in the ways in which Freud's followers used his dreams as a common property – as the coinage of psychoanalysis. The reader of *The Interpretation of Dreams* is, moreover, a Freudian in the sense that he/she, like Freud, is willing to study his/her dreams, to engage in a self-analysis. As with models of identity and identification in the text more generally, the place of the reader is not a stable one: 'the reader switches, from paragraph to paragraph, from being the censor from whom the truth must be hidden to being Freud's complicit partner' in the dream's secrets. Such shifts and instabilities make possible, however, the exchange between author and reader.

In the Preface to the first edition Freud writes: 'I can only express a hope that readers of this book will put themselves in my difficult situation and treat me with indulgence' (PFL 4, 45: SE IV, xxiv), whilst he prefaces his discussion of 'The specimen dream of psychoanalysis', the dream of Irma's injection, with these words: 'And now I must ask the reader to make my interests his own for quite a while and to plunge, along with me, into the minutest details of my life: for a transference of this kind is peremptorily demanded by our interest in the hidden meaning of dreams' (PFL 4, 180: SE IV, 105–6). Identity and identification are the most central and the most complex structures addressed by Freud in *The Interpretation of Dreams*, as identity becomes increasingly defined as the product of identifications.

In the 1925 edition of the text, Freud illustrates his claim that 'my ego may be represented in a dream several times over, now directly and now through identification with extraneous persons' by likening the multiple representation of the ego to the recurrence of the personal pronoun 'I' in such phrases as 'when *I* think what a healthy child *I* was'. (PFL 4, 435: SE IV, 323) This recalls the multiplication of the 'I' in autobiographical writing more generally – not only the 'I' as narrator and the 'I' as the object of narration, but the 'surplus articulation' of the 'I', dramatically illustrated in Rousseau's famous sentence in the *Dialogues*: 'it was necessary for me to say how, if I were another man, I would see a man like me'.[105] Freud is thus using the complex linguistic model of the paradigmatic autobiographical sentence as an analogue for the dream, and more specifically for multiple identifications in dreams – autobiography is thus not just a content in *The Interpretation of Dreams* but a structural model for the dream itself.

Freud's bodies

In the early sections of *The Interpretation of Dreams*, Freud gives pragmatic reasons for the use of his own dreams as examples. While he does in fact use his patients' dreams quite extensively throughout the text, he suggests that doing so would demand an untenable amount of background discussion of their case-histories and 'an investigation of the nature and aetiological determinants of the psychoneuroses' at odds with his desire to use dream interpretation to reach an understanding of the psychology of the neuroses:

> Thus it comes about that I am led to my own dreams, which offer a copious and convenient material, derived from an approximately

normal person and relating to multifarious occasions of daily life. No doubt I shall be met by doubts of the trustworthiness of 'self-analyses' of this kind; and I shall be told that they leave the door open to arbitrary conclusions. In my judgement the situation is in fact more favourable in the case of self-observation than in that of other people; at all events we may make the experiment and see how far self-analysis takes us with the interpretation of dreams. But I have other difficulties to overcome, which lie within myself. There is some natural hesitation about revealing so many intimate facts about one's mental life; nor can there be any guarantee against misinterpretation by strangers. But it must be possible to overcome such hesitations. (PFL 4, 180–1: SE IV, 105)

Freud's letter to Fliess of 9 June 1898 not only confirms that Freud was sending Fliess his dream book as he wrote it, but reveals that Fliess censored aspects of the work:

So the dream is condemned. Now that the sentence has been passed, however, I would like to shed a tear over it and confess that I regret it and that I have no hopes of finding a better one as a substitute. As you know, a beautiful dream and no indiscretion – do not coincide. Let me know at least which topic it was to which you took exception and where you feared an attack by a malicious critic. Whether it is my anxiety, or the *Dalles*, or my being without a fatherland? So that I can omit what you designate in a substitute dream, because I can have dreams like that to order. (F/F, 315)

Freud complied with Fliess's suggestion (though we do not know precisely why Fliess 'condemned' the dream), but continued to refer to the dream in his letters. 'I have not yet ceased mourning the lost dream', he wrote on 20 June 1898: 'As if in spite, I recently had a substitute dream in which a house constructed of building blocks collapsed ("We had built a *staatliches* house") and which, because of this connection, could not be used' (F/F, 317). Four months later, he referred again to the 'lost dream' in ways which sound very much a reproach to Fliess: 'The dream [book] is lying still, immutably . . . the gap in the psychology as well as the gap left by the [removal of the] thoroughly analyzed sample [dream] are obstacles to bringing it to a conclusion which so far I have not been able to overcome' (23 October 1898, F/F, 332). The irony is that the 'substitute' dream which took the place of the 'sample' or 'specimen' dream reveals or, rather, disguises, a scandal at the very dawning of psychoanalysis – one in which Fliess was centrally implicated.

This dream, which has attracted a host of interpreters, and is taken up in James Hopkins's and in Stephen Frosh's essays in this collection, is known as 'The dream of Irma's injection'. Occupying Chapter II of *The Interpretation of Dreams*, the dream stages the scene of a female patient examined by male doctors. As Freud's interpretation of the dream unfolds, fragment by fragment, the dream begins to cohere around a number of themes: professional responsibility and medical incompetence; women's secrecy or 'recalcitrance'; organic versus hysterical illness; self-recrimination and self-justification. In Freud's analysis, the dream is structured around a series of substitutions: 'now three similiar situations came to my recollection involving my wife, Irma and the dead Mathilde. The identity of these situations had evidently enabled me to substitute the three figures for one another in the dream' (PFL 4, 195: SE IV, 118).

The dream's structure, as a number of commentators have noted, is ternary. Anzieu explores this 'pattern' in detail, pointing to the ways in which three groups of three (women, Freud's medical superiors, his medical equals) is represented by the chemical formula for 'Trimethylamin', which Freud saw 'printed in heavy type' in the dream. The sight of the inscription is, for Anzieu, 'a reading, a decipherment', transcribing the interpretative act in the dream itself. The ternary structure of the chemical formula is matched in the theory of the three types of neurone that Freud was to use as the basis for his formula of the nervous apparatus, as outlined in the 'Project' and in the letters to Fliess. The theory, Anzieu argues, 'a triad expanding into other triads – matches the formal construction of the dream, where figures mostly appear in sets of three. In other words, the dream contains a symbolic representation of its own structure'.[106]

For Anzieu, as for numerous theorists and historians of psychoanalyis, the significance of the dream thus lies predominantly in its complex self-reflexivity. The 'specimen dream' of psychoanalysis stages the scene of patient and doctor; it also represents 'the self-analysis that Freud had been intending to carry out for some time using one of his dreams – in fact this very one'. The Irma dream not only expresses Freud's wish to carry out self-analysis but, Anzieu argues, 'makes a kind of inventory of the body'.[107] It can thus be linked with the dream of self-dissection, which I discuss below. The house–body imagery further recalls Scherner's work on dream symbolism, mentioned approvingly by Freud in Chapter I, and anticipates Freud's later discussions of 'representation by symbols', including those 'biographical' dreams in which the body and/or the 'sexual history' of the dreamer is represented in and through a continuous narrative.

If in one reading the 'body' of the dream is Freud's, in another a woman's body is simultaneously revealed and concealed by the dream. In biographical terms, the publication of the correspondence between Freud and Fliess showed that, while the Irma of the dream was almost certainly Anna Hammerschlag-Lichtheim, the daughter of Freud's former Hebrew teacher Samuel Hammerschlag and a close friend of Martha Freud, Freud's patient Emma Eckstein also lies behind the dream-figure of Irma. In 1894, Fliess had examined Emma, and determined that her 'symptoms' would be alleviated by an operation on her nose. After the operation in early 1895, Emma, Freud wrote to Fliess, was not doing well: he called in a surgeon, who discovered that Fliess had left a length of surgical gauze inside Emma's nasal cavity. Its removal caused a haemorrhage which nearly cost Emma her life. After some weeks she began to recover, and Freud, as Lisa Appignanesi and John Forrester note, 'began tentatively to entertain once again hypotheses concerning the psychic origins of her bleeding'.[108] Freud's uncomfortable manoeuvring in his correspondence at this time – his contradictory hinting at Fliess's responsibility for the near-tragedy and his insistence that Fliess was in no way at fault – is represented in the dream's alternations between self-justification and self-recrimination.

The apparent 'triumph' of self-justification in the dream is also the means by which the wish-fulfilment theory of dreams, and hence the central thesis of Freud's dream book, is validated. Freud saw the dream as foundational. 'Do you suppose', he wrote to Fliess in a letter describing a later visit to Bellevue, the house where he had had the dream, 'that some day a marble table will be placed on the house, inscribed with these words? – In This House, on July 24th, 1895 the Secret of Dreams was revealed to Dr. Sigm. Freud' (12 June 1900, F/F, 417).

The dream of Irma's injection could be read as Freud's wishful dream of the birth of psychoanalysis emerging from his relationship with Fliess, and of the overcoming of female 'resistance'. In another interpretation, the dream becomes that of the emergence of psychoanalysis out of the riddle, 'knot' or unknowable 'navel' of femininity and sexual difference. As Shoshana Felman argues, the dream 'can be said to be the very dream from which psychoanalysis proceeds, because it is also a dream about femininity, and about Freud's relationship – professional and personal – to femininity'.[109] In Felman's reading, 'the dream's wish is, precisely . . . *to conceive psychoanalysis from the female patient*', and the dream is to be understood as a 'knot' of competing pregnancies. It is pregnant with the 'birth' of psychoanalysis and with Freud's discoveries; it is pregnant with the actual rather than metaphorical pregnancy of Freud's wife, carrying the daughter, Anna, who would continue her father's legacy and devote her life to his discoveries.[110] Psychoanalysis, in Felman's account, is born out of the unknown of gender difference.

The death of his father, Freud wrote, shaped the dream-book, but the text is also haunted by the lost maternal body (as Bertram Lewin's 'dream screen' hallucinates the infant's connection with the mother's breast). *The Interpretation of Dreams* could indeed be read as a form of navigation or exploration of a woman's body, as Freud leads the reader through the narrow defiles and wooded promontories that he also represents as dream symbols for the female form. The dream's 'navel' is also the 'spot' at which the subject is connected to, and disconnected from, the maternal body, as the dream, and Freud's text, is connected to, and disconnected from, an unknowable femininity. Freud explores dreams which (anticipating Lewin's account) reconnect the dreamer to the lost mother: 'Love and hunger, I reflected, meet at a woman's breast' (PFL 4, 295: SE IV, 204), although for Freud (the desire for) the breast is also a 'screen' for 'a more serious [desire] which could not be so openly displayed' (PFL 4, 329: SE IV 233). In other dreams and their analyses, the woman's body signifies the horror of castration and of the female genitals 'as a wound' (PFL 4,

291: SE V, 201). Death and the feminine become inextricably intertwined, as the womb becomes, in the language of the dream, both birthplace and tomb. The place of the feminine and of feminine identifications in Freud's dream book are taken up more fully by Stephen Frosh and Robert Young in their chapters in this volume.

While 'the specimen dream' represents the body of a woman both opened up and resistant to male investigation, other dreams of Freud's place his own body, his person, on the dissecting table. Freud made a clear link between his dream of self-dissection and his own self-analysis: 'the task which was imposed on me in the dream of carrying out a dissection *of my own body* was thus my *self-analysis* which was linked up with my giving an account of my dreams' (PFL 4, 587: SE V, 454). Freud takes up his dream of self-dissection more than once, the last time to add a form of rider to his earlier interpretations:

> If we turn back to the dream about the dissection of my own pelvis, it will be recalled that in the dream itself I missed the gruesome feeling (*Grauen*) appropriate to it. Now this was a wish-fulfilment in more than one sense. The dissection meant the self-analysis which I was carrying out, as it were, in the publication of this present book about dreams – a process which had been so distressing to me in reality. A wish then arose that I might get over this feeling of distaste; hence it was that I had no gruesome feeling (*Grauen*) in the dream. But I should have also have been very glad to miss going grey – *Grauen* in the other sense of the word. I was already going quite grey, and the grey of my hair was another reminder that I must not delay any longer and, as we have seen, the thought that I should have to leave it to my children to reach the goal of my difficult journey forced its way through to representation at the end of the dream. (PFL 4, 615–6: SE V, 477–8)

The motif of self-dissection takes up other processes of self-referentiality – the self-dissection, the self-analysis and the dream book which is both the process and the result of this self-observation. The deferred gratification to which Freud appeals – that his children will be able to fulfil the wishes he must renounce – is in some ways belied by the performative nature of the dream and its analysis – the dream book *is* in fact the fulfilment of Freud's wish, *is* his ambition.

The self-dissection dream – which occurs in the section of the 'dream-work' chapter called 'Intellectual activity in dreams', follows on from 'Absurd dreams'. In both these sections, Freud points to dreams of death – particularly the death of fathers – dreams pointing to father–son relationships and dreams of ambition. Freud's self-dissection – his self-analysis – was in large part motivated and shaped by his responses to his father's death and this in turn shaped the writing of *The Interpretation of Dreams*. Freud suggests a further link between self-dissection/self-analysis and the representation of one's own death. He asserts that dreams in which a dead person figures in the guise of a living one means that 'the dreamer is dreaming of his own death'. But, he adds, 'I willingly confess to a feeling that dream-interpretation is far from having revealed the secrets of dreams of this character' (PFL 4, 560: SE V, 431).

The representation of death is also a particularly complex and troubling terrain in autobiographical discourse. Implicit in the search for totality in traditional autobiographical criticism is the paradox that autobiography *ex hypothesi* cannot be written from the standpoint beyond the grave which would secure a totalizing vision of the life. By extension, for the autobiographer to aim at this totalizing vision would itself be to aim for death. Recent theorists have constructed theories of autobiography in which death, as much as life, motivates or determines autobiographical discourse. The simulation of death – as in Montaigne's *Essais* – becomes a way of writing an experience which can be said to be the only experience which is properly one's own and unique.[111] Its communication constitutes the writing self as an individual subject. More generally, the distanciation from self implied by the autobiographical project has been assimilated, as in Freud's dream, to a kind of self-dissection, in which 'experience' can also take on the sense of 'experiment'.

Identity and identification

Freud's dreams are strikingly preoccupied with questions of ambition, heroism and professional advancement in a cold climate. They are, in a sense, a condensation of much of the intellectual and political history of the period, as Carl Schorske's important essay 'Politics and patricide in Freud's *Interpretation of Dreams*' was one of the first to explore.[112] The reader of *The Interpretation of Dreams* becomes aware of Freud's Jewishness, the 'denominational considerations' (PFL 4, 218: SE IV, 137) to which he alludes throughout *The Interpretation of Dreams* in the context of on the one hand emancipation and assimilation and on the other the rise of anti-Semitism and nationalisms in nineteenth-century Austria-Hungary and Germany. A number of Freud's dreams – 'The autodidasker dream', 'The Count Thun (revolutionary dream)', 'The my son the Myops dream', 'The "*non vixit*" dream' – take their meanings from these contexts.

Jacques le Rider's recent study *Modernity and Crises of Identity* is concerned with gender and Jewish identity in fin-de-siècle Vienna. Le Rider claims that all questions of identity and identification in Freud's work, and in *The Interpretation of Dreams* in particular, stem from the identity crises of this period: 'Freudian psychoanalysis is one of the theories which give an account of the human condition in the age of chronic identity crisis. Strictly speaking . . . the notion of identity fades under analysis into a more or less stable series of identifications.'[113] Le Rider points to the cultivation of private writing as a genre at the turn of the century. Hoffmansthal, Schnitzler and Musil ruminated in their diaries on the theme of identity crisis which they were putting at the heart of their work, while *The Interpretation of Dreams*, the founding text of psychoanalysis, 'comes over partly as a combination of a private notebook (accounts of dreams noted down day by day) and an autobiography'.[114] Each writer brought to bear self-narrating and self-fictionalizing elements on his identity crisis.

Sander Gilman's recent and contentious work on Freud pushes still further the reading of psychoanalysis as a specific response to anti-semitic representations.[115] In *The Case of Sigmund Freud* he makes the self/other relationship central, arguing that: 'Inherent in the very definitions of the biological and medical sciences of the day are the 'caste standards' that label Jews as unable to undertake the task of science because of their inherently pathological nature. At the same time the claims for 'universalism' made by the science of the day gave these claims a neutral face . . . The Jewish scientist was forced to deal with this claim'.[116] We thus find 'Jewish biological and medical scientists of the late nineteenth century forced to deal with what is for them the unstated central epistemological problem of late nineteenth-century biological science: how one could be the potential subject of a scientific study at the same time as one had the role of the observer: how one could be the potential patient at the same moment one was supposed to be the physician'.[117] The issues of universalism and particularism, self and other, the observer and the observed, are, in Gilman's account, determined by perceptions of race, while the pathologies that psychoanalysis identifies and seeks to remedy are in large part those that anti-Semitic society projected on to the Jew.

The tension between the universalizing desire of psycho-analysis and the particularistic charge that this discourse is merely the masked language of the Jews exemplifies, for Gilman, the burden under which the Jewish scientist of the fin-de-siècle struggled. These issues have particular saliency for *The Interpretation of Dreams*, as the question of the aspiration to a universalist scientific perspective, running concurrently with the image of the pathologized Jew, troubles the model of subject–object relations and brings to the fore the question of *what* Freud was seeing when he undertook to look at, and into, himself. In the models developed by Schorske, le Rider, Gilman and others, the self is split by historical, political and 'racial' configurations as well as psychical ones. The importance of this work is that it shows that questions of history, politics and culture are not merely a 'background' to psychoanalysis, but bound into its foundations.

For Gilman, one of the symptomatic aspects of *The Interpretation of Dreams* is Freud's use of Francis Galton's composite photography as an analogue for the processes of the dream-work, and 'condensation' in particular. The scientist and eugenist Francis Galton used composite photographs to construct images of racial and criminal 'types', including composite photographs of Jews. 'The success of the "Jewish type" convinced Galton that the future of composite photography lay largely in ethnological and genetic work', Galton's pupil and biographer Karl Pearson wrote.[118] For Gilman, the composite photographs are central to racialized images of a Jewish physiognomy and, indeed, 'of the Jew's very nature'; however, in adopting Galton's model of seeing in *The Interpretation of Dreams* (and not Charcot's, as in *Studies in*

Hysteria), Freud also sought to appropriate the gaze of science itself: 'this process of seeing that is denied to the eye of the Jewish scientist'.[119]

There could, however, be other interpretations of Freud's use of the composite photograph as analogue. Like Freud, Galton was interested in memory and visuality, but his main concern was with the placing of human knowledge on a more scientific basis. The human mind is, he wrote, 'a most imperfect apparatus for the elaboration of general ideas . . . The criterion of a perfect mind would lie in its capacity of always creating images of a truly generic kind, deduced from the whole range of its past experiences. General impressions are never to be trusted.'[120] Composite photographs are used as models for generic mental images, which are to be distinguished from our more vague and faulty general impressions.

The word 'generic', as Galton notes, 'presupposes a genus, that is to say, a collection of individuals who have much in common, and among whom medium characteristics are very much more frequent than extreme ones. The same idea is sometimes expressed by the word typical, which was much used by Quetelet . . . whose idea of a type lies at the basis of his statistical views.'[121] This is the 'mean' or 'average' man (*l'homme moyen*) posited by Quetelet (the founder of modern statistics), in whom, as in composite portraits, 'the common traits reinforce each other and the extreme ones disappear'.[122]

These debates suggest a different reading of Freud's 'universalizing' strategies. First, we could understand the 'I' of Freud's self-analytical and theoretical project not only as 'universal man' but as 'mean man'. 'I always find it uncanny when I can't understand someone in terms of myself' might then represent the conjuncture of an Enlightenment universalism and a late nineteenth-century statistical and scientific concept of 'typicality' or 'representativeness'. Second, the merger of the optical and the statistical in Galton's work, the correlation of the visible and the calculable, are closely allied, as Mark Seltzer argues, to 'the imperative of making everything, including interior states, visible, legible and governable'.[123] Freud's recurrent dreams of self-dissection could be understood as a response to this imperative – the body is turned inside out for inspection. Hence the centrality of both optics and autobiographics to *The Interpretation of Dreams* – but also the intensity of Freud's desire not to be seen, his urge to lead the reader into the darkness rather than into the rationalizing light.

'Insight such as this falls to one's lot but once in a lifetime', Sigmund Freud wrote of *The Interpretation of Dreams* some three decades after its first publication: 'It contains, even according to my present-day judgement, the most valuable of all the discoveries it has been my good fortune to make' (Preface to the third (revised) English edition, PFL 4, 56: SE IV, xxxii). Freud's dream book is widely agreed to be not only his most important work, but the one which resonates most strikingly with a whole range of intellectual and experiential preoccupations, from his own time to ours, and undoubtedly beyond. The chapters of this volume, written by representatives of a range of disciplines, as well as practitioners of interdisciplinary study, illustrate some of the most important of these concerns from innovative and illuminating perspectives.

Notes

1 The researches of historians of science suggest that Freud's claim that *The Interpretation of Dreams* was virtually ignored in the press is somewhat misleading. Hannah Decker has shown that it was widely, and fairly favourably, reviewed and discussed in the German (rather than the Austrian) press, although she acknowledges that its initial impact seems not to have been sustained. See Hannah S. Decker, 'The interpretation of dreams: early reception by the educated German public', *Journal of the History of the Behavioral Sciences* 11 (1975) 129–41. Frank Sulloway confirms this view, adding that Freud's popularizing version of the longer text, *On Dreams* (1901), was widely reviewed and translated, and that its likely success in sales figures may well have had an adverse effect on sales of *The Interpretation of Dreams* itself. See Frank J. Sulloway, *Freud: Biologist of the Mind: Beyond the psychoanalytic legend* (London: Fontana, 1980), pp. 346–50.

2 For a detailed exposition of the 'interdisciplinary' nature of Freud's project, see Patricia Kitcher, *Freud's Dream: A Complete Interdisciplinary Science of Mind* (Cambridge, Mass: MIT Press, 1992).

3 Ella Freeman Sharpe, *Dream Analysis* (London: The Hogarth Press, 1937), p. 66.

4 For papers on this theme see: Robert Fliess, *The Revival of Interest in the Dream* (New York: International Universities Press, 1953); Melvin R. Lansky (ed.),

Essential Papers on Dreams (New York: New York University Press, 1992); Sara Flanders (ed.), *The Dream Discourse Today* (New York and London: Routledge, 1993).

5 See Lanksy (ed.), *Essential Papers on Dreams*, p. 10. Lanksy focuses, in his introduction to this anthology of psychoanalytic writings on dreams on the question of self-deception and the ways in which *The Interpretation of Dreams* poses the question: 'What is the mind like such that it can deceive itself?' (Lansky, p. 6).

6 Richard Wollheim, *Freud* (London: Fontana, 1991), p. 74.

7 The issue of 'anxiety dreams' troubled Freud's dream theory from the outset, but it was not until the 1920s that the evidence of the traumatic dreams of shell-shock victims led to a revision of the wish-fulfilment theory of dreams. In 'Beyond the pleasure principle' (1920), Freud developed a theory of the mental 'compulsion to repeat', and suggested that the function of the dreams of patients suffering from traumatic neuroses, which 'lead them back with such regularity to the situation in which the trauma occured', might be 'to master the stimulus retrospectively'. 'This would seem to be the place', Freud writes, 'to admit for the first time an exception to the proposition that dreams are fulfilments of wishes' (PFL 11, 304: SE, XVIII, 32). In his essay 'Revision of dream-theory', in *New Introductory Lectures on Psychoanalysis* (1933 [1932]), Freud brought the anxiety dreams of the traumatic neuroses back into the theory of wish-fulfilment by suggesting that the thesis of dreams be redefined in these terms: 'a dream is an *attempt* at the fulfilment of the wish' (PFL 2, 58–9: SE XXII, 29–30). In this model, dreams can, in particular circumstances, fail to fulfil a wish, but, Freud suggests, this does not overturn the wish-fulfilment theory of dreaming. Freud's later theorizations of the dream also suggested that the dreams fulfils the demands of the ego (the desire to sleep) as the servant of two masters – the id and the superego. If some dreams are more like wish-fulfiments, others appear as fulfilments of a threat (punishment dreams).

8 Ernest Jones, *The Life and Works of Sigmund Freud*, ed. and abr. Lionel Trilling and Stephen Marcus (Harmondsworth: Penguin, 1964), p. 300.

9 Freud, letter to Martha Bernays, 30 June 1882. Quoted in Ronald Clark, *Freud: The Man and the Cause* (St Albans, Herts: Granada, 1982), p. 174.

10 For an account of the changes between editions, see James Strachey, 'Editor's introduction', PFL 4, 34–7: SE IV, xii–xiii, xx–xxi. The major exclusions were essays by Otto Rank (on 'Dreams and creative writing' and 'Dreams and myths), which were printed at the end of Chapter VI of the fourth, fifth, sixth and seventh editions (from 1914 to 1922), but were subsequently omitted.

11 The English translation of *On Dreams*, ed. and trans. James Strachey, is published by Norton Press (New York, 1952), and forms part of Volume V of the Standard Edition (London: The Hogarth Press, 1953).

12 'Psychoanalysis and telepathy', SE XVIII, 178. The essay is one of a number in which Freud discusses the possible applications of psychoanalytic investigation to occult phenomena. See note 31 below.

13 Didier Anzieu, *Freud's Self-Analysis*, trans. Peter Graham (London: The Hogarth Press and the Institute of Psychoanalyis, 1986), p. 124.

14 See, for example, the essays in the collection *In Dora's Case: Freud-Hysteria-Feminism*, eds Charles Bernheimer and Claire Kahane (London: Virago, 1985). For feminist critique and discussion of *The Intepretation of Dreams*, and the 'specimen dream' in particular, see Shoshana Felman, 'The dream from which psychoanalysis proceeds', in *What Does a Woman Want?* (Baltimore, MD: Johns Hopkins University Press, 1993), pp. 68–120, and Sarah Kofman, *The Enigma of Woman*, trans. Catherine Porter (Ithaca, NY: Cornell University Press, 1985), pp. 20–32.

15 Quoted in Wollheim, *Freud*, p. 44. The text of the 'Project' is given in *The Origins of Psychoanalysis: Letters to Wilhelm Fliess, Drafts and Notes, 1887–1902*, by *Sigmund Freud*, ed. and intro., Ernst Kris (London: Imago Publishing Company, 1954), pp. 347–445; and in SE I, 283–387.

16 'On the history of the psychoanalytic movement', SE XIV, 22.

17 Wollheim, *Freud*, p. 47.

18 *Ibid.* p. 55.

19 See, in particular, Jacques Derrida, 'Freud and the scene of writing', in *Writing and Difference*, trans. Alan Bass (Chicago: University of Chicago Press, 1978), and 'To speculate – on "Freud" ', in *The Post Card: From Socrates to Freud and Beyond*, trans. Alan Bass (Chicago: University of Chicago Press, 1978), pp. 411–96.

20 The word 'character' derives from the Greek *kharratein*, to engrave, and has as one of its definitions 'a distinctive mark impressed'.

21 Wilhelm Fliess was, at the time of his meeting with Freud in November 1897, a Berlin physician (an ear and nose specialist) two years younger than Freud. The relationship, personal and professional, beween the two men developed rapidly. Fliess's researches were centred on the development of a 'periodicity' thesis – the idea being that there was a male 'cycle' of twenty-three days, in addition to the female cycle of twenty-eight – and that this numerology governed much of human life. Fliess also believed that there was a correspondence between the nasal mucous membrane and the genital organs, and that neurotic symptoms were linked to nasal problems – hence the near-fatal operation on Emma Eckstein, discussed on p. 49 of my introduction. Fliess's theories have been almost entirely discredited, although his work on bisexuality undoubtedly influenced Freud's theories of sexuality. The relationship between the two men, which had in any case become strained, ended conclusively in 1904, when Fliess accused Freud (perhaps with some justice) of revealing his ideas on bisexuality to Freud's patient Hermann Swoboda, who in turn recounted them to Otto Weininger. Weininger's *Geschlecht und Charakter* (1903, trans. as *Sex and Character* in 1906), which posited a universal bisexuality, was one of the most successful and influential 'scientific' texts of the early twentieth century.

22 Freud seems to have abandoned the view that the sexual abuse (as it would
    now be termed) of children by adults was both real and widespread, in
    favour of his 'seduction theory' (the belief that stories/memories of seduc-
    tion were fantasies, the expression of incestuous infantile desires.) As he
    wrote to Fliess: 'I no longer believe in my *neurotica* [theory of the
    neuroses] . . . there are no indications of reality in the unconscious, so that
    one cannot distinguish between truth and fiction that has been cathected
    with affect' (21 September 1897, F/F, 264). This has become one of the most
    contentious aspects of Freudian theory. See Jeffrey Masson, *The Assault on
    Truth: Freud's Suppression of the Seduction Theory* (New York: Farrar, Strauss
    and Giroux, 1984); Marie Balmary, *Psychoanalyzing Psychoanalysis: Freud and
    the Hidden Fault of the Father*, trans. Ned Lukacher (Baltimore, MD: Johns
    Hopkins University Press, 1982). Nicholas Rand and Maria Torok, in their
    article 'Questions to Freudian psychoanalysis: dream interpretation, reality,
    fantasy' (*Critical Inquiry* 19 (1993) 567–94), argue that 'Freud did not simply
    face a choice – seduction or fantasy? – but that he was permanently of two
    minds' (p. 581): the issue thus remained unresolved. Ian Hacking's *Rewriting
    the Soul: Multiple Personality and the Sciences of Memory* (Princeton, NJ:
    Princeton University Press, 1995), places the debate in the context of the
    politics surrounding trauma and memory, including the recent concept of
    'false memory syndrome'.

23 Lansky, *Essential Papers on Dreams*, p. 9.

24 J.-B. Pontalis, 'Dream as an object', in Sara Flanders (ed.), *The Dream Discourse
    Today* (London: Routledge, 1993), p. 111.

25 Henri Ellenberger, *The Discovery of the Unconscious: The History and Evolution
    of Dynamic Psychiatry* (New York: Basic Books, 1970), esp. pp. 303–11.

26 *Ibid.*, p. 304.

27 Freud makes favourable reference to Sully's essay 'The dream as a revelation'
    (1893), in particular Sully's account of representation in dreams: 'Like some
    letter in cypher, the dream-inscription when scrutinized closely loses its first
    look of balderdash and takes on the aspect of a serious, intelligible message.
    Or, to vary the figure slightly, we may say that, like some palimpsest, the
    dream discloses beneath its worthless surface-characters traces of an old and
    precious communication' (Sully, 'The dream as a revelation', *Fortnightly Re-
    view* 53 (1894) 364). Sully's account bears interestingly on Freud's later model
    of the palimpsest in his 'A note upon the mystic writing-pad'.

28 *Ibid.*, p. 311.

29 *Ibid.*, p. 493.

30 *Ibid.*, p. 493.

31 Freud alludes here to the 'transvaluation of all values' posited by Friedrich
    Nietzsche in his attack on Christianity.

32 Francis Galton, *Inquiries into Human Faculty and its Developments* (London:
    Macmillan, 1883), esp. pp. 211–41. For Freud's discussion of Galton's com-

posite photographs see the following passage from *The Interpretation of Dreams*:

> Dr R. in my dream about my uncle with the yellow beard was a similar composite figure. But in his case the dream-image was constructed in yet another way. I did not combine the features of one person with those of another and in the process omit from the memory-picture certain features of each of them. What I did was to adopt the procedure by means of which Galton produced family portraits: namely by projecting two images on to a single plate, so that certain features common to both are emphasized, while those which fail to fit in with another cancel one another out and are indistinct in the picture. In my dream about my uncle the fair beard emerged prominently from a face which belonged to two people and which was consequently blurred; incidentally, the beard further involved an allusion to my father and myself through the intermediate idea of growing grey. (PFL 4, 400: SE IV, 293)

The construction of collective and composite figures is one of the chief methods by which condensation operates in dreams.

33 René Descartes, *Discourse on Method and the Meditations*, trans. F. E. Sutcliffe (Harmondsworth: Penguin, 1968), p. 27.

34 *Ibid.*, p. 28.

35 Carl Schorske has argued that Freud's use of the Virgilian legend leads us back to politics. The socialist Ferdinand Lassalle used the same words for the title page of his pamphlet *The Italian War and the Task of Prussia* (1859), a work Freud may well have read as he was completing *The Interpretation of Dreams* (see 17 July 1899 F/F, 361). Schorske comments:

> *The Italian War* contained many themes and attitudes that we have found in *The Interpretation of Dreams*: the hatred of Catholic Rome and the Hapsburgs as the bastions of reaction; the linkage of Garibaldi and the Hungarians as liberal protagonists; and, like Freud in his dream-confrontation with Count Thun, the espousal of German national feeling against the aristocratic Austrian. In intellectual strategy lay a further afffinity. Lassalle, too, played with repressed forces, in his case the revolutionary forces of the people. That is why he chose the Virgil motto for his pamphlet . . . Freud would have found it easy to appropriate Lassalle's legend, transferring the hint of subversion through the return of the repressed from the realm of politics to that of the psyche.

Carl E. Schorske, *Fin-de-siècle Vienna: Politics and Culture* (Cambridge: Cambridge University Press, 1981), p. 200.

36 The relationship between psychoanalysis and the explorations of the occult by, in particular, the psychical researchers of the late nineteenth and early twentieth centuries is a complex and fascinating one. Freud accepted membership of the London Society for Psychical Research in 1911, and wrote on a number of occasions of the sympathy between occultism and psychoanalysis, both of which had experienced the contempt of 'official science'. However,

the 'materialism' of psychoanalysis, Freud argued at other times, precluded any firm alliance between psychoanalysis and occultist or parapsychological beliefs.

A number of Freud's discussions of occultism, psychical research, etc. are focused on the question of dreams, particularly the existence of premonitory dreams and telepathic communications. See, for example, 'Psycho-analysis and telepathy' (1941 [1921]), SE XVIII, 177–94, and 'Dreams and telepathy' (1922), SE XVIII, 195–220. For further material on this theme, see *Psychoanalysis and the Occult*, ed. George Devereux (London: Souvenir Press, 1974), an anthology which contains a number of Freud's writings on occult phenomena, in addition to those of other psychoanalytic theorists. See also James Webb, *The Occult Establishment* (La Salle, IL: Open Press, 1976), esp. chapter 6, and Jacques Derrida, 'Telepathy', trans. Nicholas Royle, *Oxford Literary Review* 10 (1988) 3–42.

37 See also James Hopkins, 'The interpretation of dreams', in Jerome Neu (ed.), *The Cambridge Companion to Freud* (Cambridge: Cambridge University Press, 1991), pp. 86–141; Sebastian Gardner, *Irrationality and the Philosophy of Psychoanalysis* (Cambridge: Cambridge University Press, 1993); Donald Levy, *Freud Among the Philosophers: the Psychoanalytic Unconscious and its Philosophical Critics* (New Haven, CT: Yale University Press, 1996); Paul Ricouer, *Freud and Philosophy: An Essay on Interpretation*, trans. Denis Savage (New Haven, CT: Yale University Press, 1970).

38 John Forrester, *Language and the Origins of Psychoanalysis* (Basingstoke: Macmillan, 1980), p. 66

39 Wilhelm Stekel (1868–1940), a physician practising in Vienna, was one of the early members of the Vienna Psychoanalytic Society, and the co-founder (with Alfred Adler) of the *Zentralblatt für Psychoanalyse*. One of his central interests in the psychoanalytic field was unconscious symbolism and, in particular, dream symbolism, and he wrote a number of works on this topic. While Freud acknowledged Stekel's influence on his own thinking about symbolism, he increasingly came to see Stekel as unscientific and undisciplined in his approach, and relations between the two men were effectively broken off after 1912.

40 Wollheim, *Freud*, p. 73.

41 Rand and Torok, 'Questions to Freudian analysis', p. 575.

42 *Ibid.*, 578.

43 Kitcher, *Freud's Dream*, p. 135.

44 Malcolm Bowie, *Freud, Proust and Lacan: Theory as Fiction* (Cambridge: Cambridge University Press, 1987), p. 108.

45 William Empson, *Seven Types of Ambiguity*, (Harmondsworth: Penguin, [1930] 1977).

46 Sharpe, *Dream Analysis*, pp. 18–19.

47 *Ibid.*, p. 19.

48 *Ibid.*, p. 34.

49 *Ibid.*, p. 30.

50 *Ibid.*, p. 39.

51 Roman Jakobson, 'Two aspects of language and two types of linguistic disturbances', *Selected Writings II* (The Hague: Mouton, 1971).

52 Jaques Lacan, 'The agency of the letter in the unconscious', in *Ecrits: A selection* (London: Tavistock).

53 Bowie, *Freud, Proust and Lacan*, p. 113.

54 See Wilhelm Dilthey, *Selected Writings of Wilhelm Dilthey*, ed. H. P. Rickman (Cambridge: Cambridge University Press, 1976).

55 Jean Laplanche, *New Foundations for Psychoanalysis*, trans. David Macey (Oxford: Basil Blackwell, 1989), p. 41; Jacques Lacan, *Ecrits: A Selection* (London: Tavistock, 1977), p. 147.

56 Laplanche, *New Foundations*, p. 44.

57 See J. L. Austin, 'Performative utterances', *Philosophical Papers* (Oxford: Oxford University Press, 1st edn 1961; 2nd edn 1970) and *How to Do Things with Words* (Oxford: Oxford University Press, 1962).

58 Laplanche, *New Foundations for Psychoanalysis*, p. 45.

59 *Ibid.*, p. 45.

60 Harvie Ferguson, *The Lure of Dreams: Sigmund Freud and the Construction of Modernity* (London: Routledge, 1966), p. 88.

61 Flanders, 'Introduction', *The Dream Discourse Today*, p. 9. Flanders is discussing Erik Erikson's essay 'The dream specimen of psychoanalysis', *Journal of the American Psychoanalytic Association* 2 (1954) 5–56.

62 Georg Simmel, 'The metropolis and mental life' [1903], trans, and reprinted in Richard Sennett (ed.), *Classic Essays on the Culture of Cities* (Englewood Cliffs, NJ: Prentice Hall, 1969), pp. 47–60. Simmel's account anticipates Freud's model of the defenses constructed against stimuli and external excitations by a protective shield or crust (*Reischutz*) which forms on the surface of the mental apparatus.

63 Charles Baudelaire, 'The painter of modern life', in *The Painter of Modern Life and Other Essays*, trans. and ed. Jonathan Mayne (London: Phaidon, 1964), p. 13.

64 The original quote was by Breuer in a footnote to Section 1 of his theoretical contribution to *Studies in Hysteria*, Breuer and Freud, 1895 (PFL 3, 263 n.: SE II, 189).

65 Antonin Artaud, 'Witchcraft and the cinema', in Paul Hammond (ed.), *The Shadow and its Shadow: Surrealist Writings on Cinema* (London: British Film Institute, 1978), p. 64.

66 J.-B. Pontalis, *Frontiers in Psychoanalysis: Between the Dream and Psychic Pain*, trans. Catherine Cullen and Philip Cullen (London: The Hogarth Press and the Institute of Psychoanalysis, 1981), p. 51.

67 *Ibid.*, p. 52.

68 Pontalis quotes a letter from Freud to Stefan Zweig (20 July 1938), in which he writes that he was 'inclined to look upon surrealists, who have apparently chosen me for their patron saint, as absolute (let us say 95 per cent, like alcohol) cranks!' (Pontalis, *Frontiers in Psychoanalysis*, p. 49). In 1925 the Freudian analyst Karl Abraham was approached by Eric Neumann of Ufa about the possibility of a film exploring psychoanalytic concepts. Letters between Abraham and Freud chart Abraham's growing enthusiasm for the project and Freud's continuing resistance: 'My chief objection is still that I do not believe that satisfactory plastic representation of our abstractions is at all possible' (*A Psychoanalytic Dialogue: The Letters of Sigmund Freud and Karl Abraham 1907–1926*, ed. Hilda C. Abraham and Ernst L. Freud (New York: Basic Books, 1964), p. 80).

69 See the introduction to *Cinema and Modernism: Close Up 1927–33* ed. James Donald, Anne Friedberg and Laura Marcus (London: Cassell, 1998).

70 Stephen Heath, *Questions of Cinema* (Bloomington, IN: Indiana University Press, 1981), p. 223.

71 Constance Penley, *The Future of an Illusion: Film, Feminism and Psychoanalysis* (London: Routledge, 1989), p. 60.

72 *Ibid.*, p. 61.

73 J.-L. Baudry, 'The apparatus', trans. Jean Andrews and Bertrand Augst, *Camera Obscura* 1 (1976) 121–3.

74 *Ibid.*, p. 123.

75 Sharpe, *Dream Analysis*, pp. 76–7.

76 *Ibid.*, pp. 76–7.

77 Bertram Lewin, *The Image and the Past* (New York: International Universities Press, 1968), p. 11.

78 *Ibid.*, pp. 16–17.

79 Bertram Lewin, 'Sleep, the mouth and the dream screen', *Psychoanalytic Quarterly* 15 (1946) 419–434.

80 *Ibid.*, p. 420.

81 *Ibid.*, p. 421.

82 *Ibid.*, p. 422.

83 Bertram Lewin, 'Reconsideration of the dream screen', *Psychoanalytic Quarterly* 22 (1953) 196.

84 Lewin, 'Sleep, the mouth and the dream screen', p. 433.

85 Lewin, 'Reconsideration of the dream screen', p. 186.

86 Bertram Lewin, 'Inferences from the dream screen', *International Journal of Psychoanalysis* 29 (1948) 227.

87 Derrida, 'Freud and the scene of writing', p. 200.

88 Lewin, 'Sleep, the mouth and the dream screen', p. 429.

89 Anzieu, *Freud's Self-Analysis; The Skin Ego* (New Haven, CT and London: Yale University Press, 1989).

90 Elizabeth Grosz, 'Psychoanalysis and the imaginary body', in Penny Florence and Dee Reynolds (eds), *Feminist Subjects, Multi-media* (Manchester: Manchester University Press, 1995), p. 188.

91 Anzieu, 'The film of the dream', in Flanders (ed.), *The Dream Discourse Today*, pp. 137–8.

92 Gilman, *The Case of Sigmund Freud*, p. 141.

93 Flanders, *The Dream Discourse Today*, p. 11.

94 Pontalis, *Frontiers in Psychoanalysis*, p. 29.

95 Mikkel Borch-Jacobsen, *The Freudian Subject* (Basingstoke: Macmillan, 1988), p. 26.

96 *Ibid.*, pp. 40, 45.

97 *Ibid.*, p. 8.

98 Letter to Martha Bernays, 29 October 1882. Quoted by Ernest Jones, *The Life and Works of Sigmund Freud*, Vol. I (London: The Hogarth Press, 1953), p. 320.

99 Derrida, 'To speculate – on "Freud"', p. 305.

100 Shoshana Felman, *What Does a Woman Want?* pp. 122–3.

101 Michel Neyraut *et al.*, *L'Autobiographie*. VIes rencontres psychoanalytiques d'Aix en Provence, 1987 (Paris: Les Belles Lettres, 1988), p. 10.

102 Marthe Robert, *The Psychoanalytic Revolution: Sigmund Freud's Life and Achievement*, trans. Kenneth Morgan (London: George Allen and Unwin, 1966), p. 111.

103 See Carl Jung, *Memories, Dreams, Reflections*, recorded and ed. Aniela Jaffe (London: Collins and Routledge and Kegan Paul, 1963).

104 Ernest Jones, *The Life and Work of Sigmund Freud*, ed. and abr. Lionel Trilling and Steven Marcus (Harmondsworth: Penguin, 1964), p. 276.

105 *Rousseau judge of Jean-Jacques: dialogues*, in *The Collected Writings of Rousseau*, Vol. 1 ed. R. D. Masters and C. Kelly (Hanover, NH: University Press of New England, 1990), p. 6.

106 Anzieu, *Freud's Self-Analysis*, p. 149.

107 *Ibid.*, p. 155.

108 Lisa Appignanesi and John Forrester, *Freud's Women* (London: George Weidenfeld and Nicolson, 1992), p. 119.

109 Shoshana Felman, 'The dream from which psychoanalysis proceeds', in *What Does a Woman Want?* p. 74.

110 *Ibid.*, p. 110.

111 Louis Marin, in his article 'Montaigne's tomb, or autobiographical discourse', discusses an episode in an essay of Montaigne's in which Montaigne describes an 'experience' of 'coming close to death' in terms of death and rebirth. Marin comments: 'It is not possible to write, to transmit, to commu-

nicate death as one's own death. It is impossible, and yet it is essential, for it is the ultimate experience in which each man singularly identifies himself in his particular truth, in his propriety (*Dans son propre*)'. Marin, 'Montaigne's tomb, or autobiographical discourse', *Oxford Literary Review* 4, 3 (1981) 55.

112 Carl E. Schorske, 'Politics and patricide in Freud's *Interpretation of Dreams*', in *Fin-de-siècle Vienna*, pp. 181–207.

113 Jacques le Rider, *Modernity and Crises of Identity: Culture and Society in Fin-de-siècle Vienna*, trans. Rosemary Morris (Cambridge: Polity Press, 1993), p. 5.

114 *Ibid.*, p. 40.

115 See Sander Gilman, *Freud, Race and Gender* (Princeton, NJ: Princeton University Press, 1993) and *The Case of Sigmund Freud* (Baltimore, MD: Johns Hopkins University Press, 1993). There is a very substantial literature on Freud, psychoanalysis and Judaism, including work on a topic I have not addressed in this introduction – the relationship between Freudian and Talmudic dream interpretation. Works on Freud and Judaism include Ken Frieden, *Freud's Dream of Interpretation* (Albany, NY: State University of New York Press, 1990); Peter Gay, *A Godless Jew: Freud, Atheism, and the Making of Psychoanalysis* (New Haven, CT: Yale University Press, 1987); Marthe Robert, *From Oedipus to Moses: Freud's Jewish Identity* trans. Ralph Manheim (London: Routledge and Kegan Paul, 1977); Yosef Hayim Yerushalmi, *Freud's Moses: Judaism Terminable and Interminable* (New Haven, CT: Yale University Press, 1991). For a detailed bibliography of works on this theme, see Gilman, *The Case of Sigmund Freud*, pp. 229–32.

Gilman's work on Freud is contentious because it not only defines Freud as a Jew, but reads psychoanalysis as a 'Jewish science' in its defensive, troubled responses to pathologized, racialized representations of the Jew and Jewishness. For Peter Gay, by contrast, the two identities are distinct: 'Freud', he concludes, 'was a Jew but not a Jewish scientist' (Gay, *A Godless Jew*, p. 148).

116 Gilman, *The Case of Sigmund Freud*, p. 5.

117 *Ibid.*, p. 43.

118 Karl Pearson, *The Life, Letters and Labours of Francis Galton*, Vol. 11 (Cambridge: Cambridge University Press, 1924), p. 294.

119 Gilman, *The Case of Sigmund Freud*, p. 44; Pearson, *The Life, Letters and Labours of Francis Galton*, p. 57. For further discussion of Galton's composite photographs and racial science, see Daniel Pick, *Faces of Degeneration: A European Disorder, c. 1848–1918* (Cambridge: Cambridge University Press, 1989), esp. chapter 6.

120 Francis Galton, 'Generic Images', *Proceedings of the Royal Institution*, 25 April 1879, Vol. 1X, p. 170.

121 *Ibid.*, p. 162.

122 Pearson, *The Life, Letters and Labours of Francis Galton*, Vol. II, p. 295.

123 Mark Seltzer, *Bodies and Machines* (New York and London: Routledge, 1992), p. 95.

2

How to do things in dreams

TREVOR PATEMAN

In any professional (or, for that matter, amateur) psychoanalysis, the object of a dream-interpretation is not immediately a dream, but a dream-narrative volunteered by the person being analysed, the analysand. As often as not, the analysand as much as the analyst believes that the narrative of the dream is the narrative of something which has a hidden meaning, and that it is the job of analysis to uncover this hidden meaning and formulate it in words, guided by whatever theory is being deployed in some particular analysis – Freudian, Jungian, Kleinian, Lacanian, and so on.

In most cases, a realist assumption will be made that there really was a dream, of determinate content, which is narrated in a dream-narrative, which may thus be more or less accurate, complete, and so on. This realist assumption or presupposition is being implied every time, for example, that we write down a dream 'before we forget it'.

However, even though I think that this realist assumption is fundamentally correct, some caution is sometimes called for. People who are in the habit of narrating their dreams to friends may – consciously or unconsciously – reconstruct them with a view to saying something they want their friend to hear, but do not want to say directly. We are then dealing with a quite different phenomenon from the conscientious attempt to recall what we actually dreamt. And it is not out of the question that some dream-narratives offered to professional analysts by their patients have such a constructed, audience-directed character.

As a narrative, what the analysand says can be studied with the apparatus of narrative theory, the theory which is interested in things like point of view, and beginnings, middles and ends. But insofar as the dream-narrative is a (faithful) narrative of something which happened in another mode, in a visual dream mode, the narrative will often be disconcertingly weak or confused in structure. Structurally, it may sound like a child's early attempts at narrative, where we often look in vain for good beginnings, middles and ends, and hear instead the groping of 'and then, and then, and then . . .'.

Of course, it is partly because we often forget our dreams so rapidly that the structure of the dream-narrative is disturbed, but equally we know enough about our dreams to know that even apparently well-remembered dreams do not always have the clarity and order of a well-crafted story. There are individual differences in the completeness and distinctness with which dreams are recalled, but for many people dreams are bewildering, hard to keep track of, hard to get a grip on, both when we are dreaming them and subsequently in attempting a conscious narrative reconstruction of the experience. It is as if dreams were experimental movies which we do not quite follow.

Now there is a theory, and it is Freud's, that the manifest dreams we experience and subsequently recall can only do what Freud regards as their work of allowing expression of our dream-thoughts if indeed we do not quite follow our dreams, do not quite see their meaning. For it is that meaning which is the object of repression, and should what is hidden become open, we respond with anxiety. Dreams are things to wish with, says Freud, but the wishes expressed are ones which we are not readily able to acknowledge. In waking life, we are familiar with the idea that we may not be able to acknowledge envy or jealousy or hate or love for someone. Freud's intuition is that in a dream we may express wishes (or, more generally, thoughts) which have been subject to repression, that is, barred from conscious acknowledgement by the operation of what he calls a dream-censorship.

It is a short step to seeing dreams as, in some way, *coded* expressions of the wishes (or, more generally, thoughts) which they both express and do not express literally or in a fashion in which they could be readily recognized and acknowledged. The question then arises, whether manifest dreams code their latent content in ways familiar to us from other domains of symbolic expression, or whether there are ways of encoding which are distinctive of the dream, bearing in mind that a dream mobilizes both pictorial material (moving images, like those in film) and linguistic material (characters in a dream speak, and written words appear in books, etc.).

It is a central claim in Freud's *The Interpretation of Dreams* that although symbols with a fixed meaning, borrowed from other areas of life, may appear in dreams, there is not anything like a set of symbols constituting a specific dream-symbolism, such that a dictionary of dream-symbols could, in principle, be constructed. The hidden (underlying or motivating or literal) meanings of dream-material are meanings attaching to the explicit, manifest dream-material *on some particular occasion of dreaming*. There is no reason to proceed in dream-interpretation on any other basis than this. In the language of contemporary linguistics, dream-meaning is *pragmatic* meaning rather than *semantic* meaning, a matter of meaning in use rather than meaning in a dictionary.

By way of example, if I dream of a Painted Lady butterfly, I may on some particular occasion of dreaming really be dreaming about my friend Cynthia, who is not a butterfly but a woman. What may link them in my mind is the fact that the Linnaean name for the Painted Lady is *Cynthia cardui*. But this is not to say that every time I dream of a Painted Lady I must be reckoned to be dreaming of Cynthia, and still less that when *you* dream of a Painted Lady you are dreaming of Cynthia – you have never met her! The meaning of my dream-symbolism is pragmatic just in this, that the meaning is *indexed* to a particular occasion of use, by a particular dreamer.

If this is true, as Freud generally insists that it is, it dictates very particular strategies of dream interpretation. In particular, the only person who can link the Painted Lady to Cynthia is *me*; my analyst, in general, will not be able to do so, unless already considerably informed of people I know and my knowledge of the Linnaean taxonomy for butterflies. But the principled point is this, that although my analyst may have some pretty good ideas about how meaning is made in dreams, there cannot be any dream book which will give the analyst authority to pronounce that my Painted Lady = Cynthia. The authority is all with me, although I may be in analysis not least because to acknowledge that my Painted Lady = Cynthia may be hard for me to do, and part of a symptomatology.

But what of the analyst's 'pretty good ideas' about how things are done in dreams?

One important claim of Freud's is that things to dream with – the *dramatis personae* and props of the manifest dream – are largely taken from the residues of very recent, every-day experiences. So that if, to introduce a new example, I dream of reading the *Daily Mail* (something I have not actually done in thirty years), then I will find something in very recent experience which connects me to the *Daily Mail*. Perhaps yesterday my newsagent gave me a copy in error, and I indignantly returned it; perhaps I watched someone reading the *Daily Mail* on the train going to work; perhaps I heard the words 'the *Daily Mail*' on the radio; and so on, indefinitely. Patient investigation of the sources of dream material in recent waking experience can be startlingly productive:

> Yes, I watched someone reading the *Daily Mail* on the train; the person reminded me of my mother, who read the *Daily Mail*. She read it until she died, I had recalled, and suddenly felt her presence a grief away . . .

The original fragment of dream is well on the way to yielding itself to an interpretation, through the chain of associations which I made while awake, employed while sleeping, and am now recovering in analysis.

In this way, using free association, analysand and analyst can piece together a dream-interpretation, bringing more and more of the manifest material within the scope of an interpretation which, in classical Freudian analysis, will take the dream as eventually the expression not only of a set of thoughts, but of some definite wish or wishes. The procedure for interpretation is a traditionally hermeneutic one, in which is presupposed that the fragments of dream offered for analysis are really parts of a single jigsaw and that the jigsaw can be given, if you like, a description or a title: a dream, like a painting or a film is a dream *about* something.

Now I want to look more closely at these associative links through which one thing in the manifest dream is able to stand for another thing in the dream-thoughts (the latent dream). I will take as starting point the two examples of dream material so far deployed: the Painted Lady butterfly which stands for Cynthia, and the *Daily Mail* which stands for my mother.

A smattering of school rhetoric will allow most readers to recognize that if the Painted Lady stands for Cynthia, then it does so metaphorically; it's a visual metaphor. The routine question which follows on from this recognition asks about the aptness of this metaphor, and this may be answered in terms either of origin or effect: what made the butterfly image apt to stand for Cynthia? How effective, how resonant, is the metaphor?

The question about aptness can, in the analytic context, be answered in terms of motivation, and it is central to Freudian analysis to say that the motivation of a metaphorical dream-image is likely to be overdetermined.

That is to say, there will be more than one causally effective motive for the choice of the metaphor. In the case of my Painted Lady, I can provide an open list which would include at least the following as motives for the choice of metaphor:

(1) As an amateur lepidopterist, I know that the Linnaean name for this butterfly is *Cynthia cardui*

(2) Cynthia is a lady – a woman – who is noted for wearing lots of make-up, and so counts as 'painted'

(3) I was walking with Cynthia when the Painted Lady butterfly skimmed across the field beside us, and we both remarked on its migratory, transient qualities; and these are qualities which I feared existed in Cynthia

(4) Starting another chain of thought, I recall the Utopian philosopher Charles Fourier's idea of *the butterfly passion*, the human passion for change and variety, and recall that Cynthia and I had once discussed his work, and recognized the passion in ourselves.

The list could be extended, making the choice of the visual metaphor ever more overdetermined. Very recent connectionist theories of the mind would elucidate the idea of over-determination in terms of separate mind (or brain) modules converging on a causally effective (sufficient) 'vote' for the Painted Lady to stand for Cynthia, but always, one must add, *on this particular occasion*.

The little discussion just conducted in terms of aptness or motivation can be turned around and re-done as an analysis of the resonance of a metaphor, which it has in virtue of the number and importance of the underlying thoughts and feelings which it condenses. And where I have written of metaphor, Freud writes of processes of *condensation*, with many chains of thought and feeling condensed into the manifest dream image:

> The first thing that becomes clear to anyone who compares the dream-content with the dream-thoughts is that a work of *condensation* on a large scale has been carried out. Dreams are brief, meagre and laconic in comparison with the range and wealth of the dream-thoughts. If a dream is written out it may perhaps fill half a page. The analysis setting out the dream-thoughts underlying it may occupy six, eight or a dozen times as much space. This relation varies with different dreams; but so far as my experience goes its direction never varies. (PFL 4, 383: SE IV 279)

Metaphoric condensation could be looked at in another way. Suppose, as many theorists have argued, that all metaphors are basically similes. In that case, one gets at the aptness and resonance of a metaphor by unpacking what it condenses into a series of statements which fill out a set of *pro formas* all of which begin either 'Cynthia is like a Painted Lady in that she . . .', or else begin 'A Painted Lady is like Cynthia in that it . . .'.

Now this is undeniably part of what is done in dream-interpretation and, in the present case, filling out the *pro formas* involves not just the repetition of what has already been offered in analysis, but points readily towards formulations of underlying, latent dream-thoughts or wishes, as follows:

(1) Cynthia is like a Painted Lady in that she is or may be migratory and transient (the latent wish might then be: And I wish she wasn't).

(2) Cynthia is like a Painted Lady in that she (metaphorically) appears only in warm weather, that is, when things are easy. (The latent wish might be: And I wish she was more committed, 'for better or worse'.)

If anything like (1) or (2) can legitimately come out of analysing this dream-fragment, then it should be evident that complex and charged psychic material can be expressed and represented in an image (a butterfly for a woman) which might seem to be motivated by nothing much more than a not-very-clever association of a butterfly and a person through the accidental link provided by Linnaean taxonomy, which by naming the butterfly *Cynthia cardui* is plainly to blame for this particular dream.

Freud fully realized that apparently incidental detail in a dream could be enabling the expression and representation of powerful psychic concerns. He realized too that the analyst could not expect to cope with such material unless his or her own fund of general cultural knowledge was really very considerable, enabling him or her to follow (and occasionally, to lead) the patient's associations.

A friend narrates to me a dream in which she saw herself reading *The Tempest*, a detail recorded by her but by no means central to the manifest dream-content. But on informal analysis, it emerged that the plot of *The Tempest* was analogous to the tempestuous plot of the dream, and so in some way doubled or indicated what the plot was. Now an analyst with no knowledge of Shakespeare might to some considerable extent rely on the analysand's own knowledge – in this case considerable – to amplify the bare reference to *The Tempest*. Equally, an analyst with knowledge of the play might well be able to assist in developing the analysis past points of *resistance*. In the present case, one wish represented in the dream was the dreamer's desire to be free of guilt. Another thought that since she could not bring herself to end a relationship that she thought she was outgrowing or was otherwise unsatisfactory, she must rely on her partner to bring that relationship to a close, which he might do if he now found the relationship burdensome – alongside which chain of thought one might place the concluding lines of *The Tempest*, spoken by Prospero:

> As you from crimes would pardon'd be
> Let your indulgence set me free

Prospero's daughter is called Miranda. A week after discussing this dream, my friend remarked that one of her close friends had once rechristened her and called her 'Miranda'.

I now turn to consider in more detail my second dream-fragment, the example of the *Daily Mail*.

There was a connection between the *Daily Mail* and my mother; she read that newspaper, day in and day out. It was part of her life. Seeing someone else reading it now reminds me of her. In dreaming of myself reading the *Daily Mail*, it turns out – on analysis – that the dream thoughts underlying the manifest dream-image are thoughts about my mother and my relationship to her. In the dream, I have managed to express and represent those thoughts by substituting an image of the *Daily Mail* for an image of my mother.

In the present instance, a smattering of school rhetoric is unlikely to include the knowledge that the substitution here is called metonymy, which is elucidated as a procedure in which a part of something, or something associated with that thing, comes to stand for (substitute for) that thing itself. Freud, in *The Interpretation of Dreams*, does not use the term metonymy, but writes of *displacement*, explained as a way of handling psychically intense dream-thoughts:

> It thus seems plausible to suppose that in the dream-work a psychical force is operating which on the one hand strips the elements which have a high psychical value of their intensity, and on the other hand, *by means of overdetermination*, creates from elements of low psychical value new values, which afterwards find their way into the dream-content. If that is so, *a transference and displacement of psychical intensities* occurs in the process of dream-formation, and it is as a result of these that the difference between the text of the dream-content and that of the dream-thoughts comes about. The process which we are here presuming is nothing less than the essential portion of the dream-work; and it deserves to be described as 'dream-displacement'. Dream-displacement and dream-condensation are the two governing factors to whose activity we may in essence ascribe the form assumed by dreams. (PFL 4, 417: SE IV, 307–8)

The term 'displacement' seems absolutely right for the process being characterized: if the *Daily Mail* stands for my mother, it does so by way of displacement from her to something associated with her. The fact that she read the newspaper that she did provides a motivation for the metonymic displacement, catalysed by an experience of the previous day in which I was reminded of my mother by seeing someone else reading the *Daily Mail*.

But in the course of any day, I could – no doubt – find many things to remind me of my mother. So there is a question about why the experience in the train struck me in a particular way and, in relation to my dream, a question about why the displacement effected was apt and resonant, allowing the expression of a complex of dream-thoughts and wishes. In other words, I now want to find out at least some of the ways in which the dream-metonymy was overdetermined. Some possibilities immediately present themselves to mind, and I simply list them without seeking to prioritise them or claim that they are exhaustive. It should be reasonably clear that what is being offered is a routing from the dream-image to latent thoughts and wishes, which I may to a greater or lesser extent be able to acknowledge, prompted by the search for truth which is central to any psychoanalytic quest. And so I think:

- My mother left school in 1921, just before her fourteenth birthday; I did graduate work at several universities. Perhaps I could have stayed emotionally closer to my mother if I had stayed educationally closer. Such a wish could be represented (symbolized) by the manifest dream-image in which it is I, not my mother, who is reading the *Daily Mail*.
- There may also be a play on words in the use of the *Daily Mail* and Freud certainly believed word play endemic to the linguistic material which appears in dreams. So 'mail' is also letters through the post, and it happens that I had recently come across some of the hundreds of letters which my mother wrote to me when I was at university. I had been thinking about them, and perhaps in the dream-fragment reading them rather than the newspaper.
- 'Mail' is also homonymic with 'male'. As the only child of a woman living apart from her husband, I was for several years, by choice and default, my mother's daily male, and the dream thus expresses or represents thoughts and wishes about this excessive closeness.

In sum, the metonymic displacement from my mother on to a newspaper in the manifest dream, allows the expression of dream-thoughts and wishes which are, first of all, multiple (and thus overdetermine the choice of the image) and, second, include thoughts and wishes which when directly expressed and represented may be to various degrees anxiety-creating or uncomfortable, and liable to repression. The dream has enabled these thoughts and wishes to find expression in non-literal ways which have protected the dreamer's sleep from anxiety which might bring sleep to an end.

Our contemporary ability to see Freud's characterization of the dream-work mechanisms of condensation and displacement as characterizations of metaphor and metonymy is largely due to a remark of the linguist Roman Jakobson. In a 1956 essay, 'Two aspects of language and two types of aphasic disturbance', Jakobson wrote:

> A competition between both devices, metonymic and metaphoric, is manifest in any symbolic process, either intrapersonal or social. Thus in an inquiry into the structure of dreams, the decisive question is whether the symbols and the temporal sequences used are based on contiguity (Freud's metonymic 'displacement' and synecdochic 'condensation') or on similarity (Freud's 'identification and symbolism'). (Jakobson 1956, 80–1)

This is actually all that Jakobson has to say about Freud in his essay, and later theorists, led by Jacques Lacan in a 1957 paper 'The agency of the letter in the unconscious or reason since Freud' (Lacan 1957), have realigned Jakobson's categorization so that condensation is simply equated with metaphoric processes (which include what we normally think of as symbolism) and displacement is equated with metonymy. This realignment strikes me as fully justified, both by Freud's text and theoretical requirements. A convenient summary of all the relevant material can be found in the entries for 'Condensation' and 'Displacement' in Laplanche and Pontalis's dictionary, *The Language of Psychoanalysis* (1973).

In the preceding discussion of metaphor and metonymy, condensation and displacement, the emphasis has inevitably been on the understanding of dream-fragments – and, indeed, piecemeal reconstruction of underlying dream-thoughts and wishes from dream-fragments is central to the practice of Freudian psychoanalysis. Nothing has so far been said about the connectedness of dreams, their beginnings, middles and ends or about point of view. But this is not to say there is nothing to be said. The narrative structure of a dream or point of view can also be used to express and represent thoughts and wishes: there is no reason in principle or practice why a complicated dream should not be used as a means of expressing a wish for a complicated life, or a dream in which I am a distant observer used to express the desire for a calm life.

But it would be wrong, I think, to seek too hastily to formalize dreams and submit them to a linguistic or narratological formalization in which each individual dream would be seen as an instance of one of the possibilities licensed by, or derivable from, the formalization (such a project is attempted in Foulkes 1978). One needs first of all to take on board the realization that dreams – like the jokes and slips of the tongue also studied by Freud – are places where a very varied and rich assortment of our mental powers manifest themselves, and that it is unlikely that a theory of our mental *competences* can readily do justice to the bravura of our mental *performances*, though they may easily capture something of those performances in a fairly abstract and schematic way. By analogy, a narratology which tells us that stories have beginnings, middles and ends, but not necessarily in that order, captures all or nearly all stories, abstractly and schematically, but should give us no satisfaction if it claims to reveal the mysteries of story-making. In contrast, the narratology developed by Vladimir Propp in *Morphology of the Folktale* (1928) or Gérard Genette in *Narrative Discourse* (1980) may well provide us with a sense that stories, in their complexity and mystery, can be made to yield to narratology. This is because they offer a much more fully specified range of constraints and possibilities than the schema of beginning, middle and end. Propp, for example, is bold enough to claim that all folk-tales are built from a subset of elements taken from a full set of just thirty-one abstractly specifiable functions, and that such elements occur in the tales in more-or-less invariant narrative order. This is a very bold – and almost certainly false – claim, but in being bold (and false) it does exactly what we expect of any scientific enquiry: yields some non-obvious, non-tautological insight into the way the world is. Any scientifically interesting theory of dream-narratives must say comparably non-obvious, non-tautological things.

The contrast between competence and performance, as far as contemporary thought is concerned, is due to Naom Chomsky's linguistics, as it has developed from the time of his essay *Language and Mind* (1968). The ability to speak a language consists in part of a mental representation of that language, of its phonology, vocabulary, and of the syntactic rules by which grammatically well-formed sentences may be produced. Competence is generative of performance, though many more factors are involved in speaking than the purely grammatical. Grammar does not help us with the question of what to say, when – it helps only with the ability to say whatever it is that we do wish to say.

Likewise, the capacity to dream whatever it is we wish to dream (about), does not determine what we dream, when. That is determined, on Freud's view, by (unconscious) thoughts and wishes, given shape by what he calls the 'dream-work' which converts latent thoughts and wishes into manifest and visual content.

Now Freud's notion of the dream-work is analogous to the idea of linguistic competence. Our capacity (strictly, our liability) to dream is just our ability to do the dream-work necessary to express (unconscious) thoughts and wishes in manifest visual form. Our abilities to turn a metaphor or select a metonymy are examples of our capacity for dream-work. Freud also identifies other dream-work processes such as 'secondary revision', the capacity to tidy up a dream and give it shape and coherence, and an original need for 'figuration', to render abstract dream-thoughts in visual form. He spends many pages in *The Interpretation of Dreams* (see Chapter VI, sections F and G) discussing, for example, the figurability of abstract and logical relationships, of mathematical calculations. He regards this discussion as an important part of the work and concludes the discussion of the particular topic of absurdity in dreams with these words:

> Thus I have solved the problem of absurdity in dreams by showing that the dream-thoughts are never absurd – never, at all events, in the dreams of sane people – and that the dream-work produces absurd dreams and individual absurd elements if it is faced with the necessity of representing any criticism, ridicule or derision which may be present in the dream thoughts. (Chapter VI, section F, subsection VI)

If dream-work is thought of in this way, as the exercise of dream-competence, then – in principle – there could be impairments of the capacity to dream, analogous to the kinds of impairment of linguistic competence and performance which arise from brain or motor disorders. In principle, we can ask such questions as: Are some people unable to dream, lacking the capacity to dream? Are some people unable to do certain kinds of dream-work, lacking the capacity for metaphor, metonymy, and so on? An affirmative answer is sometimes given: in psychosis, one aspect of the general incapacity to symbolize is the incapacity to dream 'properly', and in place of dreaming the psychotic suffers from insomnia and nightmares. Such connections have been explored in some interesting writings by Masud Khan (1993), who argues that patients who cannot have a 'good dream' also cannot make appropriate use of the psychoanalytic situation. A psychotic who seeks real satisfactions rather than symbolic ones from dreaming will also seek real rather than symbolic satisfaction from the analytic situation. Likewise, a person whose overwhelming anxiety produces nightmares rather than dreams may resist any dependence in the analytic situation as too threatening. They may simply be unable to continue in analysis, or else unable to work productively with what the analyst has to offer.

Freud's problems with anxiety dreams, which appear to contradict the idea that dreams are wish-fulfilments, might find a resolution in this way. An anxiety dream is a *failed* dream – a dream which fails to symbolize the anxiety-creating wishes which it represents in such a way that the dreamer can sleep on without waking to escape the dream anxiety. Repressed material which is inconsistent with our waking self-image finds its way into an anxiety dream and obliges us to wake up in order to be rid of the threat the material poses.

This is a speculative suggestion of my own; it is not an exegesis of what Freud says. Nonetheless, it is a possibility opened up by thinking of the ability to dream as a kind of mentally represented competence, analogous to linguistic competence, and – I should add – other kinds of competence such as musical abilities.

We could also ask developmental questions about this competence, about how it grows in childhood and about how children's dreams and competences differ from those of adults. Developmental studies of dreaming have indeed been made. In a summary of an extensive project reported in *Children's Dreams* (Foulkes 1982), David Foulkes writes that the development of dreaming follows a course parallel to the stages of waking cognitive maturation:

> In the case of children's dreams, we have shown that the content seems to be more a function of what children are able to portray symbolically than, as traditional dream theory would have had it, of what their anxieties, conflicts, fixations, and so forth force them to portray symbolically. Developmentally dreams reveal more about the unfolding of human representational abilities than they do – or can do – about the sources or meanings of children's waking behaviours. This is so because, until children are reasonably capable of reflecting on and symbolically elaborating on their own waking experience and behaviours, they must remain incapable of dreaming effectively about these experiences and behaviours. Our data, as well as (waking) cognitive-developmental theory, suggest that effective nocturnal self-reflection and symbolic self-expression generally cannot occur until the consolidation of concrete-operational reasoning [that is, roughly from age seven on, TP]. (Foulkes 1982, p. 275)

I have taken it for granted that the dream-thoughts which dream-work converts into the manifest dream have a *propositional* character. That is to say, although the dream-thoughts may express wishes or feelings, they express ones which have a propositional or propositionally expressible character. This distinguishes them from bodily (somatic) sensations and from (obscure) feelings which are 'free-floating' and not attached to definite objects – just as free-floating anxiety about I-know-not-what is quite different from being anxious about tomorrow's interview. To put it precisely, Freud's assumption is that a person's dream-thoughts can be stated, in linguistic/propositional form, without loss of meaning. Dream-thoughts are, to use technical terms of philosophy, *effable* rather than *ineffable*, where the ineffable is here taken to be anything resistant to full characterization in linguistic/propositional form.

Insofar as Freudian analysis claims that the latent dream-thoughts can and do express wishes going back to earliest childhood, there is implied a presupposition that the infant (and even the pre-linguistic infant) is capable of propositional thought.

This might be put, for example, by saying that an infant boy or girl does not just need their mother's presence; they desire it – a way of putting things which implies the ability to focus the mother as an object of desire (What do you desire? I desire my mother's presence). This is not an unproblematic claim for the pre-linguistic infant, and is the subject of a great deal of philo-sophical and psychoanalytic agonizing.

Among modern philosophers, Wittgenstein in the *Philosophi-cal Investigations* (1953), as in his other writings, tries to get at the matter by considering what 'intelligent' animals are and are not capable of. By way of simplified example, it might not seem implausible to look at a dog scratching at the door, wagging its tail, and whimpering and to say of the dog, 'He's expecting his master to return.' But things would be quite different if someone tried to say, 'He's expecting his master to return on Wednesday.' For dogs do not have the concept of a week, or days of the week. What is reasonably attributable to the pre-linguistic infant by way of propositionally expressible belief has likewise to be considered and judged quite carefully.

However, one radical solution to difficulties in this domain is to argue that the (Freudian) unconscious does not come into being before the infant's acquisition of (or entry into) language, or more generally, the world of symbols, of which language is part.

On this view, repression operates on wishes and feelings which are already capable of having a propositionally expressible structure. Insofar as dream-thoughts come from that which is unconscious – the product of repression – then they will be propositional because the contents of the unconscious are propositional or propositionally expressible. The contents of the unconscious are linguistically structured or structurable without loss of meaning.

Such a position is a common enough post-Freudian one. 'The unconscious is structured like a language', is Jacques Lacan's persistent motif, and the theoretical positions of Melanie Klein (as opposed to Anna Freud) probably commit her to something like this view too. Such a view does, indeed, make sense of psychoanalysis as a 'talking cure' in which the analysand is being encouraged to avow or acknowledge linguistically expressible propositional truths. To such truths huge emotional colouring (affect) may attach, but the propositions are non-identical with their emotional charge. There is not just rage, but rage *about* something; not just anxiety, but anxiety *about* something. Proposition and affect can become detached from each other. In most psychoneuroses (and notably in the hysterias and in obsessional neurosis) the root pathological problem is the detachment of affect, of feeling, from the thoughts to which it originally and properly belonged, followed either by its complete repression or its displacement on to inappropriate thoughts (as in phobias). A psychoneurotic may be able to discourse cheerfully enough about his or her unresolved Oedipal problems, and be terrified of spiders or flying. The psychoneurotic is unable to resolve his or her Oedipal problems in part at least because the appropriate affect does not attach to the thoughts being formulated.

One use of dream-interpretation is to locate the objects to which denied or displaced affect is originally attached. 'Objects' here – following the line of Kleinian object-relations theory – may include people, parts of people (the breast, for example) and fantasies of people. However, in the content of the manifest dream, those objects may be just as much obscured as in waking life – but not always or even generally, which is why Freud calls dreams our 'royal road to the unconscious'.

A woman has an anxiety dream in which she is separated from her loved ones by King Kong. King Kong? Eventually she concedes, gorillas are her mother's favourite animal. And now it as if a mass of unresolved material is in the open: the mother who is so jealous of her daughter, and her daughter's attachment to her father, that she wishes to deny her the right to bear children and to dispossess her of those she has.

The example serves to re-emphasize a persistent theme of this chapter. For the association between King Kong and a mother is not a semantic one: there is no possible dream dictionary in which King Kong will be listed as a synonym or metaphor for a mother. The association is idiosyncratic, such that if on a given occasion of dreaming, an image of King Kong stands for the dreamer's mother, it does not do so in virtue of some code or language establishing an equivalence. Yet what the dream-work is able to do is to find a way of expressing dream-thoughts in images apt for an occasion. Free association from these images may in favourable circumstances allow us to recover the underlying dream-thoughts.

One unresolved question is why waking free association is not blocked by anxiety. After all, if someone dreams of King Kong rather than of their mother, because dream-censorship makes it impossible to dream openly of the mother, how is it possible for the connection to be made in waking analysis? A short answer is to say that 'free' association is not always easily and freely accomplished, and may only be possible if the desire to be well is strong enough. A further answer is to say that association of ideas in the 'cool' context of waking analysis is paired with avoidance of ideas in the emotionally charged world of the dream. The job of the analyst is to weave together idea and feeling, thought and affect, which repression has put asunder.

Works cited

Chomsky, N., *Language and Mind* (New York: Harcourt Brace Jovanovich 1968, rev. edn 1972).

Foulkes, D., *A Grammar of Dreams* (New York: Basic Books, 1978).

—, *Children's Dreams: Longitudinal Studies* (New York: John Wiley, 1982).

Genette, G., *Narrative Discourse*, trans. Jane E. Lewin (Oxford: Basil Blackwell, 1980).

Jakobson, R., 'Two aspects of language and two types of aphasic disturbances', in *Fundamentals of Language* (The Hague: Mouton, 1956).

Khan, M., 'Dream psychology and the evolution of the psychoanalytic situation' and 'The use and abuse of dream in psychic experience', in S. Flanders (ed.), *The Dream Discourse Today* (London: Routledge, 1993).

Lacan, J., 'The agency of the letter in the unconscious or reason since Freud', in *Ecrits: A Selection* (London: Tavistock, [1957] 1977).

Laplanche, J. and Pontalis, J.-B., *The Language of Psychoanalysis* (London: The Hogarth Press, 1973).

Propp, V., *Morphology of the Folktale* (Austin, TX: University of Texas Press, [1928] 1968).

3

Dream readers

JOHN FORRESTER

How do international scientific movements usually get started? I will take as a guide those models with which I am familiar, drawn from the nineteenth and early twentieth centuries, the first heroic age of the formation of such international networks: Quetelet and the international statistical movements from the 1830s to 1860s; Pasteur and bacteriology, in the 1860s to 1890s; Darwin and the theory of evolution in the 1860s and 1870s; hypnotism in the 1880s and 1890s.[1] Very roughly, we can expect to see emerge, not necessarily in the same temporal order: a charismatic leader or leaders (Pasteur; Charcot); a core set of doctrines and pamphleteering documents defining the ideas and practices, conformity with which determines the conditions for membership of the movement (the Normal distribution; the bacterium and its management; the idea of suggestibility); belligerent exponents and organizers (Huxley; Pearson; Bernheim); a small group of devoted followers and disciples (the X club; the Nancy group); a rudimentary organization (Office of the Registrar-General; Sections of the British Association for the Advancement of Science); a system for the preservation, handing on, emendation, expansion and consolidation of the work of the practitioners (the well-placed enthusiast engineered into a new professional post; the co-option of resources for the establishment of new institutions, such as bacteriological laboratories, dominated by the members of the movement).

The history of the international psychoanalytic movement can be told in such a way as to conform tidily to this model. The charismatic leader, Freud, set out the core theories and practices:

infantile sexuality, dream-interpretation, free association. A small group of disciples gathered around him from 1902 on, including more than its fair share of belligerent exponents (Stekel; Jung; Jones; Ferenczi); a rudimentary organization is established with the branch societies – the Vienna, Berlin, Zurich Psychoanalytic Societies – and the umbrella international association, from 1910 onwards. By the 1920s a system for training professional practitioners and for disseminating more widely psychoanalytic ideas is established: the Berlin Policlinic, the Vienna Institute, the London Institute of Psychoanalysis. Alongside these public institutions a small, secret society of close followers of Freud was set up – the ring-bearers – whose fidelity to Freud's person and his conception of orthodoxy was not dissimilar to the private machinations of Huxley's X-club.

Is this a sufficiently comprehensive account of the development of psychoanalysis? On balance I think not. Two crucial features need to be added: first, the distinctive system of training analysts, which subjects them to the same procedure as patients – undergoing an analysis themselves; second, the fact that Freud was not only a doctor and a scientist, but also a writer of immense distinction. The founding text of psychoanalysis, its pamphlet and recipe-book all in one, is also an autobiographical document. So it is Jacques Derrida who has asked most succinctly the question I want to explore in this chapter: 'How can an autobiographical writing, in the abyss of an unterminated self-analysis, give birth to a world-wide institution?'[2]

The 'autobiographical writing' in question is *The Interpretation of Dreams*. The institution is the international psychoanalytic movement, a professional body governing the practice of psychoanalysis, based on the work of Freud. Like Derrida, I think it is justified to call *The Interpretation of Dreams* 'autobiographical writing'; like Derrida, I think it is fair to regard the book as the centrepiece of Freud's self-analysis. This was also Freud's view, in the Preface to the second edition of 1909:

> For this book has a further subjective significance for me personally – a significance which I only grasped after I had completed it. It was, I found, a portion of my own self-analysis, my reaction to my father's death – that is to say, to the most important event, the most poignant loss, of a man's life. (SE IV, xxvi)

It is not clear if our agreement with Freud's own verdict should give one added confidence in this judgement of ours, or makes one wonder about its independence and objectivity. Nonetheless, the question I wish to explore is: how does this autobiographical writing which Freud allowed himself after his father's death, both in triumph and in homage, produce an international movement?

Many psychoanalytic commentators, including Freud himself, have a twofold and contradictory view of the autobiographical element in the dream book. As Freud writes in the Preface to the second edition, immediately after confessing to his readers that the book they hold in their hand is the author's reaction to the most important event in his life:

> Having discovered that this was so, I felt unable to obliterate the traces of the experience. To my readers, however, it will be a matter of indifference upon what material they learn to value and interpret dreams.[3] (SE IV, xxvi)

This book, Freud claims, however autobiographical it may be, is still a work of science: the personal dimension of the dreams and their analyses that figure in it can be discounted without loss of substance.

The second reaction, the exact obverse of the posture of indifference that Freud insists a reader should adopt in reading the book, recognizes that the book is, precisely because it is a 'portion of my own self-analysis', exemplary and originary of psychoanalysis itself: the first self-analysis in history, and the exemplar of all analyses. This was Ernest Jones's judgement on Freud's self-analysis: 'his most heroic feat – a psycho-analysis of his own unconscious . . . Yet the uniqueness of the feat remains. Once done it is done for ever. For no one again can be the first to explore those depths.'[4] Two other analysts, Anzieu and Grinstein, have devoted much research and writing to this momentous event, so intimately tied up with the writing and publication of *The Interpretation of Dreams*.[5] Freud's self-analysis is thus treated as exemplary of all analyses, and this makes *The Interpretation of Dreams* the *Principia* of psychoanalysis: *fons et origo* of all that came later – in theory, in practice and institutionally.[6]

A second contradictory set of attitudes develops from this view of Freud's self-analysis. Freud founded psychoanalysis through this first analysis, but psychoanalysis demonstrates that this act of foundation was impossible. True self-analysis, it is often argued, and more often implied, is impossible: psycho-analysis as a practice certainly utterly disdains the possibility of self-analysis being in any sense comparable with the depth of understanding and transformation achieved through analysis by an Other, by an analyst.

To cope with this contradiction, many psychoanalytic com-mentators postulate that Freud did not engage in his own analysis entirely alone. The two most obvious candidates for the histori-cally privileged post of Freud's analyst are Wilhelm Fliess, and 'Freud's patients' (a collective unity). Freud certainly regarded himself as a patient being treated by someone: 'The chief patient I am preoccupied with is myself . . . The analysis is more difficult than any other. It is, in fact, what paralyzes my psychic strength for describing and communicating what I have won so far. Still, I believe it must be done and is a necessary intermediate stage in my work' (14 August 1897, F/F, 261). Two and a half months later, in late October 1897, he writes to Fliess: 'All of what I experienced with my patients, as a third [person] I find again here – days when I drag myself about dejected because I have under-stood nothing of the dream, of the fantasy, of the mood of the day; and then again days when a flash of lightning illuminates the interrelations and lets me understand the past as a preparation for the present' (27 October 1897, F/F, 274).

It is not only the psychoanalytic orthodoxy that argued for the impossibility of self-analysis. Here is Freud writing to Fliess in November 1897:

> My self-analysis remains interrupted. I have realized why I can analyze myself only with the help of knowledge obtained objectively (like an outsider). True self-analysis is impossible; otherwise there would be no (neurotic) illness. Since I am still contending with some kind of puzzle in my patients, this is bound to hold me up in my self-analysis as well. (14 November 1897, F/F, 281)

It is remarks like these, in which Freud places himself on a par with his patients and treats in a dialectical fashion his knowledge of them and a strangely subjectless other's knowledge of himself from the outside, that tempts some commentators to see, in a proto-Ferenczi-like spirit, Freud's work of the 1890s as a form of mutual analysis. How else are we to read these forthright exclamations at the necessity of Freud's analysis and of its impossibility without an 'Other'?

The strong alternative argument runs: Fliess was that Other, and it was through his fantasied relationship to his friend in Berlin, supplemented by their occasional meetings, all mediated by Freud's writing to his 'sole audience', that Freud's analysis was achieved. The distinctive feature of the Fliessian option is that Freud's analysis was, as he himself described in *The Interpretation of Dreams*, in part based upon his methodical writing down of his dreams (SE IV, 103), whose analysis he then sends to the Other in Berlin.

Yet Freud is not only writing about his dreams and his moods to Fliess. If we scrutinise his work over the period 1897–98, we observe a number of different forms of writing fading over into one another: there are the letters to Fliess brimming with advances in clinical and theoretical ideas; there are the confessional letters about his dreams and his childhood. Then, in December 1897, Freud starts to write to Fliess in a new genre, his 'Dreckology' or Shitology, papers which have not survived – 'the Dr, in which I now deposit my novelties' (23 February 1898, F/F, 300). By early 1898, the Dreckology passes over into, or is finally superseded by, the dream book:

> I am sending you today a long, finished issue of the DR, which I will perhaps ask you to return soon because of the beautiful dream example . . . My self-analysis is at rest in favor of the dream book. (9 February 1898, F/F, 299)

Two weeks later, the Shitology has explicitly become the dream book:

> I have finished a whole section of the dream book, the best-composed one, to be sure, and am curious about what else will occur to me. Otherwise, no scientific novelties; the DR have been interrupted, since I no longer write them for you. (5 March 1898, F/F, 301)

We do not possess the Dreckology; nor are the beautiful dream examples Freud regularly passed to Fliess included in the Fliess papers bought by Marie Bonaparte, via an intermediary, from Fliess's widow in late 1936. The reason is simple and obvious:

Freud asked for the dreams and the Dreckology back from Fliess, because he then included it in the dream book. In this way, Fliess, the first reader of Freud's dreams and theories, is the exemplar for the psychoanalytic reader in general; it is probable that Freud changed very little in shifting these dream examples, written seemingly for Fliess's eyes only, on to the more public stage of *The Interpretation of Dreams*.

So, if we envisage that Fliess was, *qua* first reader, Freud's analyst, we are invited to depict the first readers of *The Interpretation of Dreams* themselves as partaking in this analytic function of Fliess. Lacan put this argument first in his discussion of 'The dream of Irma's injection':

> Freud all by himself, analysing his dream, tried to find in it, proceeding as an occultist might, the secret designation of the point where as a matter of fact the solution to the mystery of the subject and the world lies. But he isn't all by himself. Once he communicates the secret of this Luciferian mystery to us, Freud is not confronted with this dream by himself. Just as the dream is addressed to the analyst in an analysis, Freud in his dream is already addressing himself to us.[7]

The rest of this chapter will be devoted to exploring the analytic function of the readers of *The Interpretation of Dreams*, by exploring the response of the first and then of later readers of the book.

The assumption one must always guard against is that Freud was in some sense naive – that he might have been innocent of the effect of his own writing. Alongside the seeming mastery that the position of reader brings with it – the freedom that the very structure of writing accords to each reader to do what they he or she will with the text – the author in question, Freud, was well aware of the possible preconceptions, even prerequisites, a reader might bring to or with which he might combat his writing. Alongside the reader responses, from Fliess to Forrester, there is the positioning of the reader by Freud.

Fliess was not only Freud's first reader; he was also his first censor. Indeed, the very idea of the censorship, so important in Freud's theory of the dream, seems to develop hand in hand with Fliess's interventions, at Freud's invitation, in the composition of the dream book. The first hint of the idea of censorship is the graphic and textual Russian censorship, described by Freud in December 1897.

Have you ever seen a foreign newspaper which passed Russian censorship at the frontier? Words, whole clauses and sentences are blacked out so that the rest becomes unintelligible. A *Russian censorship* of that kind comes about in psychoses and produces the apparently meaningless *deliria*. (22 December 1897, F/F, 289)[8]

So the first draft of the dream book, which had started with analyses of dreams sent to Fliess, emerged in the early spring of 1898 in the wake of a clear conception of the censorship, soon to play such an important role as a component of the dream theory. By May 1898, Freud was writing at high speed, sending two chapters to Fliess in less than three weeks, with Fliess now firmly in place as the author's, if not the dreamer's, omnipotent censor:

I shall change whatever you want and gratefully accept contributions. I am so immensely glad that you are giving me the gift of the Other, a critic and reader – and one of your quality at that. I cannot write entirely without an audience, but do not at all mind writing only for you. (18 May 1898, F/F, 313)

At the congress Freud and Fliess held in early June, for which Freud had 'nothing but the dream, the dream' (24 May 1898, F/F, 315), Fliess decisively exerted his influence by censoring from the manuscript of the dream book one completely analysed dream of Freud's:

I am reasonable enough to recognize that I need your critical help, because in this instance I myself have lost the feeling of shame required of an author. So the dream is condemned. Now that the sentence has been passed, however, I would like to shed a tear over it and confess that I regret it and that I have no hopes of finding a better one as a substitute. As you know, a beautiful dream and no indiscretion – do not coincide. (9 June 1898, F/F, 315)

This act of censorship had an immediate effect on Freud: he spent four more weeks completing an unsatisfactory version of the final chapter of the book and then stopped writing. He was still 'mourning the lost dream' (20 June 1898, F/F, 317) in October 1898. By December 1898 he had decided to brave the dream literature; in May 1899 he was still dithering, but suddenly later that month he set to with eagerness and renewed confidence. A substantially revised structure of the book emerged:[9]

the dream is suddenly taking shape, without any special motivation, but this time I am sure of it. I have decided that I cannot use any of the disguises, nor can I afford to give up anything because I am not rich enough to keep my finest and probably my only lasting discovery to myself. (28 May 1899, F/F, 353)

Freud wrote fluently and with great confidence over the summer; he sent the first section to the printer at the end of June. Throughout the summer, as he produced chapter after chapter, he sent them and the proofs alternately to the printer and to the censor:

You will have several more occasions to red-pencil similar instances of superfluous subjectivity. Your looking through the proofs is indeed a tremendous reassurance to me. (27 August 1899, F/F, 368)

Why did Freud need reassuring? He himself felt he had 'lost the feeling of shame required of an author' and had thus lost control of the dialectic of revealing and concealing that formed one of the principal axes of the dream book's plot. Initially, in the years 1895–97, he had revealed himself to Fliess and acted as his own censor; now, in writing his dream book, he was revealing himself – without shame – to his public and asking Fliess to be his censor. The dialectic of revealing and concealing that so preoccupied Freud had thus been played initially with Fliess first as object – of reverence, of sustenance, later and implicitly, of criticism and contempt – and then as censor.

The dialectic then began to disseminate itself into Freud's entourage: he enjoyed the prospect of Breuer being 'appalled' by the 'abundant indiscretions' (1 August 1899, F/F, 364), just as he had confessed to Fliess his enjoyment at 'the thought of all the "head shaking" over the indiscretions and audacities it contains' (9 February 1898, F/F, 298); by the time of the book's completion, with a hint of defiant, I-told-you-so-pride, he had come to expect that all his friends would, like Oscar Rie, express the 'most serious misgivings' (4 October 1899, F/F, 377) over publication. The first response to its publication also elicited this tone of the necessity of offending the world:

The book has just been sent out. The first tangible reaction was the termination of the friendship of a dear friend, who felt hurt by the mention of her husband in the *non vixit* dream. (7 November 1899, F/F, 383)[10]

The dear friend was Sophie Schwab-Paneth, godmother of one of his daughters, widow of a friend and colleague whose reputation Freud had sacrificed in one of his own ambition dreams which culminated in the thought 'after all, I reflected, was not having children our only path to immortality?' (SE V, 487).

Thirty years later, Freud replied to André Breton's accusation, in his book *Les Vases communicants*, that, like a 'prudent bourgeois', he had deliberately withheld the sexual motives in analysing his own dreams whilst displaying such motives in the dreams of others:

> I believe that if I have not analysed my own dreams as extensively as those of others, the cause is only rarely timidity with regard to the sexual. The fact is, much more frequently, that it would have required me regularly to discover the secret source of the whole series of dreams in my relations to my father, recently deceased. I maintain that I was in the right to set limits to the inevitable exhibition (as well of an infantile tendency since surmounted).[11]

It is the infantile tendency to exhibitionism that Freud appears to denounce as underlying his virtuoso performance of self-disclosure in *The Interpretation of Dreams*. And the question of indiscretion and dissimulation emphatically does not end with the final publication of the book.

It would, at first blush, have been possible for Freud to use the dreams of others, principally his patients, as the material upon which his dream book was based. The substance of the Preface to the first edition of the dream book explained why he had not:

> The only dreams open to my choice were my own and those of my patients undergoing psycho-analytic treatment. But I was precluded from using the latter material by the fact that in its case the dream-processes were subject to an undesirable complication owing to the added presence of neurotic features. But if I was to report my own dreams, it inevitably followed that I should have to reveal to the public gaze more of the intimacies of my mental life than I liked, or than is normally necessary for any writer who is a man of science and not a poet. Such was the painful but unavoidable necessity; and I have submitted to it rather than totally abandon the possibility of giving the evidence for my psychological findings. Naturally, however, I have been unable to resist the temptation of taking the edge off some of my indiscretions by omissions and substitutions.

> But whenever this happened, the value of my instances has been
> very definitely diminished. (SE IV, xxiii–xxiv)

Freud is thus bowing to a necessity imposed on him despite
himself, and goes on to lay the onus for the view taken of these
indiscretions on the reader:

> I can only express a hope that readers of this book will put them-
> selves in my difficult situation and treat me with indulgence, and
> further, that anyone who finds any sort of reference to himself in my
> dreams may be willing to grant me the right of freedom of thought
> – in my dream-life, if nowhere else. (SE IV, xxiv)

In this way, the book opens with the dialectic of the dreamer
reluctantly revealing himself despite himself, and the reader
in consequence invited to be curious and critical, prurient and
censorious, all at once. The indiscreet dreamer (Freud) and the
censorious critic (Fliess) are immediately *mis en scène* as the
principal actors in the book itself.

At the opening of Chapter II of the book, the crucial moment
prefacing Freud's entry on stage as the principal protagonist of
his own book, the plea concerning his unwilling entry into the
spotlight and the necessity of entrusting himself to the discretion
of the reader is heard again, this time more forcefully:

> Thus it comes about that I am led to my own dreams, which offer a
> copious and convenient material, derived from an approximately
> normal person and relating to multifarious occasions of daily life.
> No doubt I shall be met by doubts of the trustworthiness of 'self-
> analyses' of this kind; and I shall be told that they leave the door
> open to arbitrary conclusions. In my judgement the situation is in
> fact more favourable in the case of *self*-observation than in that of
> other people; at all events we may make the experiment and see how
> far self-analysis takes us with the interpretation of dreams. But I
> have other difficulties to overcome, which lie within myself. There is
> some natural hesitation about revealing so many intimate facts
> about one's mental life; nor can there be any guarantee against
> misinterpretation by strangers. (SE IV, 104–5)

And the powerful theatrical effect which will, finally, justify this
self-exposure is now revealed:

> *Nun muss ich aber den Leser bitten, für eine ganze Weile meine Interessen*
> *zu den seinigen zu machen und sich mit mir in die kleinsten Einzelheiten*

meines Lebens zu versenken, denn solche Übertragung fordert gebieterisch das Interesse für die verstecke Bedeutung der Träume.[12]

And now I must ask the reader to make my interests his own for quite a while, and to plunge, along with me, into the minutest details of my life; for a transference of this kind is peremptorily demanded by our interest in the hidden meaning of dreams. (SE IV, 105–6)

Here, finally, is the bait – and the hook – by which the reader becomes interested in, fascinated by, engaged, contracted, pledged to Freud's book: he[13] is kindly requested to make Freud's interests his own, to transfer on to the dreamer portrayed in the book. The structure of Freud's sentence acknowledges that the reader must give up something in this process – his own interests – and then take on something else: Freud's own interests. How far should the reader go in this process?

Freud lets his reader know that he is well aware that indiscretions have an intrinsic interest, but is confident that this somewhat disreputable curiosity will be transformed into something else, more worthy:

it is safe to assume that my readers too will very soon find their initial interest in the indiscretions which I am bound to make replaced by an absorbing immersion in the psychological problems upon which they throw light. (SE IV, 105)

But there is an ambiguity in the evocation of these 'psychological problems' which will draw reader's attention away from Freud's personal indiscretions: he does not specify that these are *general* psychological problems that will soon absorb the reader. The implication here, and in the Preface to the second edition from which I have already quoted on p. 85, is that the reader will become preoccupied not with general problems but with specific ones – with his own dreams, following in Freud's own path. The reader will thus, by passing relatively rapidly through the stage of curiosity over Freud's indiscretions, become a Freudian.[14] And if he remains caught at the stage of prurient curiosity, if he remains caught at the stage of transference on to Freud? He may then remain another kind of Freudian, one who is identified, to all intents and purposes, with the protagonists of Freud's dreams.

We have seen how Freud's 'Other' functioned as object of indiscretion, then also as censor, then again as the invited participant in transference on to Freud's interests and inner life. Having agreed to accompany Freud on his 'imaginary walk' (6 August 1899, F/F, 365), having been led along the 'concealed pass' of the specimen dream of Chapter II, the famous 'dream of Irma's injection'[15], 'all at once' the reader, arm in arm with Freud, contemplates the next step:

> When, after passing through a narrow defile, we suddenly emerge upon a piece of high ground, where the path divides and the finest prospects open up on every side, we pause for a moment and consider in which direction we shall first turn our steps. Such is the case with us, now that we have surmounted the first interpretation of a dream. (SE IV, 122)

The trope of the walk through the country is a classical one, in both the Christian literature concerning the spiritual quest for truth, and in the secularized genre of confession and autobiography that supplanted it from Rousseau on. Freud and the reader may now engage in the journey Freud envisages: part spiritual quest, part autobiography, part account of a 'sudden discovery', a momentous event in the development of science. It is this mixture of genres that has so intrigued many of Freud's readers – 'scientific treatise, intimate diary, confession, key to dreams, fantasy journey, initiatory quest, essay on the human condition, and what is more, a vast allegorical fresco of the unconscious'.[16] But at every moment on the journey, the promised goal also recedes; as Alexander Welsh notes, 'concealment provides the drama of the dream book'.[17] Throughout the book, Freud plays a game of hide and seek with the reader. He discloses his innermost secrets, seemingly; yet, just as regularly, he peremptorily, though with apparent reluctance, closes the door on the reader. Freud entices the reader on, but just as clearly brings him up short:

> I can assure my readers that the ultimate meaning of the dream [of the Botanical monograph], which I have not disclosed, is intimately related to the subject of the childhood scene. (SE IV, 191)

In *On Dreams*, the simplified guide to the larger dream book, Freud writes:

> I might draw closer together the threads in the material revealed by the analysis, and I might then show that they converge upon a single

nodal point, but considerations of a personal and not of a scientific nature prevent my doing so in public. I should be obliged to betray many things which had better remain my secret, for on my way to discovering the solution of the dream all kinds of things were revealed which I was unwilling to admit even to myself. Why then, it will be asked, have I not chosen some other dream, whose analysis is better suited for reporting, so that I could produce more convincing evidence of the meaning and connectedness of the material uncovered by analysis? The answer is that *every* dream with which I might try to deal would lead to things equally hard to report and would impose an equal discretion upon me. (SE V, 640)

As far as the reader is concerned, the censorship will always win in the end, it seems. Yet the whole strategy of dream analysis is an implementation of techniques of circumventing the censorship. This dialectic, of the secret wish striving for expression and the censorship ensuring its suppression, is played out between dreamer and reader. Yet the roles are continually being reversed; sometimes the reader is asked to identify with the wish, only to find Freud acting as censor. Sometimes the reader is expected to repudiate the dream, as when Freud discusses the censorship of affect in dreams, and gives an account of a short dream in which Freud urinated away from the edge of an open-air lavatory 'small heaps of faeces of all sizes and degrees of freshness' – a dream 'which will fill every reader with disgust' (SE V, 468–9). Or take the footnote in which Freud refers to the sceptical response of Wilhelm Fliess, and immediately invites subsequent readers to identify with this response of the first reader and censor:

The first reader and critic of this book – and his successors are likely to follow his example – protested that 'the dreamer seems to be too ingenious and amusing'. This is quite true so long as it refers only to the dreamer; it would only be an objection if it were to be extended to the dream-interpreter. In waking reality I have little claim to be regarded as a wit. If my dreams seem amusing, that is not on my account, but on account of the peculiar psychological conditions under which dreams are constructed; and the fact is intimately connected with the theory of the jokes and the comic. Dreams become ingenious and amusing because the direct and easiest pathway to the expression of their thoughts is barred: they are forced into being so. The reader can convince himself that my patients' dreams seem at least as full of jokes and puns as my own, or even fuller. (SE IV, 297f)[18]

This passage not only links subsequent readers in a chain with the first reader, but it also is quite typical of Freud's pre-empting of the reader's response to the book, its dreamers and their dream-interpretations. It invites the reader not only to inspect the patients' dreams, but also to inspect his own – 'actual experience would teach them better', Freud remarks later in the book (SE V, 523). 'Am I', the reader is invited to ask, 'as witty a dreamer as Freud? Perhaps the lack of puns and jokes in my interpretations of them is a sign that I have not as yet found their full interpretation?' We know with what determination Freud rose to the challenge of Fliess the sceptical censor: he wrote a whole book, *Jokes and their Relation to the Unconscious*, to 'refute', or at least lay to rest, the implicit charge of the overingenuity of the dream-interpreter.

The alacrity with which Freud defended himself against Fliess's criticisms[19] – whose other principal criticism concerned anxiety dreams – is displayed throughout the book; indeed, like that other work of skilfully crafted, semi-autobiographical scientific advocacy, Darwin's *On the Origin of Species*, Freud's first priority was to elicit and then meet his reader's sceptical responses to a bold theory. Freud forestalls the reader's criticisms by voicing them on his behalf; once again, the 'censor' and the 'repressed' change places. The strategy is quite deliberate and informs the entire strategy of the book, even its principal thesis. Why did Freud put forward, as the result of the interpretation of one single dream of his own, the thesis that 'when the work of interpretation has been completed, we perceive that a dream is the fulfilment of a wish' (SE IV, 121)? Precisely in order to elicit the sceptical response of the reader. Let us consider the structure of Freud's argument in terms of the sequence of chapters, so as to examine this strategy of his.

The principal thesis of wish-fulfilment is stated at the close of Chapter II; Chapter III considers a number of dreams in order to render plausible the thesis that this is the universal characteristic of dreams. The dreams considered are confirmatory: dreams that are reasonably transparent, including a collection of children's dreams. These dreams set an engaging tone, as do the dreams of convenience: the medical student who oversleeps and dreams he is already in the hospital, the newly married woman who dreams she is having her period so as to postpone having to accept the reality of her first pregnancy. But they are not sufficient to establish the thesis, and Freud knows full well that he cannot lull his critic for long with these charming confirmatory instances. Nor does he wish to: he *needs* the sceptical critic, his reader, to become embroiled with the next step in his argument.

So, after the few pages spent showing the reader the admirable views opened up by the wish-fulfilment theory, Freud opens Chapter IV, 'Distortion in dreams', with a very different welcome for the reader.

> If I proceed to put forward the assertion that the meaning of *every* dream is the fulfilment of a wish, that is to say that there cannot be any dreams but wishful dreams, I feel certain in advance that I shall meet with the most categorical contradiction. (SE IV, 134)

You, the reader, are *certain* to deny me! There then follows a long paragraph in quotation marks in which the critic voices his categorical contradiction. Even when the 'natural' voice of Freud finally emerges from outside the quotation marks, it confesses that 'anxiety-dreams make it impossible to assert as a general proposition ... that dreams are wish-fulfilments; indeed they seem to stamp any such proposition as an absurdity' (SE IV, 135).[20]

But Freud has not lost his battle; far from it, he has simply opened up the terrain on which he will win over this sceptical critic. All he has to do is to make a distinction, here for the first time in the book, between the *manifest* and the *latent* content of the dream: the reader's critical objection is left high and dry, tilting at the windmill of the manifest content, while Freud can consolidate his discoveries by bringing to light the mysteries of the latent content. With the distinction between latent and manifest, Freud repeats the founding act of splitting of the writing of his dream book: between dream and interpretation, between writer and censor, between discretion and exposure. With the idea of 'latency' Freud both shores up, or specifies, the object of the act of interpretation: the interpreter is seeking what is latent, not what is manifest. And he also introduces the hint of secrecy which is to be such a seductive feature of the reader's progress through the book. Like Sigmund Freud, who dreamed of erecting a plaque at

Bellevue, 'where the secret of dreams revealed itself' (12 June 1900, F/F, 417) to him, each reader will go in search of the secret, not only of the dream, but also, through the 'transference' peremptorily demanded of him, of Sigmund Freud, and through him, of his own inner dream-life.

The idea of the latent is then explored through the analysis of another of Freud's dreams, a dream whose fundamental feature was the dreamer's struggle to *dissimulate from himself* his contemptuous judgement of a friend as a simpleton. Disguise in dreams – the very principle of latency – thus amounts to a defensive distortion, entirely analogous to the dissimulation practised in everyday social life by a person in the presence of someone with power over him. Freud rubs the point home: 'when I interpret my dreams for my readers I am obliged to adopt similar distortions' (SE IV, 142). That is, in the face of the all-powerful and censorious reader, Freud pointedly indicates, he adopts a disguise. Here we come upon that fundamental posture of the Freudian in relation to the world so aptly described by Paul Ricoeur: 'as a man of desires I go forth in disguise'.[21] But the very act of disguise and dissimulation has two sides: I dissimulate for the others, but I find a way of making the secret available for your eyes only. 'The stricter the censorship, the more far-reaching will be the disguise and the more ingenious too may be the means employed for putting the reader on the scent of the true meaning' (SE IV, 142). The reader switches, from paragraph to paragraph, from being the censor from whom the truth must be hidden to being Freud's complicit partner in the secret truths of the adept. What is bad news for one party to the power struggle, for instance the censoring governmental agency, will be good news for the insurrectionists plotting in disguise. In this way, the anxiety-dream of those in power is identical with the wish-fulfilment of those under their thumb.[22]

But the true sceptic is still waiting for a reply; he will not be taken in by the pleasures of collusive complicity. It is to silence this sceptic that Freud introduces a third party – the clever, wily, witty and sceptical patient, who in the course of Freud's psychoanalytic interpretations, subjects him to 'a remorseless criticism, certainly no less severe than I have to expect from the members of my own profession. And my patients invariably contradict my assertion that all dreams are fulfilments of wishes' (SE IV, 146). So, for the first time in the dream book, the patient occupies centre stage. And he – or rather she, since Freud's most sympathetically and thus critically intelligent patients seem to have been women – does so as principal critic. ' "How do you fit that in with your theory?" ' (SE IV, 146) is their insistent refrain. The 'cleverest of all my dreamers' (SE IV, 151) dreamt of spending her holiday near her hated mother-in-law:

> The dream showed that I was wrong [about the nature of dreams]. *Thus it was her wish that I might be wrong, and her dream showed that wish fulfilled.* But her wish that I might be wrong . . . related in fact to . . . [my inference that] at a particular period of her life something must have occurred that was of importance in determining her illness. She had disputed this, since she had no recollection of it; but soon afterwards it had turned out that I was right. Thus her wish that I might be wrong, which was transformed into her dream of spending her holidays with her mother-in-law, corresponded to a well-justified wish that the events of which she was then becoming aware for the first time might never have occurred. (SE IV, 151–2)

This is the model for Freud's answer to his critic's categorical contradiction: every such contradiction is not only a refutation of his theory, but embodies the *wish* that he might be wrong. In this way every possible criticism of the theory is undercut.

In 1909, and then in 1911, Freud supplemented his account of these dreams that prove Freud wrong by calling these dreams 'counter-wish dreams' (*Gegenwünschträume*): these are the dreams elicited by a person's first contact with psychoanalysis – thus explaining why he places them so strategically, immediately after the statement and confirmation of the wish-fulfilment hypothesis, as the first dreams of someone other than himself:

> I can count almost certainly on provoking one of them after I have explained my theory that dreams are fulfilments of wishes to a patient for the first time . . . or to people who have heard me lecturing . . . Indeed, it is expected that the same thing will happen to some of the readers of the present book; they will be quite ready to have one of their wishes frustrated in a dream if only their wish that I may be wrong can be fulfilled. (SE IV, 157–8, incorporating part of a footnote added in 1911)

What is so important about this strategic argument of Freud's is that it finally places the reader in the position of the *patient*, dreaming refutations of Freud's theory. The patient is always a counter-wisher (in resistance); the reader is invited to adopt this position as well.

We might call the patient's and the critic's protest against the logic of 'Heads I win, tails you lose', the principle of bloody-mindedness. But that is precisely what Freud is pointing to as a fundamental property of human relations: the critic, the censor, the counter-wish – which he called in 1915, somewhat mislead-ingly, the 'instinctive tendency to fend of intellectual novelties' (SE XV, 214).[23]

> The layman asks: 'Where is the wish-fulfilment?' And instantly, having heard that dreams are supposed to be wish-fulfilments, and in the very act of asking the question, he answers it with a rejection. (SE XV, 214)[24]

Here Freud points towards the function of negativity and noth-ingness as found in post-Hegelian philosophy – in Heidegger and Sartre – where it is intimately linked to the capacity for human freedom. Yet he wishes to disarm, to take the sting out of the 'categorical contradiction' that he has provoked – provoked delib-erately, it might seem, precisely for this end.

This provocation of absolute opposition – the staging of the confrontation between interpreter and sceptic – demonstrates the willed and deliberate character of Freud's strategy. On the one side of this confrontation, there is the reader, easily provoked into bloody-minded refusal of Freud's arguments and interpreta-tions.[25] On the other side, fully prepared there is not only the wily interpreter, but also the wily dreamer, Just as the reader is, in the very act of bloody-minded opposition, conforming to Freud's strategy, so had Freud's dream life become entirely subordinate to the requirements of writing the dream book. In May 1897, he had

> dreamed of overaffectionate feelings for Mathilde, only she was called Hella; and afterward I again saw 'Hella' before me, printed in heavy type. Solution: Hella is the name of an American niece whose picture we have been sent. Mathilde could be called Hella because she recently shed bitter tears over the defeats of the Greeks. She is

> enthralled by the mythology of ancient Hellas and naturally regards
> all Hellenes as heroes. The dream of course shows the fulfilment of
> my wish to catch a *Pater* as the originator of neurosis and thus puts
> an end to my ever-recurring doubts. (31 May 1897, F/F, 249)

Here his wish to pin down the father expressed itself as a self-
inculpation: he was dreaming a confirmation of his seduction
theory to order.[26] He wishes to see more clearly, *heller*. A year
later, when Fliess censored the complete interpretation of his big
dream and Freud mourned its irreplaceable loss, he immediately
reasserts his authority over his dream-life and asks:

> Let me know at least which topic it was to which you took exception
> and where you feared an attack by a malicious critic. . . . So that I can
> omit what you designate in a substitute dream, because I can have
> dreams like that to order. (9 June 1898, F/F, 315)

Dreaming to order – a dream-life subordinate to the requirements
of writing – had been the persistent theme of Freud's burst of
creativity in 1899:

> One day I had been trying to discover what might be the meaning of
> the feelings of being inhibited, of being glued to the spot, of not
> being able to get something done, and so on, which occur so often in
> dreams and are so closely akin to feelings of anxiety. That night I had
> the following dream [of climbing the stairs and suddenly feeling
> ashamed, inhibited and rooted to the spot]. (SE IV, 238)

And, at the height of the final spurt of writing the dream book,
Freud's dreams are nothing but commentaries – enigmatic
enough at times – on his own writing:

> My own dreams have now become absurdly complicated. Recently
> I was told that on the occasion of Aunt Minna's birthday Annerl
> said, 'On birthdays I am mostly a little bit good.' Thereupon I
> dreamed the familiar school dream in which I am in *sexta* [sixth
> grade] and say to myself, 'In this sort of dream one is mostly in sixth
> grade.' The only possible solution: Annerl is my *sexta* [sixth] child!
> Brr . . . (27 June 1899, F/F, 357)

The wilfulness of Freud the theoretician of the dream, whose
dreams become nothing but theory, is thus the match of the wilful
reader, whose first impulse on reading Freud's book, on hearing
him speak, will be to dream a refutation of him. They make a right

pair, it would seem. Indeed, that is the strategy of Freud's writing: they *are* a right pair.

We have seen how the reader of Freud's text is invited to make Freud's interests his own, to transfer entirely; we have seen how the roles of desirer and censor are apportioned out between the author and the reader, as they easily exchange roles; we have seen how the reader is expected, on the model of all Freud's interlocutors, to repudiate forcefully Freud's theories and in consequence to be drawn ever more tightly into the embrace of his theory, of an identification with him. Typical – but salutary – was the response of Freud's first serious reader after publication, a philosopher, Heinrich Gomperz, son of a patron and patient of Freud's, approached Freud in late November 1899 and started studying the method of dream interpretation with Freud:

> My philosopher, Harry G., is very amusing. Supposedly he believes nothing whatsoever, but has all sorts of beautiful and witty ideas. . . . His dreams constantly quote my dreams, which he then forgets, and so forth. (26 November 1899, F/F, 389)[27]

There are two diametrically opposed ways of characterizing this process of identification and transference: the first sees the *autobiographical* dreamer and writer as the central protagonist of the dream book, and thus views the reader's involvement with 'Freud' as a form of personal and intimate seduction, in which the reader and author perform Freud's perfectly choreographed dance of disclosure and withdrawal. In reviewing Freud's *An Autobiographical Study*, Hanns Sachs captured this fascinating autobiographical aspect of the dream book

> some of Freud's works, especially the *Interpretation of Dreams* reveal the true substance of his personality, and not his *Autobiography*. . . . Thus he had to make use of a language of his own invention, of puzzles and allusions, wherever he thought it better to cover up again for strange eyes what had been revealed; for a reader who attempts to bring to light what is hidden of his person and to join together what has been torn apart intentionally, the book can easily become a maze.[28]

This maze is more properly Freud's web, spun to capture the reader, to render him Freudian through an identification with and a driven pursuit of the person of Freud. This strategy of Freud's accounts for the personal and intimate details of the dream book, so absent from more officially autobiographical texts, for the simple reason that this is autobiography not for its own sake but for the pedagogical and analytic purpose of making readers into Freudians.

Being a Freudian has, I am stressing, a number of senses. It can mean subscribing to Freudian doctrines and theories. And this is the second way of characterising the process that the reader of the dream book undergoes: confirming or being convinced of the *scientific* (as opposed to autobiographical) truth of the theories advanced in the book. Freud's scientific strategy in this respect is resolutely universalistic: the propositions he advances are only important insofar as they have the form 'All Xs are Ys' – all dreams are wish-fulfilments. Freud's was never a statistical sensibility, despite the rise of statistical thinking, particularly in the burgeoning human sciences of the late nineteenth and early twentieth centuries.[29] The only statistics quoted in *The Interpretation of Dreams* – that 57.2 per cent of dreams are 'disagreeable' and only 28.6 per cent positively 'pleasant' – Freud put into the mouth of the sceptical critic of the hypothesis of wish-fulfilment; they are not taken seriously. A statistical law would not be serious science for Freud. His conception of 'serious science' was, however, audacious in one respect: he took as an axiom that if one could find meaning in *one* dream then it was methodologically justified to treat *all* dreams as meaningful. Similarly, he was convinced that the law that all dreams are wish-fulfilments could be adequately defended. But it never occurred to him to consider whether there might be different types of dreams specific to different subjects: that he might be a wish-fulfilling type, whereas another person might be an anxiety type. Freud assumed that one dreamer stood for all dreamers, just as contemporary physicists might assume that one substance subject to gravity stood for all substances, or biologists might assume that one sample of haemoglobin stood for all samples – and unlike those biometricians or statisticians whose object of study was the very diversity of characteristics of a field of phenomena.

In this sense, Freud behaved as modern physicists do when they accept without question – and without qualms – that the CERN laboratory is the sole place on earth capable of yielding

significant results about the next level down of sub-atomic events
– it is the sole place on earth that is capable of measuring, and of
measuring itself against, the universe. To Freud, the dreams of 'an
approximately normal person', as he described himself, were
without question a sufficient basis upon which to build a universal theory of all dreams, for all dreamers.

This is the scientific assumption, which could be contested by
critics; Ernest Jones reported one such set of criticisms to Freud,
after a meeting of the American Psychological Association that he
attended in late 1909:

> The part of my paper ['Freud's theory of dreams'] that aroused most
> opposition was, curiously enough, my statement that the *Traumge-*
> *danke[n]* were always egocentric. One wild female flourished two
> dreams at me that were 'entirely altruistic', and declared there was
> nothing selfish in her, even in her subconscious. Another one said
> you had no right to generalise that all dreams were egocentric be-
> cause you hadn't analysed all dreams; it wasn't scientific. What was
> true of Austrians might not be true of Americans! I said that experi-
> ence had shown that a man died if he was immersed in deep water
> for ten minutes. Was one not justified in generalising this statement
> before proving it on all men and in all seas? Another psychologist
> said he had been using your psycho-analysis in the study of the
> aesthetics of humour and found that the results of the analysis
> depended on the temperature of the room. As you have shamefully
> neglected to publish records of the varying temperature of your
> consulting-room, your conclusions are all worthless.[30]

To Freud and his disciples the idea that an American's dreams
might obey different laws from those of a Jewish Viennese doctor's
was preposterous – not only because it asserted in a smug and self-
serving fashion that Americans were ethically higher than the
Viennese, but principally because it imagined that an American
Freud would not be exemplary of all humanity. The autobiographical Freud could only be exemplary for all dreamers and all
readers if this axiom of universality held. It is as if Freud reversed
the principle he had enunciated to his fiancée in 1882: 'I always find
it uncanny when I can't understand someone in terms of myself.'[31]
The psychoanalytic axiom becomes: 'Understanding of myself is
both necessary and sufficient to understanding someone, anyone.
And you, dear reader, do likewise, by understanding me.'

Before we turn to look at the success of Freud's strategies, as measured by the actual responses of reviewers and disciples in the early years of this century, we can gauge his own sense of the actual reader of *The Interpretation of Dreams* from the extraordinary Preface, written in 1909, to the second edition:

> If within ten years of the publication of this book (which is very far from being an easy one to read) a second edition is called for, this is not due to the interest taken in it by the professional circles to whom my original preface was addressed. My psychiatric colleagues seem to have taken no trouble to overcome the initial bewilderment created by my new approach to dreams. The professional philosophers have become accustomed to polishing off the problems of dream-life (which they treat as a mere appendix to conscious states) in a few sentences – and usually in the same ones; and they have evidently failed to notice that we have something here from which a number of inferences can be drawn that are bound to transform our psychological theories. The attitude adopted by reviewers in the scientific periodicals could only lead one to suppose that my work was doomed to be sunk into complete silence; while the small group of gallant supporters, who practise medical psycho-analysis under my guidance and who follow my example in interpreting dreams and make use of their interpretations in treating neurotics, would never have exhausted the first edition of the book. Thus it is that I feel indebted to a wider circle of educated and curious-minded readers, whose interest had led me to take up once more after nine years this difficult, but in many respects fundamental, work. (SE IV, XXV)

Setting to one side the portrait of a misunderstood and somewhat embittered author that this Preface paints, Freud makes it clear that *The Interpretation of Dreams* has not been, and by implication will not be, read and understood by 'the professional circles to whom my original preface was addressed', 'my psychiatric colleagues', 'the professional philosophers' and the 'reviewers'; nor – and this should make us wonder somewhat – do the 'gallant supporters' count. Who counts as the readership of Freud's dream book? Only the common reader, 'a wider circle of educated and curious-minded readers', counts as constituting the appreciative and approved readership of his book. Irrespective of whether they are critics or followers, the professionals – whom we might redescribe as 'those in positions of interpretative power' – do not count; only the dreamers, the potential patients, the potential auto-analysts, the potential Freudians count. In case the reader had not bothered to read the Preface to the second edition, Freud makes the point again at the close of Chapter I:

> It [my work] has, of course, received least attention from those who are engaged in what is described as 'research' into dreams, and who have thus provided a shining example of the repugnance to learning anything new which is characteristic of men of science. In the ironical words of Anatole France, *'les savants ne sont pas curieux'*. (SE IV, 93, postscript added 1909)

The reviewers, the *savants*, were not entirely hostile to the book, nor were they few in number, as Freud often implied. Certain of them adopted the 'American' position: this holds for Freud, maybe, but not for me ('his theories compel our full agreement, provided we are not expected to subject every dream to his schematics').[32] Many found Freud 'ingenious' and 'stimulating'. Only one, Max Burckhard, set out to refute Freud's theories by analysing his own dreams in public – and it was possibly this strategy that infuriated Freud, who called it a 'stupid review, . . . hardly flattering, uncommonly devoid of understanding' (8 January 1990, F/F 394). But, we might well ask Freud, wasn't this precisely what he expected of readers? Burckhard reacts in exactly the way we saw the patients who make their entrance in Chapter IV reacted: he presented a 'counter-wish dream', and teasingly imagined what Freud would say in reply. The dream derived from one Christmas of his student days, when a romance began to blossom between him and a girl he spied sitting sewing at her window across the courtyard from him. The sighs and glances exchanged eventually led to a clandestine meeting, at which the young man discovered the pretty girl was hard of hearing. On New Year's Day, he dreamed an anxiety dream in which she and a man invaded his room through the open window, only to be chased back by his chaperoning uncle; as they retreated, they lost their grip and both, first the man, then the girl, fell to their death. When he awoke from the dream, the dreamer nailed a blanket over his window, so he would never see the girl again. 'May I ask where the wish fulfilment is in my dream?', he asks Freud:

> I suppose Dr. Freud would have me say that I was disgusted when I learned that she was hard of hearing, even if I didn't articulate it

consciously. I was then ready to get rid of her somehow, and my dream fulfilled the wish. This is the way, you must know, in which Dr. Freud artfully suggests various wishes to his patients so that he can then toss their dreams on the same pile with other 'wish-fulfilment dreams.' He says for example, 'If someone dreams about the death of his father or mother, a brother or a sister, I would never try to prove from it that he wishes their death. The theory does not need to go that far. It is sufficient to conclude that the dreamer had once wished their death, perhaps in his childhood.'[33]

No other reviewer tried to fight Freud on the field of dream-interpretation, and it is easy to see why. Freud makes it too easy to see how Burckhard had swallowed the bait.

In his self-imposed splendid isolation, Freud greeted nearly all reviews with short-tempered grumpiness over their stupidity; what grated upon him the most was their failure to recognize that he had already met all their objections in the book itself, and that their carping at wish-fulfilments or at the egoistic character of all dreams betrayed a lesser intelligence than the 'patients' who already criticized Freud in the book itself. 'You've understood nothing – go and read it again!' was his implicit rebuke of his lukewarm reviewers. His followers were to adopt similar tones with critics: in 1911 Jones recounted one Freudian's response to unenlightened professional colleagues:

> The Congress in Munich was unutterably stupid and tedious except for a few jokes that enlivened the discussions. Tromner last year read a paper on sleep, and Seif said he would give him one piece of advice – to read the *Traumdeutung*. This year he read a silly paper on, dreams, and frequently quoted the *Traumdeutung*. Seif said he was glad to find he had taken his advice about reading the *Traumdeutung* and that he would now give him another piece – to read it again.[34]

Ignorance of the *Traumdeutung* was treated by Freud's followers as a sure index of stupidity and resistance.[35] Inversely, the sure sign of being a follower was willingness to bring additional material to support the theory of dreams, and Freud dispensed acknowledgements to his growing band of followers by including their material in later editions of the book. Stekel contributed much material on symbolism and was largely responsible for the only major structural change in the book in later editions, when a new section on symbolism was added to the Chapter VI on the dream-work.[36] Ferenczi's contributions on symbolism and the question of the translatability of dreams (in particular, questions concerning linguistic usage in Hungarian and German in relation to dream-elements) were included, as were Jones's remarks about Hamlet, the relation of dreams to madness and additional individual dream interpretations. Two papers by Rank on myth and creative writing were included in the editions from 1914 to 1922, and he contributed expanded bibliographies to these editions. The most substantive theoretical contribution, which Freud included in the 1911 edition, came in the form of the 'functional phenomena' described and analysed by Herbert Silberer – and even he, a good Freudian, introduced the phenomena by analysing Freud's own dreams (SE IV, 214, n4).

The response of the followers to Freud's dreams reveals how successful Freud's specification of the reader-function had been. The simplest of these responses was permanent identification. Each follower would reread, as if to learn by heart, the original text and its later editions – for example, Jones, writing to Freud in July 1914: 'I shall look forward to the *Traumdeutung*. I have not read it since the last edition appeared, which is a long interval for me.'[37] Jones could good-humouredly spot a fellow disciple's identification in the form of a parapraxis in his learning of English when on a visit to London in 1914: 'There is only one mistake in English that I cannot cure [Sachs] of – he obstinately confounds the genders (Starfish. Tr. D. identification!).'[38] Jones knowingly concludes that Sachs refuses to correct his grammatical error by identifying with a passage in *The Interpretation of Dreams* where Freud recounts how he, on a visit to England as a young man, referred to a starfish as 'he', thus 'bringing in sex where it did not belong' (SE V, 517–18). Sachs, Jones implies, clings to his grammatical error in order to be like the Freud who confused 'he' and 'it'; like Freud, perhaps, he wants to continue to bring in sex where it does not belong. Ferenczi's letter to Freud of 1910 puts the strong case for the necessity of this identification, and thereby reveals its strength:

> Whether you want to be or not, you are one of the great master teachers of mankind, and you must allow your readers to approach you, at least intellectually, in a personal relationship as well. . . . I am convinced that I am not the only one who, in important decisions, in

self-criticism, etc., always asks and has asked himself the question: How would *Freud* relate to this?. . . . So I am and have been much, much more intimately acquainted and conversant with you than you could have imagined. . . .[39]

Even the austere and superior Ernest Jones could give Freud marks on the publication of his *Autobiographical Study* because he thus recognized the necessity of his making further personal revelations:

> I am glad you realise that . . . your mental development cannot be isolated from psycho-analysis as a whole and that you have been willing to repeat the sacrifice of your own privacy already undertaken in the *Traumdeutung*.[40]

Ferenczi was most acute, and acutely sensitive, to reading in *The Interpretation of Dreams* the signs of Freud's ambivalent relations to his readers and followers, and to what this might mean for the follower who identified too strongly with Freud. Freud had described how, after what he felt to be a poor lecture, his solitude had been invaded by an admiring member of the audience, who 'began to flatter me: telling me how much he had learnt from me, how he looked at everything now with fresh eyes . . . , that I was a very great man. My mood fitted ill with this paean of praise; I fought against my feeling of disgust, went home early to escape from him. . . .' (SE V, 470). Obviously, mindful of perpetually appearing in the guise of this unwanted flatterer, Ferenczi reminded Freud of this passage:

> I know that the many years in which you have been misunderstood have very strongly diminished your receptivity to admiration, recognition, etc. (see in connection to that the passage in *The Interpretation of Dreams* where you so morosely disdain the effusive admiration of a pupil [in the coffee house] – but you must gradually accustom yourself to the fact that times have improved, and that, without the danger of later disappointment, you can rely upon having enhanced the lives and occupations of a very large number of people who were previously striving in vain for recognition. It is my unshakeable conviction, however, that these adherents are but the predecessors of all humanity. . . .[41]

As Erik Erikson noted in 1962, when discussing Freud's 'Dora' case-history, trainee psychoanalysts of his generation knew the

dream book and the case-histories by heart.[42] Heinz Kohut gave a
somewhat different inflection to his account of psychoanalytic
training when he talked of the deep identification that arose in
him because of his use of the dream book when becoming an
analyst.[43]

This repeated evidence of the identification of Freud's followers with his person, via their reading of *The Interpretation of
Dreams*, thus shades over into the next phase I have isolated: the
use of Freud and his dreams as common property, the property of
all mankind – but for starters, of his professional followers. Nor
could these followers escape the next phase: the temptation to
analyse further the dreams of *The Interpretation of Dreams* – what
Welsh calls 'the way Freudians love to one-up Freud'.[44] In January
1908, a few months after their first meeting, Karl Abraham wrote
to Freud:

> I should like to know whether the incomplete interpretation of
> 'Irma's injection' dream . . . is intentional. I find that trimethylamin
> leads to the most important part, to sexual allusions which become
> more distinct in the last lines. After all, everything points to the
> suspicion of syphilitic infection in the patient . . .[45]

Freud knew how to reply, adopting a distinctly corrective
tone, but volunteering further 'associations' for this wild,
but entirely predictable, analytic interpretation of his would-be
disciple's:

> Syphilis is *not* the subject-matter . . . Sexual megalomania is hidden
> behind it, the three women, Mathilde, Sophie and Anna are my
> daughters' three god-mothers, and I have them all! There would be
> one simple therapy for widowhood, of course. All sorts of intimate
> things, naturally![46]

Sparingly, but with judicious timing, Freud would share self-
analytic insights with his disciples, often using elements from *The
Interpretation of Dreams* as a common code, knowing full well
the followers knew his dreams and these personal references
by heart. At the time of his final conflict with Jung, when Freud,
Jung and the other psychoanalytic leaders were gathered in
Munich for organizational discussions, Freud had fainted for the
second time in Jung's presence. Explaining this 'lapsus' to Jones,
Freud wrote:

There must be some psychic element in this attack which besides was largely fundamented on fatigue, bad sleep and smoking, for I cannot forget that 6 and 4 years ago I have suffered from very similar though not so intense symptoms in the *same* room of the Parkhotel; in every case I had to leave the table. I saw Munich first when I visited Fliess during his illness (you remember: 'Propyläeen' in the *Traumdeutung*)[47] and this town seems to have acquired a strong connection with my relation to this man. There is some piece of unruly homosexual feeling at the root of the matter.[48]

Not only were the followers tempted to conduct re-analysis of the *Traumdeutung*; so was Freud. And when it came to that new class of blood sport, fights between Freud and his estranged disciples, such as Jung in late 1912, the *Traumdeutung* was the first weapon to come to hand:

> may I draw your attention to the fact that you open *The Interpretation of Dreams* with the mournful admission of your own neurosis – the dream of Irma's injection – identification with the neurotic in need of treatment. Very significant.[49]

As might be expected, even before his open break, Jung had already presented the greatest challenge to Freud's authorial authority over the *Traumdeutung*. In 1911, when Freud asked if Jung had 'any points you would like me to consider for the addenda?',[50] the reply reminded Freud how sharply Jung had 'drilled my seminar students in the most rigorous Freudian usage', as a result of which he and his students found certain passages 'objectionable in terms of *Freudian* dream interpretation';[51] he continued:

> I also miss a specific reference to the fact that the essential (personal) meaning of the dream (e.g. Irma, uncle, monograph, etc.) has *not* been given. I insist on my students learning to understand dreams in terms of the dynamics of libido; consequently we sorely miss the personally painful element in your own dreams. Perhaps this could be remedied by your supporting the Irma dream with a typical analysis of a patient's dream, where the ultimate real motives are *ruthlessly* disclosed . . . In my seminars we always concentrate for weeks on *The Interpretation of Dreams*, and I have always found that inadequate interpretation of the main dream-examples leads to misunderstandings and, in general, makes it difficult for the students to follow the argument since he cannot conceive the nature of the

conflicts that are the regular source of dreams. (For instance, in the monograph dream the crucial topic of the conversation with Dr Königstein, which is absolutely essential if the dream is to be understood properly, is missing.) Naturally one cannot strip oneself naked, but perhaps a model would serve the purpose.[52]

Freud's reply was conciliatory but firm: as with all other attempts to demand more of his privacy than he was prepared to give, he politely declined, while throwing the pressing inquirer a small, extra smidgeon for his personal delectation:

> You have very acutely noticed that my incomplete elucidation of my own dreams leaves a gap in the over-all explanation of dreams, but here again you have put your finger on the motivation – which was unavoidable. I simply cannot expose any more of my nakedness to the reader. . . . In none do I bring out all the elements that can be expected of a dream, because they are my personal dreams. . . . (In the dream about the monograph, the crucial conversation with Königstein dealt with the very topic we touched on Munich. Cf. the Egyptian statue allegedly costing 10,000 kronen. When I was a young man my father chided me for spending money on books, which at the time were my higher passion. As you see, all this is not for the common people.) So even if the critic and the seminar are perfectly right, the author cannot do anything about it. The book proves the principles of dream interpretation by its own nature, so to speak, through its own deficiencies.[53]

And this, surely, is the point: that the complicated structure, the play of self-exposure and discretion – what Freud here nicely calls its 'deficiencies' – are what allow the reader both to be seduced by the autobiographical and personal elements while being persuaded by the scientific claims, the universality, of the book. Jung obviously already had his doubts; Freud certainly took note of his mollifying reply – 'I am convinced that the book is far from becoming obsolete.'[54]

Freud was unquestionably an ambitious man. One of the high points of interpretative virtuosity in the book, what he himself called 'my central accomplishment in interpretation' (21 September 1899, F/F, 374) was his interpretation of the *non vixit* dream, in which he accused his friends of wishing other men dead to further their own ambitions. 'As he was ambitious, I slew him' is one of the themes. Freud once again plays hide and seek with his reader, withholding a full interpretation because that would mean 'sacrificing to my ambition people whom I greatly value' (SE V, 422). But Freud did not have the self-control to withhold a more complete interpretation from his reader, which he disclosed some sixty pages after his first interpretation: he sacrificed his own friends to his own ambition – by making *public* his own ambition in the form of a successful interpretation of his dreams. Freud's dream-thoughts, preoccupied with the early death of his own brother, with the loss of his childhood playmate, asserted: 'no one is irreplaceable' (SE V, 485). As he finished writing this section of the book, he even flaunted his satisfaction to Fliess: 'In the *non vixit* dream I am delighted to have outlived you; isn't it terrible to suggest something like this – that is, to have to make it explicit to everyone who understands?' (21 September 1899, F/F, 374). As we have already seen, one of the very first readers of the book, his friend's widow, the woman who Freud would have liked to have as a patient but never did, offered Freud as explicit an interpretation as any analyst could have offered of this dream: she terminated a long-standing friendship with Freud – thus enacting the refutation of his dream-thought. 'If you think no one is irreplaceable you will have to do without *my* friendship.' By publishing the dream Freud let it be known that he cared more for readers than for friends: his wish was for immortality, no matter what the consequences.

Yet this ambition is sublimated in the final paragraph of his interpretation where he asks the rhetorical question, which corresponds to the fundamental wish of the dream: 'after all, I reflected, was not having children our only path to immortality?' (SE V, 487). It is his children, in the end, who represent the most complete and fullest satisfaction of his ambition.[55] That's what *he* says, the occasional reader might reply. With this sentence, Freud surreptitiously draws back from stating his true dream wish – the unquenched ambition for immortality – and fobs off the reader with this piece of eternal wisdom. And it is in the very act of so doing that he translates his ambition into reality: it will be the reader – not his children – who will be his guarantee of immortality. So it might have been more apposite for the final epigraph to the finest piece of dream-interpretation in Freud's book, a monument to ambition if ever there was one, to have been the following, somewhat adapted version: 'is not having readers my only path to immortality?'

Are readers in the late twentieth century in a different position from Freud's reviewers, followers or apostates? It has been my contention that the reader specified by Freud for *The Interpretation of Dreams* has three different characteristics: he is Freud's analyst; he is required to be Freudian by the structure and rhetorical manoeuvres of the text; and he is required to adopt the position of the common reader. Remember Freud's emphatic remarks about his readership in the Preface to the second edition of *The Interpretation of Dreams*, where he set to one side both ignorant opponents and enthusiastic followers as constituting his readership. The strategy of the dream book requires one to partake in the experience of analysis in both positions: as interpreter (which shades over into the almost irresistible urge to one-up Freud)[56] and as dreamer. The position of dreamer divides straight forwardly into three: insofar as the reader identifies, at his explicit invitation, with Freud, making his interests his own, he becomes the subject of those dreams of his that he analyses; insofar as the reader adopts the position of the intelligent and sceptical patient and critic, a position that Freud's strategy of argument makes very tempting; insofar as the reader takes Freud at his word, and tries out his techniques on his own dreams. ('And here I will mention a number of further, somewhat disconnected, points on the subject of interpreting dreams, which may perhaps help to give readers their bearings should they feel inclined to check my statements by subsequent work upon their own dreams' (SE V, 522).)

There is, of course, an ambiguity in this use of 'Freudian'. The Freudian that *The Interpretation of Dreams* produces is a reader who knows how to interpret – or, at the very least, what it is like to interpret – and, necessarily, by imaginative transference, knows what it is like to have his dreams interpreted. The reader of the *The Interpretation of Dreams* is not first and foremost a Freudian in the sense of *believing* – either for quasi-religious or quasi-scientific reasons – in Freud's theories, or in the sense of being professionally *qualified* to practise psychoanalysis. In contrast with the more professionally disciplined views of his disciples and colleagues, Freud maintained that self-analysis, and in particular analysis of one's own dreams, was the principal means for becoming an analyst:

> The interpretation of dreams is in fact the royal road to a knowledge of the unconscious; it is the securest foundation of psycho-analysis and the field in which every worker must acquire his convictions and seek his training. If I am asked how one can become a psychoanalyst, I reply: 'By studying one's own dreams.'

So wrote Freud in 1909, for the first grand public of psychoanalysis, in Worcester, Massachusetts. And, as ever, whenever the question of the interpretation of dreams came up, that censor and critic was always present, to be addressed in the very next sentence:

> Every opponent of psycho-analysis hitherto has, with a nice discrimination, either evaded any consideration of *The Interpretation of Dreams*, or has sought to skirt over it with the most superficial objections.[57] (SE XI, 33)

At the very least, we can assert that Freud thought that anyone who shied away from self-analysis, from the analysis of their dreams, no matter how extensive and orthodox their relations with an analyst were, did not qualify to be called 'Freudian'. 'Anyone who fails to produce results in a self-analysis of this kind may at once give up any idea of being able to treat patients by analysis' (SE XI, 145).[58] The touchstone of psychoanalysis and of the opposition to it would always remain the interpretation of dreams:

> I have acquired a habit of gauging the measure of a psychologist's understanding by his attitude to dream-interpretation; and I have observed with satisfaction that most of the opponents of psychoanalysis avoid this field altogether or else display remarkable clumsiness if they attempt to deal with it.[59]

Freud retained his sympathy for the lone dream analyst. Rebuking Jones in 1924 for wishing to dismiss a maverick writer on psychoanalysis, Pickworth Farrow, with a lightning diagnosis of dementia praecox, Freud told Jones how the man had been let down by the incompetence of two London analysts and had embarked on a self-analysis.[60] Freud felt sufficiently kindly towards Farrow to write a preface for his self-analytic writings, where he implicitly admonished analysts like Jones who thought the heroic times of self-analysis were thankfully over, replaced with an efficiently policed hierarchical system of professionally run analyses:

> The author of this paper is known to me as a man of strong and independent intelligence. Probably through being somewhat self-willed he failed to get on good terms with two analysts with whom he made the attempt. He thereupon proceeded to make a systematic application of the procedure of self-analysis which I myself employed in the past for the analysis of my own dreams. His findings deserve attention precisely on account of the peculiar character of his personality and of his technique. (SE XX, 280)[61]

The implication is clear: a reader of *The Interpretation of Dreams* may be entirely at odds with the institutions of psychoanalysis, but as long as he plants himself firmly on the privileged terrain of self-analysis, dreams, he will very likely turn out a better Freudian than otherwise.

It is true that psychoanalytic training institutions still require Freud – often introductory, intermediary and advanced – as essential elements of their courses. But it is not this that makes the psychoanalytic movement distinctive – or even Freudian – although it is a peculiar enough professional practice.[62] It is at this point that I ask you to remember my initial question, concerning the character of the international psychoanalytic movement. The true Freudians, the backbone of the psychoanalytic movement, are Freud's readers, not the psychoanalysts. No amount of policing of institutions can stem the 'wild analysis' that is unleashed by Freud's writing-effects, among which the constitution of the reader is one of the principal achievements.

Freud is consistently one of the best-selling mass paperback authors of non-fiction in the Western world today. Reading Freud is not a supplement to another source of psychoanalytic knowledge. Reading Freud is an obligatory passage point for entry into psychoanalysis: one first becomes a Freudian through reading.[63] It is this fact that differentiates psychoanalysis from other international scientific, cultural or political movements – even from the Darwinian movement, despite the clear similarities between *The Origin of Species* and *The Interpretation of Dreams*.[64] It is this fact that makes the presence of Freud in humanities departments – departments that specialize in reading techniques – so often entirely appropriate, a true reflection of the character of Freud's invention. Insofar as practitioners of psychoanalysis model their institutions and practices on those common to bacteriology, statistics or hypnosis, they inevitably distrust these other Freudians. But in their distrust and their attempts at policing the boundaries between the qualified experts and the rest, they render themselves blind to the full measure of Freud's achievement in inventing the transferential machine we know as *The Interpretation of Dreams*. Talking with students who have just read Freud for the first time – with their reactions that range from quite explicit gratitude and love for the feeling of being recognized, albeit by a figure who adopts the position of a parent of educator, to the explosive rage that does not usually prevent them picking up once again the book they repeatedly throw down – is a constant reminder of this achievement.

Notes

1 For representative substantial works on these topics, see Theodore M. Porter, *The Rise of Statistical Thinking, 1820–1900* (Princeton NJ: Princeton University Press, 1986), Bruno Latour, *The Pasteurization of France* (Cambridge, Mass. : Harvard University Press, [1984] 1988); David Kohn (ed.), *The Darwinian Heritage*, (Princeton NJ: Princeton University Press, 1985); Alan Gauld, *A History Of Hypnotism* (Cambridge: Cambridge University Press, 1992).

2 Jacques Derrida, 'Spéculer – sur Freud', in *La Carte Postale* (Paris: Flammarion, 1980), p. 325; *The Post Card. From Socrates to Freud and Beyond*, trans. Alan Bass (Chicago: University of Chicago Press, 1987); p. 305, translation modified. This is not the first time I have considered the question that Derrida so penetratingly asks; see my 'Who is in analysis with whom?', in John Forrester, *The Seductions of Psychoanalysis. Freud, Lacan and Derrida* (Cambridge: Cambridge University Press, 1990), esp. pp. 233ff.

3 Translation modified. The last sentence reads: 'Für den Leser mag es aber gleichgültig sein, an welchem Material er Träume würdigen und deuten lernt', which Strachey translates as: 'To my readers, however, it will be a matter of indifference upon what particular material they learn to appreciate the importance of dreams and how to interpret them.' This elegant translation introduces, somewhat superfluously, the term 'particular', which evokes an implicit reference to the 'general'; it is my contention later in my argument that such an implication in *not* present in Freud's text here. In addition, the translation of *würdigen* by 'to appreciate the importance', and its consequent separation off from *deuten* ('interpret') obscures the fact that Freud's German links very closely the valuing and interpreting of dreams; dreams are not

distant objects to be valued and appraised, but become valuable for what their interpretation may yield.

4 Ernest Jones, *The Life and Work of Sigmund Freud*, vol. I, 2nd edn (New York: Basic Books, 1954), p. 351.

5 Didier Anzieu, *Freud's Self-Analysis*, trans. Peter Graham (London: The Hogarth Press and the Institute of Psychoanalysis, 1986); Alexander Grinstein, *Sigmund Freud's Dreams*, 2nd edn (New York: International Universities Press, 1980); Alexander Grinstein, *Freud's Rules of Dream Interpretation* (New York: International Universities Press, 1983); Alexander Grinstein, *Freud at the Crossroads* (Madison, CT: International Universities Press, 1990).

6 An example of this attitude to Freud's correspondence with Fliess is the following judgement of Masson: '[The lost letter about a dream relating to Martha Freud] would no doubt be the most important letter of the collection, since it contains the only dream Freud ever analyzed completely.' Introduction, F/F, 10.

7 Jacques Lacan, *The Seminar, Book II. The Ego in Freud's Theory and in the Technique of Psychoanalysis, 1954–1955* [1978], ed. J.-A. Miner, trans. Sylvana Tomaseui, notes John Forrester (Cambridge: Cambridge University Press/ New York: W. W. Norton & Co., 1988), p. 170.

8 Anzieu, *Freud's Self-Analysis* p. 465, notes that this is the first use of the word 'censorship' in the correspondence with Fliess.

9 For a comparison of the first and second version of the book, see Anzieu, *Freud's Self-Analysis*, pp. 267ff.

10 For further discussion on this incident and friendship, see Lisa Appignanesi and John Forrester, *Freud's Women* (London: Weidenfeld and Nicolson, 1992), esp. Ch. 4.

11 Freud to André Breton, 26 December 1932, in *Les Rêves. La Voie royale de l'inconscient* (Paris: Laffont/Tchou, 1979), pp. 56–7; originally reproduced in André Breton, *Les Vases communicants* (Paris: Gallimard, 1932). See also Jack J. Spector, *The Aesthetics of Freud: A Study of Psychoanalysis and Art* (New York: Praeger, 1972), pp. 153–4 and Peter Gay, *Freud. A Life for Our Time* (London: Dent, 1988), p. 585.

12 Sigmund Freud, *Die Traumdeutung* (Frankfurt: Fischer Verlag, 1991), p. 119.

13 I use the pronoun 'he' to refer to the 'reader' of *The Interpretation of Dreams* throughout, partly following the masculine gender of the German word *der Leser* whose fortunes I will be following, and partly to avoid the clumsiness of the phrase 'he or she'.

14 See Alexander Welsh, *Freud's Wishful Dream Book* (Princeton, NJ: Princeton University Press, 1994), pp. 30–2.

15 The literature re-examining this dream is substantial; much of it is drawn upon in Appignanesi and Forrester, *Freud's Women*, Ch. 4, 'The dream of psychoanalysis', pp. 117–45; see in particular Erik H. Erikson, 'The dream specimen of psychoanalysis', *Journal of the American Psychoanalytical Associa-*

tion 2 (1954) 5–56; Frank R. Hartman, 'A reappraisal of the Emma episode and the specimen dream', *Journal of the American Psychoanalytic Association* 31 (1983) 555–85; Robert Langs, 'Freud's Irma dream and the origins of psychoanalysis', *Psychoanalytic Review* 71 (1984) 591–617; Carl Schorske, 'Politics and patricide in Freud's *Interpretation of Dreams*', in *Fin-de-Siècle Vienna: Politics and Culture* (New York: Knopf, 1980); Max Schur, 'Some additional "day residues" of the specimen dream of psychoanalysis', in Rudolph M. Loewenstein, Lottie M. Newman, Max Schur and Albert J. Solnit (eds), *Psychoanalysis. A General Psychology: Essays in Honor of Heinz Hartmann* (New York: International Universities Press, 1966), pp. 45–85.

16 Anzieu, 'Préface', Sigmund Freud, *Sur le Rêve* (French translation of *Über den Traum*, trans. Cornélius Heim; Paris: Gallimard, 1988), p. 10.

17 Welsh, *Freud's Wishful Dream Theory*, p. 35.

18 Note in passing Freud's challenge to the reader, when he modestly acquits himself of the charge of being a funny man in waking reality. If a reader finds his book singularly lacking in wit or charm, they will reluctantly have to agree with his argument that the ingenuity of dreams is not *his* responsibility; if the reader is, in fact, charmed and amused by the book, it is less likely that they will really hold Freud's ingenious wit against him. Nonetheless, a considerable number of the charges levelled against Freud by sceptics of dream-interpretation and psychoanalysis in general do have this form: they consist in finding Freud too clever for the good of his own claims concerning the meaning of dreams. I may have occasion to consider this argument towards the end of this chapter.

19 See 24 March 1898, F/F, 305: 'Fortunately I can answer your objections by referring to later chapters. I have just stopped before one such chapter, which will deal with the somatic stimuli of dreams. It will also touch upon anxiety dreams, on which light will be shed once again in the last chapter on "Dreams and Neurosis." But in the account you have read I shall include cross-references, to avoid the impression it gave you that the author is making things too easy for himself here . . . '

20 Note that the *Studienausgabe* edition of *Die Traumdeutung* fails to signal with quotation marks where exactly the critic's contradiction ends; in fact, Strachey in the Standard Edition closes the quotation marks exactly where the first edition of *Die Traumdeutung* does – after the long paragraph at the top of p. 135.

21 Paul Ricoeur, *Freud and Philosophy: An Essay on Interpretation*, trans. Denis Savage (New York: Yale University Press, 1970), p. 7.

22 It is not possible for me here to explore extensively the analogy between political struggle and the inner psychic world of Freud's theories; the connection between politics and psyche has been explored by Schorske (see above) and by William McGrath in his excellent *Freud's Discovery of Psychoanalysis. The Politics of Hysteria* (Ithaca, NY, and London: Cornell University Press, 1986); see also the discussion in Welsh, *Freud's Wishful Dream Book*, pp. 80ff.

23 Freud, *Introductory Lectures on Psycho-analysis*.

24 Freud, *Introductory Lectures on Psycho-analysis*.

25 See my 'Contracting the disease of love: authority and freedom in the origins of psychoanalysis', in Forrester, *The Seductions of Psychoanalysis* pp. 30–47.

26 See Jones, *The life and work of Sigmund Freud*, p. 354; Anzieu, *Freud's self-Analysis*, p. 224; Octave Mannoni, *Freud: The Theory of the Unconscious*, trans. Renauld Bruce (London: Pantheon, 1971 [1968], pp. 44–5; and Juliet Mitchell, *Psychoanalysis and Feminism* (London: Allen Lane, 1974), p. 9, n3.

27 See also Appignanesi and Forrester, *Freud's Women*, pp. 172–3.

28 Hanns Sachs, 'Review of second edition of *Autobiographical Study*', *Psychoanalytic Quarterly* 5 (1936) pp. 280–3, in Norman Kiell (ed.), *Freud Without Hindsight: Review of his Work (1893–1939)*, with translations from the German by Vladimir Rus and French by Denise Boneau (Madison, CT: International Universities Press, 1988), pp. 511–14, this quote from p. 511.

29 On the rise of statistical thinking, see Alain Desrosières, *La Politique des grands nombres: histoire de la raison statistique* (Paris: La Découverte, 1993); Ian Hacking, *The Emergence of Probability* (Cambridge: Cambridge University Press, 1975), and *The Taming of Chance* (Cambridge: Cambridge University Press, 1990); Porter *The Rise of Statistical Thinking*; Stephen M. Stigler, *The History of Statistics; The Measurement of Uncertainty Before 1900* (Cambridge, Mass.: Harvard Belknap, 1986).

30 Sigmund Freud and Ernest Jones, *The Complete Correspondence of Sigmund Freud and Ernest Jones, 1908–1939*, ed. R. Andrew Paskauskas, intro. Riccardo Steiner (Cambridge, Mass.: Harvard University Press, 1993), Jones to Freud, 2 January 1910, pp. 38–9.

31 Jones, *The Life and Work of Sigmund Freud*, p. 352, quoted letter to Martha, 29 October 1882.

32 Paul J. Möbius, 'Review of *On Dreams*', *Schmidt's Jahrbücher* 269 (1901) 271, trans. in Kiell, *Freud Without Hindsight*, p. 228.

33 Max Burckhard, 'A modern dream book. Review of *The Interpretation of Dreams*', *Die Zeit* 275 and 276, 6 and 13 January 1900, in Kiell, *Freud Without Hindsight*, pp. 103–14, this passage from p. 108.

34 Freud and Jones, *The Complete Correspondence*, Jones to Freud, 17 October 1911, pp. 117–18.

35 For example, Freud and Jones, *The Complete Correspondence*, Jones to Freud, 7 February 1909, p. 13.

36 See John Forrester, *Language and the Origins of Psychoanalysis* (London: Macmillan, 1980), Chapter 3, 'Symbolism', pp. 63–130.

37 Freud and Jones, *The Complete Correspondence*, Jones to Freud, 17 July 1914.

38 Freud and Jones, *The Complete Correspondence*, Jones to Freud, 25 May 1914, p. 282.

39 Freud/Ferenczi, *Correspondence* I, pp. 219–20, 3 October 1910, Ferenczi to Freud.

40 Freud and Jones, *The Complete Correspondence*, Jones to Freud, 17 February 1925, p. 569.

41 Sigmund Freud and Sándor Ferenczi, *The Correspondence of Sigmund Freud and Sándor Ferenczi*, vol. 1, *1908–1914* ed. E. Brabant, E. Kalzeder and P. Giampieri-Dentsch, trans. Peter T. Hotter, intro. André Haynal, (Cambridge, Mass.: Harvard University Press, 1994), p. 119, Ferenczi to Freud, 2 January 1910.

42 E. H. Erikson, 'Reality and actuality, an address', *Journal of the American Psychoanalytical Association* 10 (1962) 454–61.

43 H. Kohut, 'Creativeness, charisma, group psychology. Reflections on the self-analysis of Freud', first published in J. E. Gedo and G. H. Pollock (eds), *Freud: The Fusion of Science and Humanism, Psychological Issues*, Monograph 34/35 (New York: International Universities Press, 1976), pp. 379–425. I would like to thank Sonu Shamdasani for drawing my attention to this paper.

44 Welsh, *Freud's Wishful Dream*, p. 65.

45 Sigmund Freud and Karl Abraham, *A Psychoanalytic Dialogue: The Letters of Sigmund Freud and Karl Abraham, 1907–1926*, ed. Hilda C. Abraham and Ernst L. Freud (London: The Hogarth Press and the Institute of Psychoanalysis, 1965), Abraham to Freud, 8 January 1908, p. 18.

46 Freud and Abraham, *A Psychoanalytic Dialogue*, Freud to Abraham, 9 January 1908, p. 20; Freud's emphasis and exclamation mark.

47 The relevant discussion of 'Propyläeen' takes place in SE IV, 294–5. The details of Fliess's illness in Munich in 1894 and of Freud's reaction to it are not clear; there is an unaccountable gap in the Freud–Fliess correspondence from 13 September 1894, written before their meeting in Munich, to 24 January 1895.

48 Freud and Jones, *The Complete Correspondence* 8 December 1912, p. 182; written in English, which explains the peculiar neologism and syntax.

49 Sigmund Freud and C. G. Jung, *The Freud/Jung Letters*, ed. William McGuire, trans. R. Manheim and R. F. C. Hull (Princeton, NJ: Princeton University Press, 1974) 330J, 3 December 1912, p. 526.

50 Freud and Jung, *The Freud/Jung Letters*, 233F, 9 February 1911, p. 390.

51 All emphases in passages from Jung are in the original.

52 Freud and Jung, *The Freud/Jung Letters*, 235J, 14 February 1911, pp. 392–3.

53 Freud and Jung, *The Freud/Jung Letters*, 236F, 17 February 1911, pp. 394–6.

54 Freud and Jung, The *Freud/Jung Letters*, 239J, Jung to Freud, 8 March 1911, pp. 400–1.

55 Welsh, *Freud's Wishful Dream Book*, argues that the concept of 'wish' stands in place of Freud's 'ambition.' Whilst arguing that Freud's ambition to be acknowledged as a great discoverer and scientist is the fundamental wish of the dream book, I see no reason to substitute 'ambition' for 'wish' in the inner structure of Freud's theory; it is enough to say that ambition is the principal desire underlying many of Freud's dreams as portrayed in the book.

56 Lacan attempted to distance himself from this urge: 'I am not engaged in redoing the analysis of Freud's dream after Freud himself. That would be absurd. Just as it is out of the question to analyse dead authors, so it is out of the question to analyse his own dream better than Freud. Freud has his reasons for breaking off his associations. . . . It is not a matter of carrying out an exegesis where Freud interrupts himself but for us to take the whole of the dream and its interpretation. That's where we are in a different position from that of Freud.' Lacan, *The Seminar, Book II*, p. 152. It is a moot question whether the two seminars he devoted to the dream of Irma's injection conform to these strictures.

57 Freud, *Five Lectures on Psycho-analysis*.

58 Freud, 'The future prospects of psycho-analytic therapy'.

59 Freud, *On the History of the Psycho-analytic Movement*.

60 Freud and Jones, *The Complete Correspondence*, exchange of letters of 7 and 16 November 1924, pp. 560–2.

61 Freud 'Prefatory note to a paper by E. Pickworth Farrow' [1926]. SE XX 280.

62 As was recognized by Michel Foucault, when he noted that the movements spawned by Marx and Freud were distinctive creators of new discursive practices, who 'produced not only their own work, but the possibility and the rules of the formation of other texts': Michel Foucault, 'What is an author?', in *Language, Counter-memory, Practice*, ed. D. Bouchard (Ithaca, NY: Cornell University Press, 1977), p. 131.

63 For the theory of obligatory passage points, see Bruno Latour, *Science in Action* (Milton Keynes: Open University Press, 1987).

64 On Darwin's writing, see Gillian Beer, *Darwin's Plots* (London: Fontana, 1982).

4

Patterns of interpretation: speech, action and dream

JAMES HOPKINS

In daily life we understand one another in terms of a commonsense interpretive psychology, which is integrated with language, and through which we discern meaning and motive in one another's sounds and movements spontaneously and continually. This capacity seems to develop together with language from early childhood, and both appear to have been built up through evolution, and programmed, in Chomsky's phrase, to grow in the mind (or brain).

This interpretive understanding encompasses both language and motive, and so seems fundamental to our co-operative lives. Since most of what we know is registered and expressed in language, it also seems basic to our thought. But since this understanding is so natural to us we rarely seek to investigate it systematically, or try to see how it can have the cogency required by its fundamental role.

As is well known, Freud attempted to extend commonsense interpretive understanding, by applying it to dreams. This extension is frequently contested, particularly in the literature which seeks to contrast psychoanalysis with science; but it is rarely discussed in the context of the fundamental, natural, and apparently valid form of interpretive understanding from which it flows. So in what follows I try both to describe some of the sources of the cogency of everyday interpretive psychology, and to indicate how these relate to Freud's *The Interpretation of Dreams*.[1]

I

We can begin by considering our understanding of language in our own case, and the way this relates to our understanding of others. In doing this we invoke a familiar asymmetry, as between understanding our *selves* and understanding *others*. This is often put as a difference between the first-person perspective, which we occupy when we use the first-person pronoun 'I', and the third-person perspective, in which we regard others when we think of them as 'he' or 'she'; or again as the difference between the role we take as subject or agent of our own thoughts and actions, and the role as object which the things we think about or act on, including others, have for us.

A salient aspect of this difference is that when we ascribe thoughts or feelings to another, our judgement is characteristically mediated by perception of that person's behaviour, and usually serves in one way or another to explain this behaviour, that is, to make it intelligible to us. By contrast, when we ascribe such states to ourselves our judgements are not mediated in this way. We do not ordinarily say that we are in pain, or think or want something, on the basis of observing our own behaviour, or in order to make this behaviour intelligible to ourselves. Rather we simply take it that we feel pain, or think or want something, and can rightly say that this is so.

Thus in the case of our own minds we have, as we can say, a capacity for unmediated self-ascription. This characteristically encompasses all the states of mind which we regard as conscious, and so is remarkably sure and wide-ranging. We do not ordinarily suppose, for example, that we might be mistaken in thinking that we are in pain, or disgusted, or that we want or think something. In a great range of cases we take it that we might go wrong in ascribing these states to others, but not to ourselves. And although there are exceptions to this – including the kind of motives which are studied in psychoanalysis – it applies to many more states of mind than we ordinarily ever explicitly describe. Our thoughts and feelings on many topics occur and pass so quickly, and are so dense and numerous, that we could not seriously envisage communicating all of them to others, even if we tried.

Hence our self-ascriptions are not only unmediated, but have a unique first-person authority.

It is hard to overstate the importance of this asymmetry, and the first-person authority which goes with it; for these features partly define what we regard as consciousness, and are at the root of the epistemological tradition stemming from Descartes and including the British Empiricists and their followers. The mental events and states about which we have unmediated first-person authority include both thoughts and perceptual experiences which represent the world. As these are states of mind, they have a certain independence from the worldly things and situations they represent, and this independence, together with our first-person authority about them, makes them seem uniquely certain and free from empirical doubt.

Thus when I think I see a tree, or another person, I may be wrong as to whether there actually is a tree or other person there to be seen, for my perceptual and cognitive states are thus far independent of what they represent. But I cannot likewise be wrong that I *think* I see such things, or that *it seems to me* that I see them; for this is within the sphere of my first-person authority. Hence self-knowledge of this kind has been taken by Descartes and those who have followed him as an indubitable basis upon which the rest of human knowledge could be built or reconstructed. On this view of knowledge, each person, as we might say, thinks alone; each of us constitutes an isolated island of intellect, working his or her experience into a world-picture which is justifiable from within. So on this account the first-person perspective encompasses the foundations of our knowledge, not only about our own minds, but about the whole world.

Now among the things we know in this apparently immediate and authoritative way are the contents of our thoughts and the meanings of our sentences, and this is a particularly striking achievement. Each of us speaks and understands an idiolect, which we take to be that of a natural language that we share with others, such as English or French. So we can each combine the words of our idiolect in accord with the rules of its syntax to form an indefinitely large number of sentences; and in understanding these sentences we know the conditions in which they are true. For example each speaker of an idiolect of English knows that:

- the sentence 'Freud worked in Vienna' is true (in my idiolect) just if Freud worked in Vienna;
- the sentence 'Wittgenstein lived in Vienna' is true (in my idiolect) just if Wittgenstein lived in Vienna;
- the sentence 'The moon is blue' is true (in my idiolect) just if the moon is blue, and so on.

Thus each of us knows an indefinitely large number of truths relating the sentences of his or her idiolect to objects and situations in the world via the notion of truth. We can schematize this by saying that a person who knows how to use the sentences of a language knows indefinitely many instances of the form (using 'T' for 'truth')

T: 'P' is true (in my idiolect) just if P.

where 'P' is a schematic letter which might be replaced by any appropriate sentence of the idiolect.

When we seek to understand others, we do so by characterizing their environments, minds and actions in terms of our own idiolects, and in a particular way. In interpreting others we make use of a vocabulary of words like 'desires', 'believes', 'hopes', 'fears', etc., each of which admits of complementation by a further sentence. So we speak of the desire, belief, hope, fear, etc., *that P*, where 'P' can be replaced by any sentence suitable for specifying the object, event or situation towards which the motive is directed. In this we, as it were, recycle our sentences for describing the world, thereby creating new sentences for describing the mind. Our finite stock of basic psychological words thus becomes the basis for a potential infinity of ascriptions of desire, belief, hope and so forth. This practice implements our conception of the mental as having *intentionality*, that is, a kind of causal and logical directedness upon the world; for any description of this *that P* kind perforce represents the mind as engaged with whatever aspect of the world the embedded sentence 'P' serves to describe. Since we can ascribe a desire *that P* corresponding to any describable situation which a person might desire, a belief *that P* corresponding to any describable situation a person might think obtains, and so forth, this mode of specification is extraordinarily flexible and precise.

The practice of describing motives in this way is central to psychological understanding. To see something of its working, imagine that we watch someone reach out to get a drink, and assume (hypothesize) that she does this because she saw the drink, wanted it and so reached for it. Then we might try to spell out what was involved in such explanation in the following way. Using 'A' to name our agent, and underlining sentences so as to indicate patterns among them, we have:

(1) *There is a drink within A's reach.*
(2) A sees that *there is a drink within A's reach.*
(3) A forms the belief that *there is a drink within A's reach.*
(4) A forms the belief that *if she moves her hand in a certain way then she will get a drink.*
(5) A desires that *she get a drink.*
(6) A desires that *she move her hand in that way.*
(7) *A moves her hand in that way.*
(8) *A gets a drink.*

Of course, we have spelled out this sequence in a way which is unnaturally full and explicit, but this makes it easier to see underlying patterns. Thus for example we would not ordinarily say that someone desires *that she get a drink*; but this brings out, as the idiomatic *to get a drink* does not, that the agent's desire is that she, herself, get a drink; and this in turn makes more explicit the connection between the desire in (5) and the belief in (4) with which it interacts, and between the same desire and the situation which fulfils it in (8).

We can bring these patterns out more clearly by replacing the sentences which articulate the various desires and beliefs in the sequence by schematic letters. Then, and taking some liberties with pronouns and tenses, we have:

(1) P [there is a drink within A's reach].
(2) A sees that P [that there is a drink within A's reach].
(3) A forms the belief that P [that there is a drink within A's reach].
(4) A forms the belief that if Q then R [that if she moves her hand in a certain way then she will get a drink].
(5) A desires that R [that she get a drink].
(6) A desires that Q [that she moves her hand in that way].

(7) *Q* [A moves her hand in that way].
(8) *R* [A gets a drink].

Clearly this pattern could be discerned in the explanation of many different actions with a similar underlying structure; and such patterns can be applied predictively, and to actions as we watch them unfold. Thus we might have seen the agent above notice the drink, and guessed from the way she looked that she would want to get it. This, in effect, would constitute a hypothesis that the sequence described in (1)–(3) had already taken place, and that described in (5)–(8) was about to occur.

The same sort of patterned explanation also applies to speech. Thus consider someone uttering 'The day is warm' because she wants to say that the day is warm. In this case we have:

(a) A desires that *P* [that she say that the day is warm].
(b) A believes that if *Q* then *P* [that if she utters 'The day is warm' she says that the day is warm].
(c) A desires that *Q* [that she utters 'The day is warm'].

This, as we can see, involves the same pattern as (4)–(6) above, with the sentences in a different order.

The patterns in psychological ascription here marked by schematic letters have a notable feature. They are on the one hand *causal*, and on the other also *correct*, *rational* or *logical*. Thus, speaking roughly, we can take what we describe by (1) as a cause of what we describe by (2), what we describe by (2) as cause of what we describe by (3), and so on through the sequence. For, as we know, the transition between (1) and (2) marks the place at which light reflected by objects described in (1) strikes the eyes of the agent described in (2), and causes the changes in the retina, optic nerve, visual areas of the brain, etc., involved in seeing; and perception as described in (2) is a cause of belief, as described in (3); and so on. But also the use of the same schematic letter in (1)–(3) indicates that the perception and belief described there are *correct*, and *correctly formed*. For in describing a perception *that P* as caused by a situation *that P*, we mark that the perception is *veridical*, that it accurately reflects the situation which it is a perception of; and in describing the resulting belief as a belief *that P* we mark that the belief is both *true*, as beliefs ought to be, and also caused by the situation which renders it true, and so *well grounded*. Likewise, the pattern displayed in (4)–(6) describes a formation of desire in light of belief which is both *causal* and *rational*; and (5)–(8) describe intentional action which is *successful*, that is, which is not only *caused by* desire, but in which desire is *satisfied*. So these patterns, as we can say, are both *causal* and *normative*: they are patterns of causal functioning which are in one way or another correct or as they should be.

We are thus dealing with a number of patterns of interpretive / causal explanation, some of which we can briefly describe, write and label as follows. These include:

(i) A pattern of *well-founded belief*:
B: P {causes}→ A bels that P.   (cf. (1) and (3) above)

(ii) A pattern of *practical reason* (the rational formation of desire in light of belief):
PR: A des that P and A bels that if Q then P {causes}→ A des that Q.   (cf.(4)–(6) above)

(iii) A pattern of the *satisfaction of desire*:
D: A des that P {causes}→ P.   (cf. (5) and (8) above)

These patterns, which can be represented in deeper and more detailed ways than sketched here, can be discerned in intentional action of all kinds. They seem to constitute a part of the underlying 'grammar', or logical and causal structure, of our natural and intuitive way of understanding one another. Bringing them out in this way enables us to see how our *that P* mode of description of motives makes use of *hermeneutic connections* – connections in sentential description – to mark *motivational causal connections*, that is, connections between motive and motive, or motive and world, such as are sketched in (1)–(8). In these cases, as we can say, relations of *linguistic coherence*, such as obtains among the sentences we are considering, systematically mark relations of *causal coherence*, as between motive and motive, motive and action, or motive and world generally.

This alloy of linguistic and causal coherence flows from the *that P* mode of description itself. When we describe a desire by a sentence 'P', we tacitly lay it down that the desire is to be regarded as satisfied in the circumstances in which 'P' is true; and these are the circumstances in which we understand the desire as functioning to bring about in successful action, as registered in D. Likewise when we describe a belief by a sentence 'P' we lay it down that the belief is true in the same conditions as the sentence; and these are the conditions which we take the belief as serving to reflect, as registered in B, or again as serving to bring into the satisfaction conditions of desires, as registered in PR. In these cases our norms for the truth of sentences, as registered in T, become norms for the proper working of perception, belief, and desire, as schematized in B, PR, and D. Something similar holds for other motives and mental states which we describe in this way. This systematic reuse of world-describing sentences in characterizing the objects of desire, hope, fear, etc., in effect fuses our conception of *the truth of sentences* with that of *the causal role of motives*, so yielding a natural system for the hermeneutic (or linguistic) discernment of motivational causal role.

Recognizing the way that we naturally use relations of linguistic coherence to map relations of causal coherence enables us to reduce dissonance between hermeneutic and causalist approaches to interpretation, or to the psychological explanation of behaviour generally. Schematically, hermeneutic approaches to these fields emphasize that understanding persons is a matter of finding relations of meaningful coherence or fit – as between motive and motive, motive and action, and so forth – while causalist approaches emphasize that such cohering factors can serve to explain thought or behaviour only insofar as they bear upon them causally.[2] Each of these claims represents a genuine insight into the nature of interpretive understanding. Advocates of each, however, have tended to ignore the way in which we naturally register relations of causal coherence among motives in terms of linguistic or logical coherence, as we have been illustrating; hence both have tended to *contrast* finding meaning or coherence with discerning causes.

This has led to disputes in which advocates of each approach reject the insight of the other. Causalists have tended to deny the explanatory relevance of hermeneutically detected relations of coherence or fit, while hermeneutic thinkers have tended to deny the causal role of reasons or the relevance of causality to explanation generally. What we see in the case of desire, belief, and the like above, however, is that commonsense interpretive thinking naturally registers causal connection (and causal coherence) by way of hermeneutic (sentential) coherence. Hence, and as we

shall see in more detail shortly, the finding of appropriate relations of coherence, or connections in sentential content, can be
a way of supporting causal hypotheses, and hence a way of
finding causes. Thus we can see that both parties to causalist/
hermeneutic disputation are mistaken in their negative claims
against one another, while in their positive claims both are stressing something correct, which, as their dispute indicates, might
otherwise be denied.[3]

II

Now to go further into both commonsense and psychoanalytic
explanation we must observe that the working of desire, which
we can take as the central motive which we invoke in explaining
action, is more complex than we have so far indicated. This is
because we take it that desire not only prompts (causes) action,
but also ceases to operate in response to the perception that action
has been successful. We take it that someone who wants a particular drink will, after drinking, realize that she has had the drink she
wanted, and so cease to want it. (She might now want *another*
drink, or even to drink that drink *again*, but these are different
matters.) Let us describe this by saying that we normally expect
that when an agent *satisfies a desire* (that is, when A des that
P {causes}⟼ P), and in consequence *believes that this is so* (that is ,
when P {causes}⟼ A bels that P), then this results in the *pacification* of the agent's desire (that is, that A's des that P is pacified.) So,
abbreviating as above, we have

> (iv) A fuller pattern of the role of desire in commonsense psycho-
> logical explanation, including the *pacification (ceasing of opera-
> tion) of desire*, produced by belief in its satisfaction.
> D*: A des that P {causes}⟼ P {causes}⟼ A bel that
> P {causes}⟼ A's des that P is pacified.

This pattern D* represents, as it were, the life-cycle of a single
desire in successful intentional action. (It clearly contains within
itself both D (the pattern of the satisfaction of desire) and B (the
pattern of well-founded belief) above.) Thus in thinking that a
person, A, is (intentionally) going to get a drink, we in effect
frame a predictive hypothesis, which could be put into words by

using the sentence 'A gets a drink' in all four positions in an instance of D*. We think, that is, that A desires that A get a drink, and we predict *first* that this will result in A moving her body in such a way that she gets a drink, *second* that she will come to believe that she has done so, and *third* that this will pacify her desire, so that she turns to something else. (Of course, again, we do not formulate such predictions, or anything like D*, explicitly to ourselves. But that we make such predictions shows in the ways in which we would be surprised if the agent's action unfolded differently from the way we expect.)[4]

As this example suggests, our tacit explanatory and predictive use of patterns like B, PR, and D* is far more frequent and complex than we are aware. Indeed, we commonly see intentional actions as informed by very many more desires and beliefs than we can perspicuously represent by listing the desires and beliefs as above. We can, however, *begin* to show some of the complexity involved by making use of another sort of diagram, of a kind familiar from linguistics. Thus for the explanation of the speech-act above, we have the following, as shown in Figure 4.1.

In this diagram we display the structure of our hypotheses about the constituent structure of an agent's goals in action by a tree diagram, which grows from an aerial root down through a series of branching nodes. Such a tree will have an agent's overall goal in acting at the top (root), and will go down from this motive through the ordered series of other goals which the agent takes as requisite to securing the root. We can take each of these subordinate goals to give rise to a further tree of the same kind, until we reach goals which are simply the performing of various desired

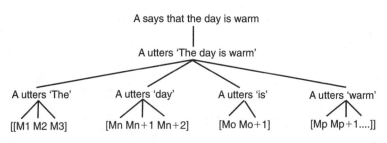

Figure 4.1

bodily movements in sequence, which we can label by M1, M2, etc.[5] In this way we can indicate the overall structure of actions or projects approaching everyday complexity, such as getting cash from a till (Figure 4.2).

Each such tree relates the sentence at its root to a sequence of hypothesised effects, which, if all goes correctly, should also ultimately be describable as a bringing about of the situation, and thence of the belief, and thence of the pacification of the desire, described by that same root sentence. The same holds for each subsidiary sentence likewise, and in the order marked by the tree. The whole hypothesis thus fixes for each goal and for each intentional movement by which that goal is executed a place in a determinate order of satisfaction and pacification. This imposes a complex bracketing or phrasing on behaviour, which segments the flow of movement upon which the hypotheses is directed into the series of units and sequences, groups and sub-groups, which we perceive as the unfolding rhythm of intention in action. The whole, moreover, can be seen as consisting of iterations of simpler parts which correspond to each aspect of this segmentation, that is , to instances of D* governed by instances of PR. So we can see each goal-specifying sentence in a tree as applied repeatedly, now to articulate a motive as hypothesis, now to describe predicted (or cohering) effects of that motive as test, as in the simple case spelt out above. In such a tree, therefore, we find the basic normative and hypothetical structure of D* both repeatedly and in the large.

We can thus see our commonsense practice of interpretation as one in which we tacitly and intuitively hypothesize such tree-like structures of motive as explaining both speech and action.

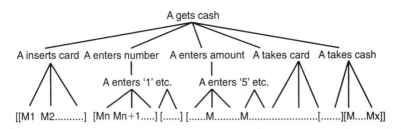

Figure 4.2

Accordingly, the patterns specified in such trees have an epistemic status worth noting. We interpret behaviour in accord with them naturally, and hence spontaneously, rapidly and continually. In this sense we use them more frequently, and rely on them more deeply, than any generalizations of science. (But of course we have no need to realize that this is so.) We learn such patterns together with language, so that their use is in a sense *a priori*. Also, however, we find them instantiated, and hence supported in a way which is both empirical and *a posteriori*, in instances of successful interpretive understanding too dense and numerous to register. This indicates that our practice of interpretation can be considered to have the kind of strength possessed by a well-confirmed empirical theory, and this serves to explicate its potential cogency.

III

We have so far considered how in interpretation each of us systematically maps the sentences of his or her own idiolect on to the utterances and actions, and thence on to the mind, of others. We can see that language also plays a central role in the first-person case. For when I consider, say, my own belief that Freud lived in Vienna, I use a sentence from my own idiolect (the sentence 'Freud lived in Vienna') to describe the circumstances in which my belief is true; and something similar holds for the other sententially described states of mind which I ascribe to myself. So it seems that all my understanding of sententially described states of mind – my understanding of my own mind, as well as that of others – presupposes my grasp of my own idiolect.

This again is a consequence of our *that P* practice of describing motives. Since in this practice we use sentences to articulate the states of mind we ascribe to ourselves as well as to others, we can see that our grasp of the mind presupposes that of these sentences. But this, as the schematization in T makes clear, encompasses a potential infinity of beliefs, in accord with which each of us relates his or her sentences, and so his or her linguistically apprehended thoughts, to the world. This is a massive claim to empirical knowledge, about which it seems we could in principle be wrong. So we can ask: How can we be sure that we use the sentences of our idiolects in a way which is coherent and correct? How can each of us know that the sentences in our idiolects – and hence the desires, beliefs, thoughts and feelings which we articulate by means of these sentences – *really* relate to the world in the way we *think* they do?

This question applies to everything in the scope of our first-person authority. So once we ask this question, I think it is plain that there is a sense in which we cannot answer it.[6] When we occupy the first-person perspective – when we think, speak or act *as subjects* – then we *use* our idiolects, either overtly or in thought; but we do not at the same time fully *evaluate* our uses for correctness, and it is clear that we could not do so without begging the question. If I am asked how I know that I hold the sentence 'Freud worked in Vienna' as true in my idiolect just if a certain person (Freud) performed a certain activity (worked) in a certain place (Vienna), there is nothing to the point which I can reply. For if I were mistaken about how my words relate to the world – if unknown to myself I actually used 'Freud' to speak of Jung, and 'Vienna' to speak of Zurich, so that on my lips and in my mind the sentence 'Freud worked in Vienna' was true just if Jung worked in Zurich – then I would not know what my thoughts were, and so would be unable to think reflectively at all. So this knowledge is in a sense the foundation of my articulate thinking, without which I would be lost; and that I have this knowledge is something I *assume*, but not something I can justify – or even *think* about justifying – without begging the question in the sense of assuming or presupposing that I have it.

This indicates, I think, both how our understanding of language is as at the basis of our cognitive lives, and also how we cannot justify this understanding from within the first-person perspective or by reference to first-person authority. But, of course, the fact that I cannot justify my own use of language from within does not show that this use is not correct. For when *another* understands my language and action, that other can see from outside my perspective that my language relates to the world as I take it to, and also that my first-person ascriptions of thought and feeling are correct. But then so far as another, who takes me as object, could thereby be justified in holding that my mind and language are as I take them to be, I am justified as subject as well.

So even if the first-person perspective cannot be justified from within it can still be justified from without, and this justification is both interpretive and social.[7]

IV

We can now see more clearly how interpretive understanding is basic to our thought. Contrary to the Cartesian/empiricist tradition mentioned at the outset, the first-person perspective itself stands in need of justification and so cannot provide the foundations of knowledge. Interpretive thinking provides the required further justification. So our capacity to think and speak about ourselves is constituted as knowledge by a possible relation to others, which shows in our being such as to be interpretable by them.

This, however, provides a further challenge. How are we to understand our interpretive practice as sufficiently powerful to justify our first-person authority about mind and meaning, which includes the precision and certainty with which we understand language itself? I think we can begin to see the outlines of the kind of justification which is required by attending to the contrasting role in interpretation of speech as opposed to non-verbal action.

Speech seems a kind of action which we can interpret with particular clarity and certainty; and it is through understanding speech that we attain precise and extensive understanding of the motives of others. But it is worth noting that speech is a kind of behaviour which we could *not* understand in isolation from the rest of the behavioural order of which it is a part. If we could not regard people's productions of sounds or marks as part of a larger pattern of action and relation to the environment, we could not interpret these sounds or marks, or regard them as language at all. (One can get a sense of this point imagining trying to interpret radio broadcasts of foreign speech, without, however, being able to know anything about what the programmes are about.)

By contrast, we can understand a lot of non-linguistic behaviour without relying on language, at least up to a point. We can generally see the purposive patterns in people's behaviour in terms of their performance of commonplace intentional actions, as in accord with the patterns above. But unless we can link such actions with language, we cannot, in many cases, know the precise contents of people's beliefs and desires; and in the absence of language it would be doubtful how far we could ascribe precisely conceptualized thoughts to people at all.

Interpretive understanding encompasses both words and deeds (verbal and non-verbal behaviour). But we now find that words with no relation to deeds are unintelligible, and deeds with no relation to words are inarticulate. It follows that the understanding of people we actually attain, in which we take their deeds to spring from motives with determinate and precisely conceptualized content, requires us to integrate our understanding of verbal and non-verbal action, and hence to correlate and co-ordinate the two. It is some such integration which enables us to tie the complex structure of utterance to particular points in the framework of action and context, and thereby to interpret language; and this in turn enables us to interpret the rest of behaviour as informed by experience and thought which, like that expressed in language, has fully articulate content.

I think that the particular mode of integration which we use involves what we can regard as a process of interpretive triangulation. This turns on the fact that in interpreting speech we do not merely assign meanings to sounds; rather we characteristically take utterances as expressions of desire, belief, intention and other motives. (Thus we regularly take assertions as expressing beliefs, questions as expressing desires to know something, requests or orders as expressing desires that something be done, and so forth.) This enables us to interpret the motives which we take to be expressed in this way with precision, and also to relate such interpretation to the speaker's ability to express such motives with first-person authority. Clearly, however, we could not take utterances as such expressions of motives with any degree of accuracy and certainty unless we also had independent means of determining what the agent's operative desires, beliefs or intentions really were. Evidently, the means we use are the interpretation of further actions, including non-verbal ones.

In general, we are able to regard utterances as accurate or authoritative expressions of motives because doing so enables us to interpret other actions, and with cogency, as stemming from those same motives, or others related to them. In understanding persons in this way, therefore, we in effect correlate their utterances with their other actions, as effects of a set of common causes (motives). Schematically, insofar as we take an utterance of 'P' as an expression of a desire, intention, or belief that P, and then confirm this by independently interpreting further actions as flowing from that same motive, we thereby correlate utterance and action as effects of that desire, intention or belief. By this means we triangulate from episodes in speech and non-verbal action to focus upon their common causes, that is, motives which can be specified by relation to both verbal and non-verbal behaviour.

In this we constantly and tacitly cross-check the motives we assign via speech against those we assign via non-verbal action; and this method becomes particularly powerful where the interpretee also has first-person authority. Roughly, the more an interpretee can put his or her goals and beliefs into words – the more the interpretee exhibits first-person authority – the better an interpreter is able to use those words to understand both the interpretee's speech and other actions. But the better an interpreter is able to understand the interpretee's speech and other actions, the more fully the interpreter can check the interpretee's first-person authority. So in favourable circumstances an interpreter can cross-check his or her understanding of an interpretee's verbal action, non-verbal action and first-person authority together, and in such a way as simultaneously to confirm all three.

We can see this in a kind of situation which is extremely common in everyday interpretive understanding. Suppose that I frame hypotheses as to the motives upon which you are presently acting, and also about what the sounds in your idiolect mean. Then suppose that you also make sounds which, according to my understanding of your idiolect, constitute authoritative expressions of the motives upon which I take you to act, and your further behaviour bears this out. Questions of sincerity aside, this tends to show both (i) that my hypotheses about both the meanings of your utterances and the motives for your present behaviour are correct, and (ii) that you have first-person authority about these things. (The principles underlying this kind of inference are discussed further in the appendix on p. 154.)

In such cross-checking of interpretive hypotheses everything is confirmed empirically, so that nothing is merely assumed or taken on trust. As I test my understanding of your non-verbal actions against my understanding of your expressions of motive, my confidence in my interpretations is based upon their success in explaining and predicting what you do and say, and my confidence in your first-person authority is based upon its coinciding with my own independent understanding of the actions and utterances in which it is expressed. So the more instances of your verbal and non-verbal behaviour I understand in this way, the greater confidence I can gain about my interpretations of your actions and utterances, and also your possession of first-person authority.[8]

The same, of course, also holds for your understanding of me. So given that each of us is both a competent interpreter and an authoritative interpretee, it seems that by this method we may attain mutual understanding which is highly precise and certain. Of course, an interpreter will not always interpret accurately, and there are circumstances in which an interpretee's first-person authority will fail. Still, an interpreter can correct faulty interpretations in light of evidence provided by an interpretee, can check how far the interpretee's first-person account is accurate, and can try to correct it where it is not. Interpreter and interpretee can thus together continually explore the assumptions and presuppositions of interpretation of this kind, in a process which admits of continual extension and refinement.

This particularly applies to the understanding of language. For each of us can, in principle, take any of our countless interpretations of another's non-verbal actions, and seek to pair it with an appropriate self-ascription from the other; and by this means each interpretation of non-verbal action, provided it is correct, can also be made to test and improve each's understanding of the other's use of language. This potentially infinite correlation between verbal and non-verbal action can thus be exploited indefinitely and often, to drive confirmation of the hypothesis that each understands the language of the other steadily upwards. This process exploits first-person authority about language in such a way as to provide it with continuous testing and ratification, and so bridges the justificatory gap noted above. So by this means, it

seems, we can come to regard our possession of mutual understanding, and in particular mutual linguistic understanding, as
confirmed in the way our intellectual practice requires.

V

This sketch of our commonsense practice of interpretation is of
course very incomplete, but it suggests that interpretation proceeds most surely where an interpreter can constantly match
his or her own account of an interpretee's motives with the
interpretee's own potentially authoritative expression of these
motives in speech. These theoretically ideal conditions for interpretation are in fact actually approximated in the therapy devised
by Freud, which provided the background for his interpretation
of dreams. In this an interpretee (analysand) provides an interpreter (analyst) with the fullest possible verbal specification of
the motives which both are seeking to understand. Also the
analysand engages in free association, reporting the contents of
consciousness as they occur, without seeking to censor them, or to
render them logical or sensible. This enables the analyst to frame
hypotheses (interpretations) as to further motives on the part of
the analysand, which both can then consider on the basis of the
maximum of shared relevant data.

Above we discussed the everyday practice of the explanation
of action by reference to desires (goals) and beliefs. As is familiar,
psychoanalysis extends this practice by relating dreams, symptoms and other phenomena to desires or goals as well. The nature
of this extension can partly be seen in very simple examples. Thus
Freud found that when he had eaten anchovies or some other
salty food, he was liable to have a dream *that he was drinking cool
delicious water*. After having this dream, or a series of such dreams,
Freud would awake, find himself thirsty and get a drink. Probably many people have had this dream, or its counterpart concerning urination. And anyone who has such a dream will
naturally regard it as a *wish-fulfilment* in Freud's sense; that is, as
(i) caused by, and (ii) representing the satisfaction of, the desire to
drink felt on waking.

This natural reasoning is clearly cogent, and it turns upon the
fact that the dreamer's desire is so clearly and closely *related in*

sentential content to the dream. This is more or less obvious, but let us spell it out. The dreamer's desire is for a certain sort of situation (that in which the dreamer has a drink), and the dream represents that situation as real (the dreamer is having a drink). To put the point schematically, the dreamer's desire is *that P*, and the dream is *that P*, and this striking similarity gives good reason to suppose that the desire brought about the dream. Also it seems that such a dream has a pacifying influence – perhaps only a fleeting one – on the desire which prompts it. The dream-experience of drinking seems to provide a form of temporary relief or check on the underlying thirst, the insufficiency of which is indicated by the dreamer's waking to get a real drink.

Such an account assimilates the dream to wishful thinking or imagining, and this, and its role in the pacification of desire, are also familiar. We are aware in many other cases that our response to a desire or wish that P is in one way or another to imagine, suppose or make believe that P (or something related to P) is the case. We know that people day-dream in this way regularly, and often more or less deliberately; and such episodes of imagining may give pleasure, and seem partly to pacify the desires which they represent as fulfilled. The same applies to the kind of make-believe found in children's play, or again to the suspension of disbelief or imaginative immersion involved in the theatre, cinema, video games and the like. In these and many other cases, it seems, people make use of forms of imaginative representation to pacify desires which they cannot or would not actually satisfy by representations of their satisfaction. In using imaginative representation in this way, moreover, people regularly falsify reality – represent things as other than they are – in two connected ways. They misrepresent the state of *their own mind* in representing themselves as experiencing the satisfaction of some desire which, in fact, remains frustrated. And they misrepresent the state of *their own activity* in representing themselves as satisfying a particular desire, while in fact they are at best pacifying that desire with a false representation of its satisfaction. (The dreamer represents himself as actually drinking, while in fact he is only dreaming of doing so.)

Above we described intentional actions as sharing a common schematic pattern, and we can see that the episodes of wishful imagining we are now considering share a common pattern as well. In all these cases a desire (or wish) that P leads to a form of imagining or making-believe that P, which in one way or another serves (perhaps only partly or incompletely) to pacify the desire.[9] If we call the kind of belief- or experience-like representation involved in such cases 'b-representation', then we can write their common pattern as:

> W: A des (wish) that P -[causes]→ A b-reps that P -[causes]→ A's des (wish) that P is pacified.

This pattern is evidently closely related to D* above. Both are patterns in which desire is pacified, and via representation; for belief, as it figures in D* can be taken as the limiting case of belief-like representation which figures in W. The kinship shows in the fact that W can be regarded as a version of D* in which the role of reality is left out, so that an instance of W can be seen as a kind of *short-circuiting* of the full cycle described by D*. In the example of drinking by which we illustrated D* above, the agent's desire produced a real action resulting in a real drink, and thence in a pacifying belief that she was drinking. In a dream of drinking, by contrast, the mind (or brain) by-passes the path through reality which might result in real satisfaction, and produces the pacifying representation directly and by itself. (This shows in that fact that W is like D* except for the omission of '-[causes]→ P -[causes]→'; that is, except for the production of the real action which satisfies desire and renders the pacifying belief true and justified.)

Since we are already familiar with many ways in which people use forms of imaginative representation to pacify their desires, pattern W appears to be one which we already tacitly use and understand, even if we rarely make it explicit. And it is certainly intelligible that such a pattern should exist, and that it should be so closely related to that of action. For, as D* already makes clear, action is aimed not only at satisfaction, but also at the pacification of desire; and in successful action the mind (or brain) achieves this pacification by way of belief, that is, by way of representation. Since such representation is the key to pacification in the case of successful action, it is not surprising that a related form of representation – familiar in various forms of imagination, make-believe, suspension of disbelief, and the like – should also play a role in pacifying desire and motives related to it. Human desire far outruns the possibilities of successful action. So it is natural that desire should admit of pacification by other means, and that there should be forms of desire, or motives related to desire, which are characteristically pacified by representation alone.

To see something of the role of W in psychoanalytic interpretation let us consider the example with which Freud begins *The Interpretation of Dreams*, his own dream of Irma's injection (SE IV, 104ff). In this dream Freud met Irma, a family friend and patient, whom he had diagnosed as hysterical and treated by an early version of psychoanalysis. He told Irma that if she still felt pains, it was her own fault, for not accepting his 'solution' to her difficulties. As she continued to complain, however, he became alarmed that she was suffering from an organic illness which he had failed to diagnose, and this turned out to be so. Freud examined Irma, and then she was examined by some of Freud's colleagues, including his senior colleague M; it became manifest not only that she was organically ill, but also that her illness was caused by a toxic injection given by another of Freud's colleagues, his family doctor Otto. Thus he sets out the parts of the dream with which we shall be concerned as follows:

> numerous guests, among them Irma. I at once took her on one side, as though to answer her letter and to reproach her for not having accepted my 'solution' yet. I said to her, 'If you still get pains, it's really only your fault.' She replied: 'If you only knew what pains I've got now in my throat and stomach and abdomen – it's choking me' – I was alarmed and looked at her ... I thought to myself that after all I must be missing some organic trouble ... I at once called in Dr. M., and he repeated the examination and confirmed it ... M. said, 'There's no doubt it's an infection, but no matter; dysentery will supervene and the toxin will be eliminated.' ... We were directly aware, too, of the origin of the infection. Not long before, when she was feeling unwell, my friend Otto had given her an injection ... Injections of that sort ought not to be made so thoughtlessly ... And probably the syringe had not been clean. (SE IV, 107)

Unlike the simple dream of drinking this dream does not appear to be wish-fulfilling: in fact it dealt with topics which were not pleasant to Freud. It concerned the continued suffering of a patient who was also a family friend, and for whom, therefore, the question of his responsibility was particularly acute; it was also about the possibility that he had misdiagnosed an organic illness as hysteria, which he described as 'a constant anxiety' to someone offering psychological treatment. But Freud systematically collected his free associations – the thoughts and feelings which occurred to him – in connection with each element of the dream, and in light of these we can see that the treatment of these topics in the dream is in fact wishful, and in a way which is radical.

The topics of the dream had arisen on the day before. Otto had just returned from visiting Irma and her family and had briefly discussed Irma with Freud, commenting that she was looking 'better, but not yet well'. Freud had felt something like a reproof in this, as though he had held out too much hope that Irma might be cured; and in consequence he regarded the remark as thoughtless, and felt annoyed with Otto. (Also, as it happened, Otto had been called on to give someone an injection while at Irma's – cf. the topic of the dream – and Freud had just had news indicating, as he thought, that another of his female patients had been given a careless injection by some other doctor, and had been contemplating his own careful practice in this respect with a degree of self-satisfaction.) That night, in order to justify himself, Freud had started to write up Irma's case to show to M, who was respected by both himself and Otto, and who appeared in the dream as diagnosing Irma's illness and becoming aware that it was Otto's fault.

In considering the dream Freud noted that his desire to justify himself in respect of Irma's case, and in particular not to be responsible for her suffering, was apparent from the beginning, in which he told Irma that her pains were now her own fault. Also, he felt that his alarm at her illness in the dream was not entirely genuine. So, as Freud realised, it seemed that he was actually *wishing* that Irma be organically ill: for as he undertook to treat only psychological complaints, this also would mean that he could not be held responsible for her condition, by Otto or anyone else. This theme, indeed, seemed carried further in the rest of the dream, in which M found that Otto, not Freud, bore responsibility for Irma's illness. The whole dream, in fact, could be seen as a wishful response to Otto's remark. According to the dream, and contrary to what Freud had taken Otto to imply, Freud bore no responsibility whatever for Irma's condition. Rather, Otto was the sole cause of her suffering, and this was a result of Otto's bad practice with injections, a matter about which Freud himself was particularly careful.

The contrasting role of desire in action and wish-fulfilment shows here particularly clearly. Freud's intentional action in response to his desire to be cleared of culpable responsibility was to write up a case history to show to his respected senior colleague M., whose authoritative judgement might serve to clear him. This is an action in potential accord with pattern PR, and so also with D*. His dream apparently shows the same motive at work, but in a very different way. There the desire to be cleared produced no rational action, but rather gave rise directly to a (dreamt) belief-like representation of a situation in which Freud was cleared of responsibility in a whole variety of ways, some involving M. These are instances of b-representation produced in accord with pattern W.

We can think of the process by which we specify these instances, and thus represent the material of a dream in terms of pattern W, as follows. The dreamer's free associations, which range over intimate details of his or her life and thought, give information about incidents and emotions (Otto's giving someone an injection while at Irma's, his remark about Irma, Freud's annoyance) which appear to have influenced the content of the dream. These apparent connections between associations and dream are data which require to be explained. The explanation needed is one which specifies how the material from the associations is causally related to the content of the dream.

Inspection of Freud's dream and his associations reveals many such apparent connections. We might start in a preliminary way to list some we have considered as shown in Table 4.1. The list is incomplete but illustrative. It seems hard to deny that the relation of elements on the left to those on the right requires explanation in terms of a causal connection. This being so, the question arises as to what kind of causal hypothesis would provide the best explanation. Freud's hypothesis is in effect that these data are linked by *wishful imaginative representation*, and hence in

Table 4.1

Data from the associations	Data from the dream
Freud wants not to be responsible for Irma's suffering.	Freud says to Irma 'If you still get pains, it's really only your fault.'
Freud wants not to be responsible for Irma's suffering.	Irma is suffering from an organic complaint, for the treatment of which Freud is not responsible.
Freud is annoyed with Otto for his remark implying that Freud was in some way at fault in his practice with Irma.	Otto is at fault in this practice with Irma.
Otto had given someone an injection while at Irma's, and Freud has been contemplating that his injections never cause infection.	Otto gives Irma an injection which caused an infection.
Freud desires to clear himself of responsibility for Irma's suffering.	Otto bears sole responsibility for Irma's suffering.
Freud hopes that M's opinion of his treatment of Irma will clear him of responsibility.	M observes Otto's bad practice and recognises that Otto bears full responsibility for Irma's suffering.
Freud considers Otto's remark to him thoughtless.	Otto's injection of Irma is thoughtless.

accord with pattern W. We can represent this hypothesis in relation to the data as shown in Table 4.2.

Now Table 4.2 represents only a fraction of the data from the association and dream which bear on the hypotheses advanced in it, but examination of further data will also be found to fit with these. Freud's interpretation thus serves to explain data which are clearly discernible by bringing them under an hypothesis whose

Table 4.2

Data from the associations	Hypothesis: the data from the associations are linked with those from the dream by wishful imaginative representation.	Data from the dream
Freud wants not to be responsible for Irma's suffering.	Freud wishfully represents Irma's suffering as not his fault, but her own.	Freud says to Irma 'If you still get pains, it's really only your fault.'
Freud wants not to be responsible for Irma's suffering.	Freud wishfully represents Irma as suffering from something for which he is not responsible.	Irma is suffering from an organic complaint, for the treatment of which Freud is not responsible.
Freud is annoyed with Otto for his remark implying that Freud was in some way at fault in his practice with Irma	Freud wishfully represents the situation as the reverse of that implied by Otto, so that it is Otto, not Freud himself, who can be accused of fault connected with Irma's suffering.	Otto is at fault in his practice with Irma.
Otto had given someone an injection while at Irma's, and Freud has been contemplating that his injections never cause infection.	Freud uses elements from reality to represent wishfully the situation as one in which Otto, not Freud himself, should be accused of fault connected with Irma's suffering.	Otto gives Irma an injection which causes an infection.
Freud desires to clear himself of responsibility for Irma's suffering.	Freud wishfully represents the situation as one in which he has no responsibility for Irma's suffering.	Otto bears sole responsibility for Irma's suffering.
Freud hopes that M's opinion of his treatment of Irma will clear him of responsibility.	Freud wishfully represents M as finding that Irma's suffering was Otto's fault.	M observes Otto's bad practice and recognises that Otto bears full responsibility for Irma's suffering.
Freud considers Otto's remark to him thoughtless.	Freud wishfully represents Otto as thoughtless.	Otto's injection of Irma is thoughtless.

pattern is represented by W. The application of this pattern, however, carries a commitment to a range of hitherto unacknowledged mental states and processes. The processes are those of the wishful imagining which give rise to the manifest content of dreams; and the states are those desire-like states which give rise to the wishful imagining, and which, therefore, we call wishes, but in a theoretical and extended sense. These here include Freud's wishing that Irma's suffering be her own fault, that it be organic, that it be Otto's rather than Freud's responsibility, and so forth. Thus in Freud's conception a dream-wish is an entity introduced by hypothesis, to account for an episode of apparently wishful imagining (or pacifying representation more generally). Such wishes stand to the process of wishful imagining manifest in a dream or day-dream, partly as desires stand to the actions they are cited to explain. Hence, just as a desire can be read in part from the intentional action which the desire is hypothesized to explain, so the wish can be read in part from the episode of imagining – from the dream or day-dream – which it is hypothesized to explain; and just as the action serves to pacify the desire, so, apparently, the imagining serves to pacify this wish.

This indicates that the wishes introduced in the psychoanalytic explanation of dreams in accord with W are comparable, from a methodological perspective, with the desires introduced in the explanation of action in accord with D*. In particular, we can see that psychoanalytic hypotheses admit of testing, and hence of confirmation, in the same sort of way as those advanced in the commonsense explanation of action, which in general we regard as capable of a high degree of cogency. In this case, however, the hypotheses concern motives (dream wishes) of a kind which are capable of explaining phenomena which are unexplained in commonsense psychology, and whose contents are different and more extreme.

We can mark this difference by noting that the wishes which Freud has here uncovered – even in this most superficial layer of interpretation – already stand in striking contrast to motives standardly acknowledged in waking life. By everyday standards, for example, these wishes are highly egoistic, ruthless and extreme. We should regard someone who acted on *desires* with these contents – who, to escape an imagined reproach, arranged for a friend and patient to be seriously ill, and for revenge threw the blame for this on another friend, the author of the supposed reproach – as criminal or worse. Likewise, the way of thinking shown in the dream is radically defective: the reversal of Otto's reproach, for example, seems like a transparently childish 'It's not *me* that's bad – it's *you*' (projection). Also, the dream-wishes are sharply at variance with Freud's other motives, so that the representation of their fulfilment seems alarming rather than pleasant, and the acknowledgement of them, even as mere dream-wishes, is not entirely easy. Thus take the wish that Irma be physically ill. Since she was Freud's friend and patient, this would have been a source of considerable distress in real life, and the situation was one of some alarm in the dream. Accordingly, in acknowledging the wish Freud says that he 'had a sense of awkwardness at having invented such a severe illness for Irma simply in order to clear myself. It looked so cruel . . .' So even in this first example, we begin to find a significant extension of commonsense psychology.

And clearly, even in this first example, the extension goes further. We have been considering Freud's dream in relation to events of the day before, and his apparent wishes (i) not to be responsible for Irma's suffering and (ii) to turn the tables on his imagined accuser, Otto. But it is clear from Freud's associations that the dream also related to deeper matters of responsibility, and in particular to Freud's role in the death of one of his patients and one of his friends. Thus he associated as follows to the element of the dream in which he called in Dr M to examine Irma:

> *I at once called in Dr. M., and he repeated the examination* . . . This re-minded me of a tragic event in my practice. I had on one occasion produced a severe toxic state in a woman patient by repeatedly prescribing what was at that time regarded as a harmless remedy (sulphonal), and had hurriedly turned for assistance and support to my experienced senior colleague . . . My patient – who succumbed to the poison – had the same name as my eldest daughter . . . Mathilde . . . (SE IV, 111, 112)

In addition, this touches on the theme of thoughtless medication, which was also connected with the death of one of Freud's friends, as well as some lesser matters, which, however, also seem likely causes of guilt. As Freud introduces this topic:

What I saw in her throat: a white patch and turbinal bones with scabs on them . . . I was making frequent use of cocaine at that time to relieve some troublesome nasal swellings, and I had heard a few days earlier that one of my women patients who had followed my example had developed an extensive necrosis [area of dead tissue] of the nasal mucous membrane. I had been the first to recommend the [medical] use of cocaine, in 1885, and this recommendation had brought serious reproaches down on me. The misuse of that drug had hastened the death of a dear friend of mine . . . I had advised him to use the drug internally [i.e. orally] only, while morphia was being withdrawn; but he had at once given himself cocaine *injections*. (SE IV, 111, 115)

So the figure of Irma in the dream was linked in Freud's mind with that of three persons to whom he had done some damage in his medical interventions, including two who had actually died as a result of them. These cases are apparently alluded to in the dream in a number of ways, for example in M's statement above that 'the toxin will be eliminated'. Their role becomes clearer if we consider Freud's associations to the final elements of the dream, which were quoted above:

Injections of that sort ought not to be made so thoughtlessly. Here an accusation of thoughtlessness was being made directly against my friend Otto. I seemed to remember thinking something of the same kind that afternoon when his words and looks had appeared to show that he was siding against me. It had been some such notion as: 'How easily his thoughts are influenced! How thoughtlessly he jumps to conclusions!' – Apart from this, this sentence in the dream reminded me once more of my dead friend who had so hastily resorted to cocaine injections . . . I noticed too that in accusing Otto of thoughtlessness in handling chemical substances I was once more touching upon the story of the unfortunate Mathilde, which gave grounds for the same accusation against myself . . .

And probably the syringe had not been clean. This was yet another accusation against Otto, but derived from a different source. I had happened the day before to meet the son of an old lady of eighty-two, to whom I had to give an injection of morphia twice a day. At the moment she was in the country and he told me that she was suffering from phlebitis. I has at once thought it must be an infiltration caused by a dirty syringe. I was proud of the fact that in two years I had not caused a single infiltration; I took constant pains to be

Table 4.3

Data from the associations	Data from the dream
Freud accidentally caused the death of a patient by prescribing her a toxic substance	Otto misuses toxic substances.
Freud advised a friend to take cocaine, and the friend's death was hastened by cocaine injections.	Freud reproaches Otto with the thought that injections of that kind ought not be made so thoughtlessly.

sure that the syringe was clean. In short: I was conscientious. (SE IV, 117, 118)

Thus, on examination, Freud's associations indicate further apparently non-coincidental connections with his dream, which we can represent as shown in Table 4.3.

It seems clear that, just as Freud wished to avoid culpable responsibility for Irma's suffering, so he might well have wished that he could avoid such responsibility in these cases as well. So if we apply Freud's form of hypothesis to this data, we can represent it as shown in Table 4.4.

These hypotheses are deeper than those which touch merely on the day before the dream and the figure of Irma herself. They involve further figures, the more distant past and deeper emotions. What Freud took to be in question in Otto's remark was responsibility for Irma's continued neurotic suffering. What was in question in the case of his friend and patient, however, was responsibility of a graver kind: that for causing death. Hence the deeper emotion involved is guilt. This is coherent with the wish not to be responsible for Irma's suffering shown more explicitly in the dream; for although Freud does not make the point explicit, this too would be a source of guilt.

To accept these further hypotheses, therefore, is to see the dream as wishfully related not only to persons and events of the day before the dream, but also to persons and events from the past. To put the point in terms of some of Freud's theoretical terminol-

Table 4.4

Data from the associations	Hypothesis about wishful imagining which connects associations and dream	Data from the dream
Freud accidentally caused the death of a patient by giving her a toxic substance.	Freud wishfully represents Otto rather than himself as responsible for the misuse of toxic substances, as in the case of the patient whose death he caused.	Otto misuses toxic substances.
Freud advised a friend to take cocaine, and the friend's death was hastened by cocaine injections.	Freud wishfully represents Otto rather than himself as responsible for thoughtless injections, as were given in the case of his friend who died.	Freud reproaches Otto with the thought that injections of that kind ought not be made so thoughtlessly.

ogy: in these hypotheses the image of Irma in the dream is seen as a *condensation*, involving not only Irma herself, but also the friend and patient from the past, in whose cases Freud would like to be free of guilt; and the dream effects a wishful *displacement* of the kind of guilt Freud felt in respect of these cases too on to the figure of Otto. The dream is thus shaped by persons and events from the past, which are linked in the mind of the dreamer with those from the day before, but have a deeper emotional significance.

In seeing the dream in this way, moreover, we also have reason to see Freud's conscious feelings and actions in a different light. For we can now see, for example, that Freud was so sensitive to Otto's remark, and so ready to regard Otto as thoughtless, for the reason that Otto's remark touched upon issues of medical responsibility which were particularly significant for Freud, even though he was not aware of them at the time, and would not have become aware of them had he not analysed the dream. (Likewise for Freud's action of writing up Irma's case-history, his contemplation of his own care with respect to injections, and so forth.)

The point is not that these thoughts, feelings, and actions are not to be seen partly as Freud consciously represents them; it is rather that the dream and associations indicate that they are also to be seen in another way, that is, as related to the past, and to guilt, in ways the conscious representation alone tells us nothing of.

V

Although our discussion has touched on only a few of the relevant topics,[10] it suggests that we can see Freud's reasoning in this paradigmatic example as an extension of the kind of patterned interpretation we find in everyday life, and one which admits of potentially strong confirmation in the same way. We noted above that in everyday interpretation an interpreter could cross-check the interpretation of a variety of verbal and non-verbal actions, and so both confirm and explore the limits of the interpretee's first-person authority. From our example we can see that cross-checking in psychoanalysis also plays a distinct but complementary role. The example shows that the interpretation of wish-fulfilments in accord with W can introduce new desires and wishes – such as Freud's desire to be free from blame for thoughtless injections – whose ascription can be cross-checked against both the explanation of actions in accord with D*, and the explanation of further wish-fulfilments via W.

Interpretation in accord with W thus has the capacity both to discover new (or previously unacknowledged) motives and to contribute to confirmation of their role in human psychology. So Freud's discovery of this mode of interpretation has the power to extend commonsense psychology in ways which are potentially radical, cumulative and sound. Radical, because the interpretation of dreams (or other wish-fulfilments) evidently leads quickly to the ascription of wishes very different from those acknowledged in everyday life, and also to the discernment of new mental mechanisms, new kinds of dependence of present mental life on the past and so forth. Cumulative, because the kinds of wishes we can discern by this means depend upon the desires we take people to have in waking life, and our hypotheses about these, as we have just seen in the case of Freud, tend to be strikingly enriched as a result of considering dreams. So the discovery of dream-wishes might lead to further hypotheses about waking motives, and these to the finding of further dream wishes and so on, in rapid succession. (Something of this may be visible in Freud's consideration of the Oedipus complex in *The Interpretation of Dreams*.) Finally, even such a radical and cumulative extension might be sound, in the sense that each further hypothesis about new wishes, desires, etc., might be thoroughly cross-checked via the interpretation of very many dreams (or other wish-fulfilments) and verbal and non-verbal actions, and hence be intuitively confirmed to a high degree.

Freud and his successors have in effect claimed that this is so. The argument here suggests that while this would be very difficult to demonstrate, it might nonetheless be true. If this is so there is at least some case for regarding psychoanalysis, as Freud intended, as an interpretive science. Still we should recognize that even a cogent interpretive discipline could never fully *seem* like a real science. For any interpretive discipline must be one in which the tacit and intuitive testing of hypotheses outruns our capacities to make the relevant data, claims and inferences fully explicit and communicable. Whether we choose to call psychoanalysis a science or not, it seems to be such a case; and hence, however well psychoanalytic hypotheses are confirmed, we must expect them to remain in dispute.[11]

Appendix: Cross-checking the interpretation of language and action

To represent the points discussed in the text more schematically, let us imagine that we have an interpreter A and an interpretee B, and that the sentences of their idiolects are numbered, so that A's sentences include P1, P2 . . . Pn . . . and B's include Σ1, Σ2, . . . Σn . . . Then in trying to understand B's language A will be trying to devise a correlation in his own idiolect whose instances might be represented as:

'Σ1' is true (in B's idiolect) just if P1
'Σ2' is true (in B's idiolect) just if P2
'Σ3' is true (in B's idiolect) just if P3
'Σ4' is true (in B's idiolect) just if P4

and so on. We may call this the Σ/P correlation, and it could be effected by a theory of truth for B's language.

Let us suppose that A has a hypothetical understanding of B's utterances which includes these interpretations, and also that A is able to interpret some non-verbal action of B's, by a tree such as shown in Figure 4.3. Since A also has a tentative understanding of B's idiolect, he can use this to translate this tree into B's sentences, that is, as shown in Figure 4.4. Now suppose also that A can get B to explain what he is doing, or otherwise to express the desires and beliefs upon which B is acting, so that B's own use of sentences gives us a further tree. This gives us two trees in B's idiolect, the first supplied via A's interpretation of B's language and action, the second via B's own exercise of first-person authority. Given these materials, A can now test his understanding of B's language and action by comparing these trees. If (i) A has understood B's action correctly, and (ii) A's translation of A's hypothetical tree into B's idiolect is correct, and (iii) B has first-person authority, then the translated tree, and that produced by B, should match sentence for sentence.

This is a very precise and antecedently improbable prediction, so, if it is correct, A can regard his understanding of B's sentences and action, and A's possession of first-person authority, as simultaneously confirmed. (Alternatively, if the trees fail to match at any point, A has reason to hold that his interpretation of B's speech or action was mistaken, or that B's first-person authority is defective at this point.) More fully, a match between the trees should raise A's confidence in his initial tree, towards whatever level he associates with B's first-person authority in the case, while also confirming B's possession of this authority, by showing a correlation between self-ascription and the results of interpretation by another. Finally, the match offers support for A's under-

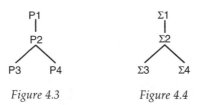

Figure 4.3   Figure 4.4

standing of B's idiolect, with regard to all the sentences which figured in the trees, for it indicates that A maps B's sentences on to the same actions and situations as B himself. Repeated support of this kind would thus constitute confirmation of A's hypothesis as to the Σ/P correlation generally.

It thus appears that insofar as we hold that this kind of match with the speech of an interpretee obtains for an interpreter's trees for actions generally, we thereby hold (i) that the interpretee has a degree of well-founded first-person authority about her goals and beliefs; (ii) that the interpreter can enjoy a degree of confidence in ascribing these goals and beliefs which tends to approach that of the interpretee; and (iii) that the interpretation of any action can be turned to the testing, and hence to the confirmation, of the interpreter's understanding of the interpretee's sentences. So systematic triangulation between utterance and action of the kind we have been considering can tend simultaneously to render interpretation cogent, first-person authority credible, and our interpretive grip on the meanings of sentences as firm as any we possess.

Notes

1 This chapter continues a line of exposition developed in my essay 'The interpretation of dreams', in J. Neu (ed.), *The Cambridge Companion to Freud* (Cambridge: Cambridge University Press, 1991) and 'Psychoanalysis, interpretation, and science', in J. Hopkins and A. Savile (eds), *Psychoanalysis, Mind, and Art: Perspectives on Richard Wollheim* (Oxford: Basil Blackwell, 1993).

   The general approach to interpretation is partly based on work by Donald Davidson. See his *Essays on Actions and Events* (Oxford: Clarendon Press, 1982), and *Inquiries into Truth and Interpretation* (Oxford: Clarendon Press, 1984). Davidson discussess Freud in 'Paradoxes of irrationality' in R. Wollheim and J. Hopkins (eds), *Philosophical Essays on Freud* (Cambridge: Cambridge University Press, 1982).

2 An example of what I am calling a hermeneutic approach would be that of Klein, *Psychoanalytic Theory* (Chicago: International Universities Press, 1976). A contrasting causalist approach is found in Adolf Grunbaum, *The Foundations of Psychoanalysis: A Philosophical Critique* (Berkeley: University of California Press, 1984) and *Validation in the Clinical Theory of Psychoanalysis* (Madison, CT: International Universities Press, 1993). For a discussion of Grunbaum's critique of Freud in these terms see my 'Epistemology and depth psychology', in Peter Clark and Crispin Wright (eds), *Mind, Psychanalysis, and Science* (Oxford: Basic Blackwell, 1988), in particular pp. 50ff. In general, attempted critiques of Freud's thinking have failed to grasp

the role of sentential coherence in the intuitive discernment of causal role. Thus the present exposition can be compared with the criticisms in Ch. 1 of E. Erwin, *A Final Accounting* (Cambridge, Mass.: MIT Press, 1997).

3 The present approach also enables us to understand dispute of this kind at a deeper level. Our natural interpretive practice enables us to grasp and inter-relate various causes of our behaviour (motives) through what we apprehend and describe as relations of sentential coherence. This mode of understanding is basic, capable of accuracy and, at present, the only one we can apply to ourselves in any detail. These same causes, however, admit of study in other ways, say through their realization in the brain, and this would be part of culturally developed physical science. We thus have two ways of thinking and speaking about the same set of causes, and since the ways of thinking are different, it is natural to forget that they are ultimately ways of thinking about the same things, and hence to take them as in competition. But we have good reason to think both ways of thinking capable of accuracy, and insofar as this is so, we can be sure that their results will coincide.

4 Thus there are many sorts of cases in which expectations which are predictive in accord with D* are falsified. For example: (i) an agent may do something we do not expect (instead of drinking the water she pours it on the flowers) so that we conclude that we were wrong about her desire (we were wrong about the sentence 'P' in des P); (ii) an agent may try to do what we did expect but fail (des P was present but failed to cause P); (iii) an agent may not succeed but think she has succeeded and so stop trying (des P produces something something besides P, which yet causes bel P); (iv) an agent may succeed but not notice that she has and keep trying (des P causes P, which fails to cause A bels P); and other variations from the predicted norms are possible. Finally, an agent might recognize her own success, but nonetheless be unable to stop trying to achive her goal (this would a case in which bel P failed to pacify des P). Given the many ways in which the hypotheses in D* may be falsified, we may also reasonably take them to be confirmed when things go as we expect.

5 This kind of representation is intuitively fairly clear, but it may be worth spelling out what is involved a little more fully. Suppose we have a goal G connected by branches to sub-goals G1 to Gn, and these by further branches to further sub-goals G1,1, G1,2, etc., as in Figure 4.5.

The top tree corresponds to a desire that G and a belief that if G1 and G2

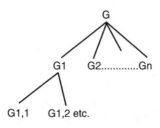

Figure 4.5

and . . . Gn (in that order) then G. This tree constitutes a complex instance of PR, as does the tree down from G1, which corresponds to a desire that G1 and a belief that if G1,1 . . . then G1; and so on down the tree. When we spontaneously interpret an agent's movements in terms of intentions and reasons, we tacitly relate these movements to such a tree, or to a series of such trees. (Ordinarily we do not fill these out consciously, but if pressed we can do so in more or less detail; and in this we are not introducing further hypotheses, but making explicit what we already tacitly took to be the case.)

6 This line of questioning, and the answers provided in the next section, are derived from Wittgenstein's celebrated treatment of following a rule. For a discussion of this topic, also related to Freud, see James Hopkins, 'Wittgenstein, interpretation, and the foundations of psychoanalysis', *New Formations: Special Issue on Psyconanalysis and Culture*, autumn (1995) 54–73.

7 To spell this out a little more fully, we can say generally:

> (i) The claim that A has a certain belief, desire or other mental state is justified insofar as this claim provides, or is part of, the best explanation of what A says and does, that is, the best explanation of A's behaviour overall.

And since we are taking such explanation to characterize the causes within us of what we say and do, we also have:

> (ii) The claim that A has a certain belief, desire or other mental state is justified insofar as this claim provides, or is part of, an accurate and explanatory characterization of the causes within A of what A says and does, that is, the (neural) causes which serve to explain A's behaviour overall.

These criteria of justification are objective in the sense that they are uniform with those which we apply in scientific understanding generally. So this indicates a solution at least to the problem of justifying the claim of first-person authority made by, or on behalf of, a given individual, A. We can say that A has first-person authority insofar as A has the ability to say and think things about A's own mental states and behaviour which are not interpretively mediated by observation of A's own behaviour, but which nonetheless are justified by the objective criteria provided by (i) and (ii). Since this applies to A's beliefs about his or her own idiolect, it covers language as well.

8 Comparison of this type can be made between any two hypotheses which purport to locate the same motives or mental states, and so, e.g. among successive interpretations which we might make of successive bodily move-ments as a pattern of action unfolds, or those we might offer for a succession of speech acts related to the same objects or events. It is part of our everyday understanding to integrate the ascriptions which cover various actions in such ways, and so check each against the others. Nonetheless, the case taken here, which involves comparing the interpretation of non-verbal action with authoritative expression, has a special role. In this kind of case the interpreter can cross-check his construal of verbal and non-verbal action with the

interpretee's first-person authority, and this makes it possible, as illustrated, simultaneously to confirm all three.

9 Such pacification may not be as deep or permanent as that achieved by satisfying action, but the effects can be genuine nonetheless. In *Sleep and Dreaming* (London: Harvester Wheatsheaf, 2nd edn, 1993), Jacob Empson reports an experiment in which dreamers were deprived of water for twenty-four hours and given a salty meal before going to bed. On these nights their dream-reports included more water-related imagery, such as lakes or snow, as well as some explicitly thirst-satisfying objects, than on nights when they had been allowed to drink as they pleased. Also, subjects reporting gratifying dreams including themes of eating and drinking during the course of the night drank less in the morning, and rated themselves as less thirsty, than those who had not.

10 In particular it should be noted that we have said nothing about symbolism, which can, however, naturally be added to this account. There is some discussion of this in my essay 'Psychoanalysis, metaphor, and mind', in M. Levine (ed.), *The Analytic Freud* (London: Routledge, forthcoming).

11 The comparison between psychoanalysis and fully communicable science is developed in my 'Psychoanalysis, interpretation, and science'.

5

The other day:
the interpretation
of day-dreams

RACHEL BOWLBY

It almost seems to go without saying that dreams in *The Interpretation of Dreams* are creatures of the night. Shady, enigmatic, mysterious, they draw unto them all the accumulated metaphorics of a symbolic division between darkness and light. They belong to a nether world which has no place on the surfaces of daytime life – as in the following passage leading up to the famous identification with a legendary literary conqueror:

> In waking life the suppressed material in the mind is prevented from finding expression . . . but during the night . . . the suppressed material finds methods and means of forcing its way into consciousness.
>
> Flectere si nequeo superos, Acheronta movebo. (PFL 4, 768–9: SE V, 608)

Freud cites Virgil in the original Latin, as though to emphasize not only the epic connection, but also the sense of strangeness in the movement from one world to its underworld, from day to night: 'If I cannot move the higher powers, I will move the lower.' But the separation itself seems to be a sure one. Sleep and 'night' go together as surely as 'waking life' and the day. Dream, sleep, night-time, darkness all come to shade into one another to the point that they appear to be inseparable. As though to acknowledge that there is something about this obscurity that is more than the evidence allows – since it is obvious that sleep, and dreams, can occur in daylight as well as at night – Freud sometimes uses the expanded term 'night-dreams'. Without darkness, without the night, dreams would carry no mystery; there would be nothing to interpret.

Yet the day is far from being absent from these nocturnal phenomena. It enters into Freudian night-dreams in two regular manifestations, each of which is considered at some length in *The Interpretation of Dreams*. First, the use of the term 'night-dreams' is partly, of course, a way of marking the existence of day-dreams. And second, there are those ubiquitous features known as 'day's residues'.

At first sight, day-dreams and day's residues appear rather different – day-dreams are comparable with night-dreams, while the day's residues contribute to their making. But this initial division is complicated by the fact that day-dreams themselves can also appear as part of the content of dreams. In this instance, day-dreams function as ready-prepared, unobjectionable material that can be used by the dream without more ado, in this respect like the day's residues. The other case, that of the comparison of dreams to day-dreams, is itself used for two opposite purposes: day-dreams show something about dreams either because they are like them, or because they are not. This is partly because different features of dreams and day-dreams are being utilised in each instance, but also because there are important variations in how Freud conceives of the relative importance of each.

The day's residues are subject to other ambiguities of deployment. Freud states unequivocally that in every dream there is something left over from the previous day. That something is there, however, not because it has any significance in itself, but because it does not: being recent and new, the day's residues qualify under the purely negative condition of being insignificant, free of associations. It is this that gives them the capacity to act as a 'cover' for the real thoughts of the dream, which cannot obtain free expression by itself. The day is of merely passing significance, in two senses: the obvious one, whereby it matters only while it lasts, until it is past; and a second, whereby it enables the night-dream's thoughts to 'pass', to appear to be as trivial and innocuous as the day's are supposed to be.

These enigmatic and elusive appearances of the day, in a context for the most part resolutely nocturnal, can themselves easily pass unnoticed. In this chapter I shall pursue in more detail some of these peculiarities that attach to the day in the dream, and the dream in the day. What is the significance of the day's actual ubiquitousness but alleged insignificance in the Freudian dream? With this question in mind, Freud's reference to a story by the nineteenth-century French novelist Alphonse Daudet in one of his discussions of day-dreams offers a minor road which ends with a different view.

Day's residues, night's survivals

Freud insists that all dreams find some material out of 'day's residues', from the thoughts and activities of the very day before. All dreams, it is claimed, make use of impressions from the day that immediately precedes the sleep of the dream; their usefulness is premised on the need for a cover or surface of indifference to hide dreams' real motives and meanings. This, day's residues are uniquely suitable to provide:

> Both groups of impressions satisfy the demand of the repressed for material that is still clear of associations – the indifferent ones because they have given no occasion for the formation of many ties, and the recent ones because they have not yet had time to form them.
>
> It will be seen, then, that the day's residues, among which we may now class the indifferent impressions, not only borrow something from the *Ucs.* when they succeed in taking a share in the formation of a dream – namely the instinctual force which is at the disposal of the repressed wish – but that they also offer the unconscious something indispensable – namely the necessary point of attachment for a transference. (PFL 4, 717: SE V, 564)

As the language of borrowings and offers suggests, a kind of deal is struck. The deal depends on a negotiation between the ephemeral in quest of continuation and the permanent in search of short-lived daylight. The day's residues gain some temporary continuing role when they get to participate in a dream, and the dream acquires a means of gliding its instinctual disturbances into an acceptable form. In what we shall see is a persistent attribution in many contexts, that which belongs to the day is taken to be transitory and thereby also trivial, while that which belongs to the night is durable to the point of timelessness, loaded with a pressure of meaning that must out into the temporal.

It is significant that, in contrast to the usual emphasis in his outlining of this kind of structure – in relation, for instance, to the formation of neurotic symptoms – Freud here suggests not so much the negative aspect of a compromise, where a bargain is struck by each contributor making concessions, but the positive gains associated with a move that is beneficial to both parties. In the neurotic structure, the repressed wish gets itself out in the form of a symptom, but not as a fulfilment; while the ego keeps the wish from coming out openly, but only by allowing the symptom. The day's residue, on the other hand, has nothing to lose, being destined only to get lost. Its lack of significance is indicated in numerous phrases of dismissal, to the point that this characteristic shades over into utter worthlessness – no value, and a corresponding quality of encumbrance insofar as it is not disposed of: 'unimportant details . . . worthless fragments of waking life' (PFL 4, 260: SE IV, 174); 'remnants of trivial experiences' (PFL 4, 264: SE IV, 177); 'the "dregs" of daytime recollections' (PFL 4, 264: SE IV, 178); 'indifferent refuse left over from the previous day' (PFL 4, 746: SE V, 589).

The rhetoric of rubbish apparent here is linked sometimes to an idea that such detritus has to be disposed of, as it were, by a daily refuse collection. Freud rejects this theory in relation to dream-content only because it posits an impossible task of working over for dreams to accomplish, not because he thinks that there is no disposal to be done:

> The night would not be long enough to cope with such a mass. It is far more likely that the process of forgetting indifferent impressions goes forward without the active intervention of our psychical forces. (PFL 4, 264: SE IV, 178)

What is revealing about the form of this refuse-refusal is its premise of rational order: the night, with the dreams that take its time, is conceptualised as a given period for the achievement of necessary work, rather than – for instance, and as elswhere – as a phase in which the normal, social orders of time and reason are suspended altogether.

The treatment of the remains of the day as superfluous waste for throwing out puts them at the opposite extreme from the dream-thoughts. These latter stay put come what may; are full of significance whereas the day's impressions have none whatever; and are virtually indestructible whereas the day's remains are (literally) ephemera, lasting only for a day and with no enduring value. A further radical distinction is suggested by the 'mass' of indifferent impressions in the passage quoted above. 'Crowds of such impressions enter our minds and are then forgotten' (PFL 4, 262: SE IV, 176), he says a little earlier: on one side, teeming in from the day, is a number so large, it is implied, that it could not possibly be incorporated or assimilated; on the other, the small, select and well-defined group of the repressed wishes. Such polarization is typical of the way in which Freud establishes his two-tier systems – in this instance, as often, contrasting a surface (of transient dailiness) with the underlying depths of timeless significance and potency.

The day's residues serve primarily as only the veil or excuse for the dream-thoughts, the wishes to which they offer a means of muffled expression. For although Freud does discuss the possibility of a contribution to dreams of thoughts and worries and wishes from daily life in their own right, as independent instigators, he nonetheless affirms that they are not sufficient in themselves to get a dream going: 'In my view, therefore, wishful impulses left over from conscious waking life must be relegated to a secondary position in respect to the formation of dreams' (PFL 4, 705: SE V, 554). In this connection, daily life seems to be at once crucial and trivial: necessary to give the unconscious wish a hearing or a sighting, but of merely passing significance in relation to the psychical interests that are older, more deeply established. This accords, as we shall see, with one of the ways in which day-dreams are differentiated from dreams.

Day-dreams, night-dreams

Day-dreams flit in and out of *The Interpretation of Dreams*, in various guises and various kinds of connection and disconnection with the night-dreams that form the ostensible focus of the book's enquiry, its 'royal road' to the unconscious. They are protean and contradictory in their appearances – sometimes just a bit of a dream, sometimes similar to night-dreams and sometimes their antithesis. In the later, theoretical parts of the book, Freud deliberately draws on day-dreams as both counter-example and analogy to elucidate his claims for the significance of night-dreams in their relations to unconscious wishes. As we shall see, these passages resonate with others in essays of the following years, in the course of which day-dreams gradually come to serve as adumbrations or exemplary modes of what he is now exploring under the term 'phantasy'.

In *The Interpretation of Dreams*, then, day-dreams appear on one side as extensions or analogues of dreams. In this connection, Freud makes a minor argument out of their shared name. In the German, a footnote glosses the term *Tagtraum* – a conscious translation of the English 'day-dream' – with both French and English: *'rêve, petit roman – day-dream, story'*.[1] The connection here has to do with narrative form: the unity which characterizes the stories of day-dreams resembles the surface appearance of night-dreams produced in the process of secondary revision (we shall come back to this aspect of the comparison). In a passage from the eighth of the *Introductory Lectures* (1916–17), Freud again makes the point about linguistic continuity. In this instance, he even goes so far as to refer to dreams as 'nocturnal day-dreaming', thereby making the day-dream into the default mode of which the night-dream would be just a special case. Here the point of similarity is not the story as a whole, but the happy ending attributed to day-dreams: 'Linguistic usage, therefore, has a suspicion of the fact that wish-fulfilment is a chief characteristic of dreams' (PFL 1, 162: SE XV, 130).

The clearest and largest claim for the importance of day-dreams in *The Interpretation of Dreams* makes them an alternative 'royal road', a kind of *Autobahn* to the unconscious constructed after the first arrival at the destination:

> They share a large number of their properties with night-dreams, and their investigation might, in fact, have served as *the shortest and best approach* to an understanding of night-dreams. (PFL 4, 632: SE V, 492; my emphasis)

And in a footnote later in the same section, this considerable overlap of features becomes, unequivocally, 'the complete analogy between night-dreams and day-dreams' (PFL 4, 635: SE V, 494).

The usefulness of day-dreams to the study of dreams on the grounds of shared components is emphasized in later writings. In 'Hysterical phantasies and their relation to bisexuality' (1908), we read:

> They are justly called 'day-dreams', for they give us the *key* to an understanding of night-dreams – in which the *nucleus* of the dream-formation consists of nothing else than complicated day-time phantasies of this kind that have been distorted and are misunderstood by the conscious psychical agency. (PFL 10, 88: SE IX, 159–60; my emphasis)

And in the *Introductory Lectures*, in a long section on day-dreams, Freud summarizes:

> We know that such *day-dreams are the nucleus and prototype of night-dreams*. A night-dream is at bottom nothing other than a day-dream that has been made utilizable owing to the liberation of the instinctual impulses at night, and that has been distorted by the form assumed by mental activity at night. (PFL 1, 421: SE XVI, 372–3; my emphasis)

Running through these passages are the two models of part and paradigm. On the one hand, day-dreams contribute to dreams: they form a nucleus, provide materials that go into the composition of the night-dream. On the other hand, day-dreams resemble night-dreams. They could equally well have been used as a key to understanding that which night-dreams enable us to understand, since they are similar in psychical function – 'the complete analogy', no less. Let us look first at the second of these aspects.

Day-dreams, like night-dreams, are narratives which lead to satisfaction by representing the fulfilment of wishes:

> Incidentally, if our experience in dreams is only a modified kind of imagining made possible by the conditions of the state of sleep – that is, a 'nocturnal day-dreaming' – we can already understand how the process of constructing a dream can dispose of the nocturnal stimulus and bring satisfaction, since day-dreaming too is an activity

> bound up with satisfaction and is only practised, indeed, on that
> account. (PFL 1, 162: SE XV, 130)

Such wishes, for both kinds of dream, are long-lasting, dating
back, apparently, to the earliest period of life. From *The Interpretation of Dreams*:

> Like dreams, they are wish-fulfilments; like dreams they are based to
> a great extent on impressions of infantile experiences; like dreams,
> they benefit by a certain degree of relaxation of censorship. (PFL 4,
> 632–3: SE V, 492)

Day-dreams can also be unconscious, Freud goes on to say – as far
from waking awareness as dreams themselves. They too may
point towards something that is constantly undermining the apparent unity and singularity of daytime consciousness and aims.
Like dreams, they are a piece of normality which verges on being,
and is structured like, a neurotic symptom. They may be the
immediate forerunners of a hysterical attack (a suggestion made
in 'Hysterical phantasies' (PFL 10, 88: SE IX, 160), as well as in *The
Interpretation of Dreams* (PFL 4, 632: SE V, 491), or they may pre-
cede a dream that is itself interchangeable with a hysterical attack
(a suggestion made in *The Interpretation of Dreams* (PFL 4, 635: SE
V, 494).

But day-dreams are also said to resemble not so much dreams
in general as one particular aspect of their form and function: that
of secondary revision. The longest section on day-dreams in *The
Interpretation of Dreams* occurs in the part dedicated to that fourth
feature of the dream-work; in it, the unifying, reconstructive effect is said to be epitomized by day-dreams:

> The function of 'secondary revision', which we have attributed to
> the fourth of the factors concerned in shaping the content of dreams,
> shows us in operation once more the activity which is able to find
> free vent in the creation of day-dreams without being inhibited by
> any other influences. We might put it simply by saying that this
> fourth factor of ours seeks to mould the material offered to it into
> something like a day-dream. (PFL 4, 633: SE V, 492)

Here too, Freud both makes an analogy of day-dreams and, at
the same time, offers them as component parts of dreams. He
continues:

If, however, a day-dream of this kind has already been formed within the nexus of the dream-thoughts, this fourth factor in the dream-work will prefer to take possession of the ready-made day-dream and seek to introduce it into the content of the dream. There are some dreams which consist merely in the repetition of a day-time phantasy which may perhaps have remained unconscious. (PFL 4, 633: SE V, 492)

The alleged likeness of day-dreams to dreams thus subtends very different – and conflicting – emphases. Day-dreams are considered either as touching on the unconscious, repressed thoughts that are the origin of night-dreams, or as resembling only the not-dream part of the dream – its presentable, outside, external face as formed in the process of secondary revision.

In later writings, this point slides into the suggestion of an obviousness that attaches to day-dreams; it is this which might have made them a more accessible, less twisting road to the understanding of wish-fulfilment as the primary feature of dreams. The word that tends to be used here is 'transparent'. In the fifth *Introductory Lecture*, Freud states: 'The content of these phantasies is dominated by a very transparent motive' (PFL 1, 127: SE XV, 98). And in the eighth: 'at one point we hoped to approach an understanding of the problems of dreams from the fact that certain imaginative structures which are very transparent to us are known as "day-dreams"' (PFL 1, 162: SE XV, 130).

These references to transparency (*Durchsichtigheit*) may be compared with a pair of architectural similes that occur in the course of the discussion of day-dreams in *The Interpretation of Dreams*. Here is the continuation of Freud's enumeration of the points of similarity between day-dreams and night-dreams:

> If we examine their [day-dreams'] structure, we shall perceive the way in which the wishful purpose that is at work in their production has mixed up the material of which they are built, has rearranged it and has formed it into a new whole. They stand in much the same relation to the childhood memories from which they are derived as do some of the Baroque palaces of Rome to the ancient ruins whose pavements and columns have provided the material for the more recent structure. (PFL 4, 633: SE V, 492)

In addition to its derivative, remake status, the Baroque comparison functions to suggest the ornateness, the complexity and above all the finished appearance of a day-dream, as of a dream which has been through the process of secondary revision. But here, when the 'complete analogy' is still being considered, the structure is opaque rather than transparent: this is a front which obscures what lies behind it, rather than serving as a window on the wish.

In the other instance, we move once again from the analogy to the component part, as day-dreams are considered in their capacity to furnish one of the elements – the outward front – for the total building which will make up the dream:

> Now there is one case in which it [this fourth factor – secondary revision] is to a great extent spared the labour of, as it were, building up a façade for the dream – the case, namely, in which a formation of that kind already exists, available for use in the material of the dream-thoughts. (PFL 4, 631: SE V, 491)

This ready-made formation is then described as a 'phantasy', which is in turn elucidated as being like a 'day-dream' (the inverted commas signifying a new concept in the first instance, and a new linguistic coinage, as we have seen, in the second).

It is here that the use of day-dreams as counter-comparison, rather than as analogy, begins to appear more sharply. Unlike the dreams of sleep, day-dreams in this instance are said to show their meaning on the surface: there is no subterranean layer to be plumbed. As such, they can provide the varnish on a dream, appearing as a gloss for the unpresentable materials underneath. In themselves, they are what they seem: straightforward – unified and unidirectional – stories of wish-fulfilment. This leads to further differences, some of them mentioned more than once, some only implied and some where there is no consistency – what Freud states as a difference in one place, he may assume as a common feature in another.

Minimally, the dream occurs during sleep, the day-dream when the subject is awake. The distinction is barely more than physiological; what is interesting is the way that it comes, surreptitiously, to be mapped on to others, in particular the opposition of night and day. Freud assumes, without question, that day-dreams are unlike night-dreams because 'their relation to sleep is already contradicted by their name' (PFL 1, 128: SE XV, 98–9). As natural, in appearance, as the difference between sleeping and being awake, this opposition takes on the greatest symbolic importance and makes way for others, some explicit and some not.

A contrast regularly stressed by Freud concerns the dreamer's belief in the dream. Where dreams carry conviction, daydreams do not: they 'are *thought*, even though vividly imagined, and never experienced as hallucinations' (PFL 1,162: SE XV, 130). You are always aware of day-dreaming, so that in some sense you are knowingly in two places, two times, at once, with the difference between the orders of reality clearly maintained: 'we do not experience or hallucinate anything in them but imagine something, we know that we are having a phantasy, we do not see but think.'

Another marked difference is that the dreamer has no control over the dream, but some control over the day-dream. (However, in a passage added to *The Interpretation of Dreams* in 1909 – the year after 'Creative writers and day-dreaming' – Freud provided an interesting qualification to this by granting some control to some dreamers. There are those 'who thus seem to possess the faculty of consciously directing their dreams. If, for instance, a dreamer of this kind is dissatisfied with the turn taken by a dream, he can break it off without waking up and start it again in another direction – just as a popular dramatist may under pressure give his play a happier ending' (PFL 4, 727: SE V, 571–2).) There are also alleged differences of form and medium. Drawing together a number of these distinctions, Freud states that 'dreams differ from day-dreams . . . in the fact of their ideational content being transformed from thoughts into sensory images, to which belief is attached and which appear to be experienced' (PFL 4, 683: SE V, 535). He goes on to qualify this by a caveat based upon personal experience: not all dreams make ideas into images, witness one of his own discussed earlier in the book. The criterion of conviction is not, however, affected, he says; it is just that the normal pattern puts seeing with believing.

This claiming of Freud's own difference from the norm of experiencing hallucinatory images in dreams is also made in a footnote added in 1909 to the principal discussion of day-dreams in *The Interpretation of Dreams*. It comes immediately before the declaration of 'the complete analogy between night-dreams and day-dreams', and reads:

> Incidentally, I underestimated the importance of the part played by these phantasies in the formation of dreams so long as I was principally working on my own dreams, which are usually based on discussions and conflicts of thought and comparatively rarely on day-dreams. (PFL 4, 634–5: SE V, 494)

Here, the assumption about the predominance of sensory images in dreams, as opposed to day-dreams, seems to be reversed, or at least re-inflected. For most people, not for Freud, day-dreams, as bearers of what is not discursive or ideational, would be more dream than the dream – the key to dreams because they are hyperdreams, not milder versions. (A further incidental autobiographical detail of this kind occurs in another day-dream context of *The Interpretation of Dreams*; we shall come to it in a moment.)

A further apparent difference between dreams and daydreams concerns the temporal direction of the wishes represented in day-dreams; this direction is inseparable from the nature of their wishes, which, it turns out, is both constant and restricted. For although Freud says in *The Interpretation of Dreams* that daydreams, like dreams, are derived from and resuscitate childhood wishes, nonetheless when he comes to talk about them in the essays of subsequent years, the two wishful modes that he names as being those that are typically expressed in day-dreams are both turned towards the future, rather than returning to an image of ancient satisfactions. These two wishful modes, of which there will be more to say, are ambition and love.

Sometimes the difference of temporal orientation disappears, when the fulfilment of the future-directed wish is interpreted as being, in effect, a return to the securities or supremacies of the idealized early years. So a man seeking work who dreams, as he walks to a job interview, of marrying the boss's daughter and inheriting the business himself, elicits, in 'Creative writers and day-dreaming' (1908), the following interpretation:

> In this phantasy, the dreamer has regained what he possessed in his happy childhood – the protecting house, the loving parents and the first objects of his affectionate feelings. You will see from this

example the way in which the wish makes use of an occasion in the present to construct, on the pattern of the past, a picture of the future. (PFL 14, 136: SE IX, 148)

But even if a Freudian future can always be found to hark back, at some level, to a memory or an ancient desire, still in the case of the day-dream the wishes are resolutely forward-looking in their mode of return, seeking to find a replacement, a new story, even if it does take as its model the older one.

And indeed at other moments, the forward orientation of the day-dream appears unequivocal. For Freud also states that day-dreams are modified throughout the subject's life: they do not remain fixed once and for all at the time of their origin, or by reference to an earlier period. A passage from the *Introductory Lectures* states:

> In other respects these day-dreams are of many different kinds and pass through changing vicissitudes. They are either, each one of them, dropped after a short time and replaced by a fresh one, or they are retained, spun out into long stories and adapted to the changes in the circumstances of the subject's life. They go along with the times, so to speak, and receive a 'date stamp' which bears witness to the influence of the new situation. (PFL 1, 128: SE XV, 98–9)

This adaptability of the day-dream according to changing circumstances is also mentioned, with the same image of recorded dating, in the 'Creative writers' essay (on which Freud manifestly drew for his recapitulation a few years later in the *Introductory Lectures*):

> We must not suppose that the products of this imaginative activity – the various phantasies, castles in the air and day-dreams – are stereotyped and unalterable. On the contrary, they fit themselves in to the subject's shifting impressions of life, change with every change in his situation, and receive from every fresh active impression what might be called a 'date-mark'. (PFL 14, 135: SE IX, 147)

'"Date stamp"' and '"date-mark"' translate the same word, *Zeitmarke* – a 'time-branding', or trademark of the time. Freud puts it in inverted commas as though to patent a new expression, one which itself offers a suitably modern image for fantasy's way of keeping up with what's new, of never passing its 'sell-by' date. Although the earlier passage does go on to refer to the present occasion's capacity to make a connection with an older experience of wish-fulfilment, in neither of them is there mention of a kernel or core phantasy that would remain the same from the beginning. The day-dreams are modified in relation to a changing outside 'situation' or 'circumstances'. They seem to have no necessary continuity, but merely 'fit themselves in', 'go along with the times', malleable to the mark of each new impression encountered.

Something comparable with this outward impressionability is going on in the categorization of the changing wishes as either ambitious or amorous, despite the inner continuities that such specification might suggest. The two modes are differentiated by the sex of the day-dreamer: women's dreams are of love, men's are ambitious. But at the same time, Freud regularly subsumes each of the two into the other, so that an ostensibly ambitious outcome in a man's day-dream should be understood as secondary to a primary aim, which is that of pleasing a woman, while a woman's love-dreams are in reality the only expression allowed to her ambition.

This extract from the fifth *Introductory Lecture* gives a typical summary of these attributions and their mobility, beginning with the factor of obviousness or transparency that is consistently associated with the meanings of day-dreams:

> The content of these phantasies is dominated by a very transparent motive. They are scenes and events in which the subject's egoistic needs of ambition and power or his erotic wishes find satisfaction. In young men the ambitious phantasies are the most prominent, in women, whose ambition is directed to success in love, the erotic ones. But in men, too, erotic needs are often enough present in the background: all their heroic deeds and successes seem only to aim at courting the admiration and favour of women.

It is common enough, not to say standard, for Freud to find that binary distinctions – as here, between male and female wishes, and correlatively between the erotic and the ambitious – turn out to be not so distinct after all. What seems unusual in this instance is that the solution, or the further complication, of the initial situation – ambition and love, one assigned to each sex – is itself said to be social: 'women, whose ambition *is directed* . . .' The usual structure would be for a socially specific situation to turn out to be the outward appearance only, to have an underlying reality or cause classified in some way as non-social or pre-social. This claim for the social determination of the day-dream accords with the inversion of the habitual Freudian structure in the 'date-stamp' passages cited above: for once, the date or the 'moment' – historical or daily – is what matters.

Daydreaming in fiction

There is a further occasion in *The Interpretation of Dreams* when Freud is led to adopt his analogy of dreams to day-dreams. He is arguing that in dreams, 'the thought is represented as an immediate situation with the "perhaps" omitted' (PFL 4, 682: SE V, 534), and that dreams thus adopt the present tense in representing their wish as fulfilled, replacing the hesitation of the optative grammatical mood – 'would that . . .' – with a straightforward declaration:

> We need not linger long over this first peculiarity of dreams. We can deal with it by drawing attention to conscious phantasies – to day-dreams – which treat their ideational content in just the same manner. (PFL 4, 683: SE V, 534)

Here, as with other points of correspondence, the likeness to the day-dream is assumed, not argued; the day-dream is brought in not for itself, but because it serves just as well as a dream for illustration.

This is one elision; a second one is that the day-dream offered as an example is neither Freud's nor anyone else's, but is taken from a work of fiction. The passage continues:

> While Daudet's Monsieur Joyeuse was wandering, out of work, through the streets of Paris (though his daughters believed that he had a job and was sitting in an office), he was dreaming of developments that might bring him influential help and lead to his finding employment – and he was dreaming in the present tense. Thus dreams make use of the present tense in the same manner and by the same right as day-dreams. (PFL 4, 683: SE V, 535)

We shall return to the themes of this paraphrase. For the moment, though, there is a different lead to follow. For although Daudet's novel is the named source here, the example does turn out to have a peculiar connection with a real day-dream – one of Freud's own.

In *The Psychopathology of Everyday Life* (1901), Freud describes a near error in his redaction of this section of *The Interpretation of Dreams*. When he drafted it, he was away on holiday, without his books. He describes how he misremembered the name of Daudet's day-dreamer, substituting Jocelyn for Joyeuse, and also changed the plot of the day-dream in Daudet:

> I imagined I had a distinct memory of one of the phantasies which this man – I called him Monsieur Jocelyn – hatched out on his walks through the streets of Paris; and I began to reproduce it from memory. It was a phantasy of how Monsieur Jocelyn boldly threw himself at the head of a runaway horse in the street, and brought it to a stop; how the carriage door opened and a great personage stepped out, pressed Monsieur Jocelyn's hand and said: 'You are my saviour. I owe my life to you. What can I do for you?' (PFL 5, 200: SE VI, 149)

There are in fact other mistakes that Freud retains in his revised remembering of the literary episode, and there will be more to say about them. But the mistake in the name turns out to be a significant one: ' "Joyeux", of which "Joyeuse" is the feminine form, is the only possible way in which I could translate my own name, Freud, into French' (PFL 5, 201: SE VI, 149).

The suppressed identification and the substitution of a different story then suggest to Freud that the day-dream was in fact his own, which leads to a quite fabulous evocation of himself as youthful *flâneur*:

> Perhaps I invented it myself in Paris where I frequently walked about the streets, lonely and full of longings, greatly in need of a helper and protector, until the great Charcot took me into his circle. (PFL 5, 201: SE VI, 149)

Here we have the classical scene of masculine day-dreaming: the modern city street. In this setting, anonymity of view (you are not known by sight) licenses the departure into another mental world, as well as reinforcing the typical plot structure, whereby the day-dreamer's present situation as anyone or nobody is replaced by another, in which he acquires a name for himself. In this day-dream of Freud's, that element is compounded by the actual naming of great names that become, in effect, the dreamer's new

family. First there is 'the great Charcot'; then, finally, the inter-
fusion of fiction and reality in day-dreams as wish-fulfilment,
inside and outside the pages of novels, seems to be complete
when Daudet himself makes a (literally) guest appearance. With
touching irrelevance to his argument, Freud adds a concluding
sentence to his happy ending: 'Later I more than once met the
author of *Le Nabab* in Charcot's house.'

But that is not all. Until the 1924 edition of the *Psychopathology*, Freud went on to make further personal confessions:

> But the irritating part of it is that there is scarcely any group of ideas
> to which I feel so antagonistic as that of being someone's protégé.
> What can be seen in our country of this relation is enough to rob one
> of all desire for it, and the role of the favourite child is one which is
> very little suited indeed to my character. I have always felt an un-
> usually strong urge 'to be the strong man myself'. (PFL 5, 201: SE VI,
> 149–50)

A first point about this is its curiously unpsychoanalytic mode of
argument: you do not wish to be a protégé for the commonsense
reason that any objective observer can see that it is a bad position
to be in. Second, the passage takes up the ambitious aim which
was to acquire such a prominent place in subsequent accounts
of day-dreams; yet it assumes, equally curiously and perhaps
unpsychoanalytically too, that the fantasy as given – of saving a
great man who then offers a favour in return – is passive rather
than active, the inversion of an ambitious desire, rather than the
example of one. Only the later elucidation, that a great man of this
type would be like the 'helper and protector' that Charcot represented, makes this explicitly a protégé structure at all, in effect by
completing the story to suggest what kind of favour would be
involved. In the account of the misremembered day-dream, the
strengths would seem to be all on the side of the rescuer, not the
rescued man.

The structure of this Freudian day-dream thus in one way
turns the emphasis from physical to social powers. The act of
saving a life is both reciprocated and replaced by symbolically
offering a better one. Insofar as this is a day-dream of ambition, it
seems to involve an unstable rotation between two men's positions of dependence and superiority in relation to one another, as

the initiative and the power move from one to the other. Freud's readiness to make this into an issue of activity versus passivity, with negative connotations attached to the latter and activity appearing to be straight away threatened by the possibility of slipping into its opposite, may be connected with his initial repudiation of the name 'Joyeuse' that he identifies as the feminine version of his own.

'Hysterical fantasies and their relation to bisexuality' features a feminine version of the 'great man' urban day-dream. A woman finds herself in tears in the street from imagining a story in which she has an affair with a locally celebrated musician, who abandons her to poverty when she has his child. In this negative version, the culmination leaves the woman with neither love nor money, a fall made the more pronounced by her temporary acquisition of both during her relationship with the pianist. This story in turn suggests links to another of the basic day-dreams or fantasies outlined by Freud: the rescue of the fallen woman.

A version of this is discussed in some detail in the essay of 1910 entitled 'A special type of object-choice made by men'. Here, the initial focus is on male fantasies of 'rescuing' women who are sexually involved with another man. This represents, Freud argues, a repetition of the situation of the boy with his parents, since the mother whom he desires is already attached to his father. The force of the image of the fallen woman is also related, both by contrast and by assimilation, to what he calls the mother-complex. As the boy learns about adult sexuality, he is first unable to connect it with his own parents, who seem so remote from such things; but 'when after this he can no longer maintain the doubt which makes his parents an exception to the universal and odious norms of sexual activity, he tells himself with cynical logic that the difference between his mother and a whore is not after all so very great, since basically they do the same thing' (PFL 7, 238: SE XI, 171).

In addition to the fantasy of rescuing a fallen woman, there is also, however, a parallel fantasy in relation to a father-surrogate:

> When a child hears that he *owes his life* to his parents, or that his mother *gave him life*, his feelings of tenderness unite with impulses which strive at power and independence, and they generate the wish

> to return this gift to the parents and to repay them with one of equal
> value. It is as though the boy's defiance were to make him say: 'I
> want nothing from my father; I will give him back all I have cost
> him.' He then forms the phantasy of *rescuing his father from danger
> and saving his life*; in this way he puts his account square with him.
> (PFL 7, 239–40: SE XI, 172)

Such a calculated equalization – a life for a life – applies in this
hostile mode only in relation to the father; it can be modified into
other, milder forms:

> This phantasy is commonly enough displaced on to the emperor,
> king or some other great man; after being thus distorted it becomes
> admissible to consciousness, and may even be made use of by crea-
> tive writers. In its application to a boy's father it is the defiant
> meaning in the idea of rescuing which is by far the most important.
> (PFL 7, 240: SE XI, 172)

Here, then, is the meaning that Freud subsequently gave to the
fantasy of rescuing a great man that he describes as his own
distortion of the passage from the Daudet story.

Rescuing a man seems to have to do with power, rescuing a
woman with her sexuality: respectively, ambition and love in
their more naked forms. The great man rescued in Freud's fantasy
is momentarily fallen – from his horse, literally, and thereby also
from the power he normally wields. The woman in a rescue
fantasy is sexually 'fallen', to be redeemed by the unconditional
love offered her by the man who takes her up in spite and because
of her situation. It is now he who falls for her, in both senses: falls
in love and falls on her behalf.

Yet the differences are not nearly as clear-cut as this summary
would suggest. In 'A case of female homosexuality' (1920) , the
falling is made literal in the would-be suicidal act of a young
woman who throws herself down the side of a railway cutting.
She has 'fallen for' an older woman, who is promiscuous and
whom she adores and wants to rescue. As Freud points out, this
is the 'special type of object-choice' situation. He interprets the
woman's love as masculine, because its object is the feminine
'special type'; yet in this case, and presumably only because the
man in the affair is a woman, he interprets the fall in sexual, not
social, terms.

Another incident from the works of Daudet which is also about the inseparability of sexual and social inversions appears earlier on in *The Interpretation of Dreams*. This time, the association is to the opening part of Daudet's *Sappho* – in which, in Freud's précis:

> A young man carries his mistress upstairs in his arms; at first she is as light as a feather, but the higher he climbs the heavier grows her weight. The whole scene foreshadows the course of their love-affair, which was intended by Daudet as a warning to young men not to allow their affections to be seriously engaged by girls of humble origin and a dubious past. (PFL 4, 391: SE IV, 285–6)

The dream, in Freud's interpretation, involves a woman's sexual and thereby also social rise and fall, and a man's social rising and falling, in relation to the dreamer's brother – all of which features he sees as being intimated by the Daudet parallel. Peculiarly enough, the idea of this particular source-text for the dream is Freud's own; but the dreamer accepts its relevance by making a connection to a further work (a play he had seen the evening before) that involved similar themes of the upward and downward mobility of the sexual and social career of a young girl.

Some other misrememberings in Freud's deployment of the Joyeuse story from *Le Nabab* are pertinent here, in adition to the one about the name that he identifies himself. For one thing, the story simply does not prove the main point claimed for its illustrative value at this stage in *The Interpretation of Dreams*. Freud wants it to demonstrate that day-dreams, like dreams, are immediate and therefore appear in literature in the present tense; but in the Daudet story, they are as often in the imperfect, while the narrative of what is really happening, as opposed to the day-dream, is frequently in the present tense.

A second point is related to Freud's interest in day-dreams of masculine rescue. In the *Psychopathology*, as we have seen, Freud claims that his first draft of the passage included a fantasy for M. Joyeuse which turned out, when he later checked it, to have been a complete invention: his stopping a runaway horse and thereby rescuing a 'great personage'. Yet in fact such a rescue scene does occur in the day-dreams of Daudet's character, who sees himself saving a child from a similar street accident involving a horse and carriage. Only the sequel is different, in that M. Joyeuse has his imaginary heroism followed up not with grateful promises from an important man, but with a scene in which, having been injured himself, he is surrounded by his anxious and adoring family waiting to see if he will be all right.

So Freud in this instance forgot that he had not forgotten. The rescue fantasy of horse and carriage is present, after all, in the source-text. But it is used to very different ends: in Freud's case, in relation to a question of ambition, with a rejection of the position of beneficiary; in M. Joyeuse's, as a means to return to the un-questioned love of the family fold. Daudet's hero rather desires the situation of childish dependence and centrality, which he seems to have taken as a reward from the child he has just saved, whereas Freud analyses himself as rejecting anything that smacks of the dependent and feminine passivity of the protégé.

In Daudet's story, day-dream and reality are hard to differen-tiate. This is first because, contrary to one of Freud's criteria for day-dreams as distinct from dreams, M. Joyeuse's rêveries are convincing, like dreams, to the point of complete immersion. He forgets his surrounding reality until it brings him back abruptly. He is walking about, and he lets out a cry at a crucial point in his fantasy, which then 'awakens' him from it.[2] The overlap is also because what he dreams of is never more than what he has or what, during the course of the story, he loses. He has, and contin-ues to have, a doting family of daughters; he has, loses and then recovers a job with which to support them. While he is out of work, he has to 'play-act' at home, making up stories about the day at work when in reality he has been wandering the streets in search of work. In the end, he is really rescued by the intervention of a friend of a friend who offers him a job at the same salary as the one he lost.

So while M. Joyeuse's day-dreams do indeed conform to the themes of ambition and love, inseparable as they are in Freud, they could hardly be more modest: apart from averting the acci-dent with the horse, or taking vengeance on the imaginary attack-ers of one of his daughters, his day-dream wishes extend to no more than a Christmas bonus from his boss, while he is still in work. The figures of the rescuer or the protégé – those that Freud refuses for himself – are, in their small way, common to the plots of the day-dreams and the story itself. Daudet's is a story of the day-dreamer as ordinary man, employee in the modern city; and of the day-dream itself as an outlet for underused mental capacities; he describes the surprisingly large number of 'those waking sleepers [*dormeurs éveillés*] in whom too restricted a fate pushes down unemployed forces and heroic faculties'.[3] At the same time, the story of M. Joyeuse is itself an idealized representation of the lovable, decent, honest chap, for whom all comes right in the end.

Freudian day-dreams, whether grandiose or humble, are recognizably social stories – the upwardly or just horizontally mobile wish-fulfilments of modern life, as it is lived and as it is promoted. It is thus appropriate that when Freud writes about the relationship between day-dreams and creative writers, he makes a point of dealing with mass-market authors who flatter their reader with an identification with 'His Majesty the Ego, the hero alike of every day-dream and of every story' (PFL 14, 138: SE IX, 150). Day-dreams fit the comparison with novels of modern life, of recognizable aspirations. For ambition and love sound, in fact, less like the dangerous instincts of an anti-social, repressed but irrepressible unconscious, than like the acceptable driving forces that openly move the plots of the standard nineteenth-century novel or personal biography. Freud's confident attribution of a morally educative purpose to Daudet when he discusses the introduction to his *Sappho* – 'intended by Daudet as a warning to young men not to allow their affections to be seriously engaged by girls of humble origin and a dubious past' (PFL 4, 391: SE IV, 286) – would seem to accord with this view of a simple communication from writer to reader, in which the text presents no difficulty of interpretation.

One swiftly reported night-dream of *The Interpretation of Dreams* actually involves the author Daudet, along with two other contemporary novelists, as participants:

> A young woman had been cut off from society for weeks on end while she nursed her child through an infectious illness. After the child's recovery, she had a dream of being at a party at which, among others, she met Alphonse Daudet, Paul Bourget, and Marcel

Prévost; they were all most affable to her and highly amusing. All of the authors resembled their portraits, except Marcel Prévost, of whom she had never seen a picture; and he looked like . . . the disinfection officer who had fumigated the sick-room the day before and who had been her first visitor for so long. Thus it seems possible to give a complete translation of the dream: 'It's about time for something more amusing than this perpetual sick-nursing.' (PFL 5, 205: SE IV, 126)

From modern writers, complex meanings are not to be sought; to drive the point home, the next sentence goes on: 'These examples will perhaps be enough to show that dreams which can only be understood as fulfilments of wishes and which bear their meaning on their faces without disguise are to be found under the most frequent and various conditions.'

These considerations seem to have something to do with Freud's repeated assertion that day-dreams, and the stories that are like them, wear their meaning on the surface. All the better, once again, to separate the supposed obviousness of everyday modern life – its moments, its residues, its routines – from the darker depths of the night and the unconscious. It is to Greek tragedy that Freud turns, not to a contemporary novel, when he is seeking a literary analogue for those other, less manifest wish-fulfilments that are revealed by the analysis of night-dreams: Sophocles, not Daudet. It is there, below and not on the surfaces of daily life, of public spaces and of commonplace dreams of ambition, that he sees the turbulent forces of mental life to lie. In the process, the other day can be casually forgotten.

Notes

1 Freud, *Die Traumdeutung* (Frankfurt am Main: Fischer Taschenbuch Verlag, 1977), p. 401.

2 See Alphonse Daudet, *Le Nabab* [1877], *Oeuvres*, Vol. II, ed. Roger Ripoll (Paris: Gallimard, 1990), Ch. V, p. 544.

3 Daudet, *Le Nabab*, p. 545, my translation.

6

Freud's dreams, Dora's dreams

STEPHEN FROSH

The origins of psychoanalysis

There is a sense in which the origins of psychoanalysis can be said to lie in the tension between masculine reason and feminine expressiveness, felt particularly as hysteria. Psychoanalysis is constructed on this knife edge: it plays with the borders of reason, refusing to give up its search for meaning but also showing how unreason is an intrinsic element in the human condition, and will never disappear. Not surprisingly, therefore, even when psychoanalysis is at its most masterly and apparently clearly scientific, it can also be obscure and uncomfortable with itself, suggesting a state of inner unease.

This situation becomes particularly poignant when the implicit parallel between femininity and the unconscious is brought into the open. Translated into gender terms, the apparently 'masculine' activity of knowing and ordering phenomena is always in a relationship with the supposedly 'feminine' activity of embodiment and disruption. When it speaks, in its many contradictory voices, of sexual difference, psychoanalysis delineates concepts that help in the struggle to find meaning and to make sense of the way in which gender insinuates itself into people's psychic lives. But the speech of psychoanalysis also *expresses* this presence of gender. In the texts of psychoanalysis, just as in the discourse of patients, can be found the voices of sexual difference, channelling, influencing and undermining the narratives which unfold. Indeed, because of its concern with sexuality and subjectivity, the language of psychoanalysis is a particularly sexed language, marked by the slipperiness of its identificatory positions and its playfulness when faced with issues of reference. Whenever it speaks in an apparently 'masculine' voice, it also raises the question of femininity: as the word of the master is put forward, so the subversion of that word appears in the background.

In this chapter, I explore this ambiguity in the gender position of psychoanalysis as it appears in Freud's *The Interpretation of Dreams*. At various points, I will juxtapose this with a kind of counterpoint to be found in the dream analyses in the 'Dora' case, properly known as the 'Fragment of an analysis of a case of hysteria' and originally intended (as a piece provisionally entitled 'Dreams and hysteria') to supplement *The Interpretation of Dreams* and demonstrate its utility for clinical psychoanalysis. 'Dora' has become a feminist source-book, liberating not only a critique of psychoanalysis, but also a challenging debate about the nature of feminine sexuality when it encounters the (male) analytic eye. Frequently, it has been examined on its own in relation to Freud's emerging practice, his blind spots and (as one of these) his incipient theory of feminine sexuality. When seen as a kind of commentary on *The Interpretation of Dreams*, however, it enhances that text's capacity to work with conventional categories of masculinity and femininity in such a way as to reveal both sides of a characteristic tension: both how sexual difference works as an organizing principle central to personal identity, and how its constructed character makes transgression of conventional gender categorization possible.

Psychoanalysis is an unusual science in that its early body of knowledge was built up in considerable part on the basis of Freud's personality and self-scrutiny. His famous 'self-analysis', carried out in the closing years of the nineteenth century, is commonly represented (particularly by Jones (1955) in the first 'official' biography) as the heroic founding act of psychoanalysis; given that it is explicitly concerned with Freud's subjective impulses and internal struggles, this means that his own conscious and unconscious desires are set up as the marker from which all analysis takes its stance. Freud's self-analysis subsequently became the prototype of the training analysis undergone as part of the process of becoming a psychoanalyst, producing a dynastic sequence begun with the act of self-creation. Already here can be found some structural ambiguities paralleling those encountered in sexual difference. Much as in the biblical Genesis tale, the original creator contains within his one being all that is necessary for generating life, both male and female elements; later on, the divisions occur, differentiation begins and no one can manage the creative analytic task on their own.

If one regards 'Dora' as a companion piece to *The Interpretation of Dreams*, however, it becomes apparent that the self-sufficiency of Freud's own creativity is also uncertain and fragile. It has always been recognized that he needed male partners – primarily, in the early stages, Wilhelm Fliess – to help with the scaffolding of psychoanalysis, while later it was women who supported him most, looking after him and reflecting back his glory (Marie Bonaparte, his daughter Anna, and others – Ernest Jones was a male exception to this, interestingly taking the feminist position in the debates on feminine sexuality). But 'Dora' demonstrates the way the problem of the woman and what to do with her – how to survive her challenge – surfaces right at the start and heart of psychoanalytic theorizing. To force the metaphor as far as it will go, there is a Lilith aspect to both 'Dora' as a text and Dora as a person: so much of Freud's energy goes into mastering them both, into excluding the latter by dictating her fate in the former. The dream book makes scientific claims, 'Dora' is meant obligingly to show their truth; but the woman will not stay still long enough nor do what she is told, she is an irritant instead of a support. Freud may have created the enchanted garden of psychoanalysis, but his chosen helpmate refused to play her part, so drawing attention to the way the apparently certain masculine mastery of Freudian thought is premised on an ambivalent exclusion of feminine experience. This is one reason why 'Dora' drifts so much, supposedly being an account of a case but gradually turning into a description and evocation of Freud's own thought processes, as he comes up against the recalcitrance of his chosen subject. From her to him: analysing Dora's second dream, he writes, 'I shall present the material produced during the analysis of this dream in the somewhat haphazard order in which it recurs to my mind' (PFL 8, 134), and in the analysis of the first dream it is Freud's theories concerning the origins of bedwetting which are pushed to the fore. The woman's voice is not the one he wants heard: rather than complementing *The*

Interpretation of Dreams by offering an application of dream theory to another subject, he keeps on talking about himself, appropriating Dora's voice and trying to make it his own.

As one might expect, the attempt to repress the feminine in 'Dora' does not work; the repressed has kept on returning, in the text itself and in the numerous feminist commentaries which it has provoked. Looking at *The Interpretation of Dreams* in this light, for evidence of the repression of femininity, something else appears: the way expressions of feminine identity – or, more properly, identifications – can be found in the interstices of the text, in its structure, its silences and in the way it moves. It is partly the energy produced by this disconcerting presence that makes *The Interpretation of Dreams* such a fragmenting and productive work.

The body of the dream

Lacan (1955) gives the following rule for analysis, whether of dreams or of patients:

> You must start from the text, start by treating it, as Freud does and as he recommends, as Holy Writ. The author, the scribe, is only a pen-pusher, and he comes second . . . Similarly, when it comes to our patients, please give more attention to the text than to the psychology of the author – the entire orientation of my teaching is that. (153)

Start with the text and assume that every element within it has significance: this is a principle of psychoanalytic practice. In relation to the dream of Irma's injection, Lacan also comments that 'this dream is not only an object which Freud deciphers, it is Freud's speech (162) – precisely, then, the kind of text upon which psychoanalysis operates most freely. Anzieu (1975) reads the Irma dream even more grandiosely, as a kind of template for psychoanalysis itself, in which can be found a crucial motivational complex for Freud's endeavours. Irma's injection is:

> a programme dream for the whole series of subsequent discoveries that were to constitute psychoanalysis. It spells out the identity of both the body of the dream and the dream of the body. Freud experiences the unconscious, whose corpus he has set out to estab-

lish, as the body of the crime from which he must exculpate himself,
for it represents symbolically, and contains metonymically, the
desired body of the unpossessed mother. (155)

This quotation immediately raises the issue of the status of
dreams in relation to unconscious motivations. The dream and
the unconscious: the two things are related, but not the same.
Behind the dream is the unconscious, and for Freud this is associated with the feminine principle, the secret thing, mastery of
which he craves – 'the desired body of the unpossessed mother'.
The dream is not itself unconscious, but reflects the workings of
the unconscious, it is the 'royal road' to it, the way in. It is Irma's
throat, or the woman's vagina. It is also a body of text marked by
something else, something outside the awareness of the author/
dreamer, a 'symptom' (PFL 4, 174), a text, then, like any other. The
author is just the scribe; her or his intention and personality are
part of the text, not its origin. 'The author, the scribe, is only a pen-
pusher, and he comes second . . .'

The body of the text: subjecting the dream to scrutiny, it
becomes located in the conventionally feminine position as something looked at, an object of desire. Yet, like femininity, it has its
own sexuality, its own passion and life: it slips in and out of being,
transgressing boundaries, ignoring formal demands, inscrutable
and disruptive. It is seductive, playful and self-contradictory,
attempting to subvert all attempts to control it from outside. It is
largely this ability to express all these tensions, between knowing
and being known, desiring and being desired, that makes *The
Interpretation of Dreams* such a remarkably disruptive text – all its
loose ends showing, but full of life.

As Anzieu (1975) documents, resolution of Freud's relationship with Wilhelm Fliess may have been a cogent precipitating
motivation for much of the dreamwork recorded in the book;
nevertheless, it is not the deepest biographical cause. The most
important identification with which this text engages is that of the
father, and Freud himself is absolutely explicit about the significance of this strand. In the Preface to the second edition, he writes:

this book has a further subjective significance for me personally – a
significance which I only grasped after I had completed it. It was, I
found, a portion of my own self-analysis, my reaction to my father's

death – that is to say, to the most important event, the most poignant
loss, of a man's life. (PFL 4, 47)

Much of the self-justification to be found in the dreams is related
to legitimizing himself to his father, even if there is often a screen
of other people – colleagues and opponents – who are in the
foreground. Indeed, it is a psychoanalytic platitude that dreams
of rivalry and triumph can be read Oedipally as triumph over the
father, and such dreams pervade the text with extraordinary
regularity and ferocity. Uncle Josef with the yellow beard (PFL 4,
218ff) has Freud denigrating a friend in order to find a way of
surpassing him professionally; the Botanical Monograph 'turns
out to have been in the nature of a self-justification, a plea on
behalf of my own rights' (PFL 4, 259), and Irma's injection has
exoneration of the self in the face of criticism and farce. In his
analysis of the Count Thun dream, Freud disavows the significance of his paternity, identifying the dream-thought as, 'It is
absurd to be proud of one's ancestry; it is better to be an ancestor
oneself' (PFL 4, 564). In relation to the same dream, Freud recollects his father's prediction that he will 'come to nothing' and
shows how his dream represents a triumph over it – not just
proving the father wrong, but humiliating him as well by imagining him micturating in front of him and needing Freud's help
with a urinal. Most explicitly, in the context of the 'Rome' dreams,
Freud recalls his father's passivity in the face of anti-Semitic abuse
(PFL 4, 286) and contrasts it with his own heroic identifications
(although, as Anzieu points out (1975, 200–1), all the heroes docu-
mented by Freud in the commentary on the dream eventually
failed to achieve their aspirations). In so doing, Freud is also
asserting his own power now: in this book, he writes his success
and leaves behind something permanent, including an indelible
trace of his father's humiliation.

Commenting on the dream of the bird-beaked figures (PFL 4,
740–1), the last of Freud's own dreams presented in the text,
Anzieu makes the following comment, linking the working-
through of the relationship with the father with the production of
this new 'body' of knowledge:

By placing the interpretation of the dream at the end of his book,
[Freud] was confirming that he had taken back his beloved mother

from his father and regained possession of her; but, more than that, he was indicating that he now had the last word on death, the last word on anxiety, the last word on separation from the primally loved object. (1975, 309)

The sexual curiosity so evident in the dreams, but fairly consistently and consciously suppressed by Freud in his interpretations ('It will rightly be suspected that what compels me to make this suppression is sexual material', PFL 4, 307), comes into play as an antagonism between paternal and maternal principles, between the prohibitive presence of the father and the attainment of access to the body of the mother. This is straightforwardly Oedipal, but it is also an integrative and generative process; as dreams unfold, as the unconscious is made available for inspection, so sexuality slips into view and makes itself known. What this brings into view is the way the disruptiveness of this text, as with many or perhaps all great works, lies in the erotization of language which it allows to be felt.

Throughout the text of *The Interpretation of Dreams*, Freud unproblematically positions himself and the general subject of knowledge as masculine, using 'us' to refer uncomplicatedly to males all the time:

It is the fate of all of us, perhaps, to direct our first sexual impulse towards our mother and our first hatred and our first murderous wish against our father. Our dreams convince us that this is so. (PFL 4, 364).

But Freud is too honest to suppress completely the feminine identifications in which he also engages, the elements in the dreams and their interpretations that show the slippage between gender positions which is a characteristic of the unconscious. These feminine identifications within *The Interpretation of Dreams* can be found in numerous places, although usually their recognition depends on agreement with the argument of some particular commentator – that is, they usually require some kind of analysis before they become apparent. For example, Resnick (1987), in an intriguing reversion to what might be called a 'pre-Freudian' account of dreams in terms of their prophetic quality, suggests that there is a 'premonitory' element in the dream of Irma's injection. In this reading, the discovery of diseased organs in Irma's mouth is to be taken not just as a symbolization of sexuality, but as an anticipation of Freud's future illness, the cancer of the mouth that was to cause him so much agony and distort his speech. Resnick comments on Freud's search for origins and for the 'guilty' organ at the root of each illness – looking in the throat to find the source of disturbance, unravelling the symptom to find its pure cause. Then he comments, in a footnote, that Freud

> is also looking, 'without knowing it', for an anticipated memory of his own future. 'Freud's cancer' is already speaking in the present, or in any case his worries and 'tissular' fantasies are being summoned in his transference with Irma, a transference that he was later to call 'countertransference'. (Resnick 1987, 119, n. 8)

Before looking in more detail at the Irma dream, it is worth considering this point as a moment of transference or cross-sex identification. Freud looks into Irma's mouth and sees his own physical future; he sees her organ as his own. Anzieu makes a similar observation, in relation to the discovery of a 'dull area low down on [Irma's] left', that Freud had been suffering from heart trouble and had himself been examined for this. 'Thus the dreamer was doubly present in his dream, both as the theoretician of the sexual aetiology of neuroses and as a patient suffering from a possibly fatal cardiac complaint' (Anzieu 1975, pp. 136–7). Again, Freud slips across the gender boundary to see himself in the woman, to feel himself the object of concern and wonder.

This transference, as Resnick calls it, or at least this identification with femininity, is important theoretically in psychoanalysis as it underpins the notion of the 'negative' Oedipus complex and also shows the sustained impact of what Freud terms 'bisexuality' past the Oedipal period and into adulthood. Without it, too, there would be even more of a question than there already is over the analyst's capacity to stand in as a transference object of either sex for the patient; that is, transference depends on the possibility of confusion and linkage across any number of structural differences, particularly that of gender. The male analyst must be able to take up the position of the maternal container; the female must have the fantasized capacity to say 'no'. But there is something even more powerful than this operating at this moment of the origin of psychoanalysis. Freud looks around in his dreams and finds himself everywhere; as Lacan (1955) notes, this is one of the major discoveries in this text. Unexpectedly, though, for one who places sexual difference at 'the bedrock' of analysis, the point beyond which analysis cannot go, he discovers himself in the woman as well as the man. Here he is, then, denying or transcending difference, fascinated by it (sexually curious), but also slipping in and out of subject positions, not allowing difference to get in the way. This is not simply a matter of being able to understand the other; it is a process of being, of taking on the sexual identity of the woman.

In interesting agreement with the Lacanian position on femininity, Anzieu takes up the verbal opposites *Auf Geseres/Auf Ungeseres* in the 'My son the Myops' dream (PFL 4, 572) and interprets them as an indication of the negativity of femininity, its non-being:

> The verbal opposites . . . are determined specifically by the person to whom each of them is addressed – a woman in the first case, a man in the second. They therefore represent the difference between the sexes: the man is *Geseres*, in other words the cause of something imposed or doomed to occur (the first meaning of *Geseres*) as well as the cause of weeping and wailing (the second meaning of *Geseres*); the other sex is defined negatively, by the lack or absence (*Un-*) of the first. Freud, in his analysis, describes *Auf Ungeseres* as being 'quite meaningless'. (Anzieu 1975, 262)

Freud rejects femininity, that much is clear. But he is also fascinated by it and finds himself inside it, part of it. The denial of sexual difference is closely linked up with hysteria, which in turn is a condition in which the body replaces the word, in which, therefore, the traditionally feminine sphere occludes the masculine. Freud's hysteria, the male hysteria of which he speaks in his interpretation of the dream of the town council (PFL 4, 568), is in part his creative capacity to slip across from one subject position to the other, and find them both full of meaning. *Ungeseres* it may be, but not nonsense, not an empty state of existence. Looking into the mouth of the other, one finds oneself; what is taken as fixed in the position of subject or object, masculine or feminine, is again revealed in its actual instability.

Perhaps this makes some sense of, and is clarified by, the terrible struggle for control expressed in 'Dora'. At some level, it is clearly the case that Freud wants Dora to do his bidding, and his counter-transference towards her – the source of so many commentaries – is partly governed by his irritation at her intractability. 'He does not like her', comments Marcus (1974):

> He does not like her negative sexuality, her inability to surrender to her own erotic impulses. He does not like 'her really remarkable achievements in the direction of intolerable behaviour'. Above all, he does not like her inability to surrender herself to him. (90)

But Freud's difficulty with Dora is not just dislike; it is a much fuller problem concerning the recognition of his part in her story, and of the way his identifications with various players and characters disturb his own equanimity and apparently scientific distance. Lacan (1952) sees Freud's unrecognized counter-transference as having been the obstacle to appreciation of the strength of Dora's homosexual desire for Frau K; others have used it to account for aspects of Freud's own 'really remarkable achievements in the direction of intolerable behaviour' – his presumptuousness, his disparagement and silencing of Dora, his inability to take her at her word. *Ungeseres*: the danger to Freud is of looking too fully at the face of femininity and finding himself there, and of it being something he does not want – something with a lack at its heart.

Hertz (1983) is one of several commentators to draw attention to the similarities between Freud and Dora in 'Dora' – for example, in the way they each struggle for control, and how the theme of gaining knowledge applies both to Dora (for instance in the question of who is doing what to whom in the family drama and in the symbolism of the encyclopaedia in the second dream, representing the whole question of sexual knowledge) and to Freud, writing 'Dora' as a way of knowing Dora and perhaps himself. Hertz then asks:

> Suppose what went wrong between Freud and Dora was not just a matter of unrecognised transferences (and countertransferences) but also of an unrecognised – or refused – identification? Suppose what Freud missed, or did not want to see, was not that he was drawn to

(or repelled by) Dora, but that he 'was' Dora, or rather that the question of who was who was more radically confusing than even the nuanced accounts of unacknowledged transferences and countertransferences suggest? (1983, 225)

This issue of identification with the other – with the feminine – is central not only to 'Dora', but to the whole gender fabric of psychoanalysis, for it suggests that the certainties of masculine identity at least are based on a willed repudiation of femininity. What is at the heart of this repudiation will be explored a little more later; but some more textual support for the presence, denial and potential fertility of the transgressive identification that finds the feminine in the man, can be found in *The Interpretation of Dreams* itself. It is not for nothing that the core dream of that book is a dream by Freud that has a woman at its source.

The dream of Irma's injection

It is in Freud's 'specimen dream', the dream of Irma's injection, that the recurrent uncertainty over gender identity and sexual difference finds its clearest expression. Freud presents this dream and its analysis as an opportunity to demonstrate his 'method of interpretation' (PFL 4, 180), but it is clear from the detail and energy of the analysis that he is engaged in work on it for more than just pedagogic reasons. Indeed, it is in commemoration of the dreaming of this particular dream that Freud wonders to Fliess about a marble tablet being placed on the house in which he dreamt it – a tablet inscribed with the words, 'In this house, on July 24th 1895, the secret of dreams was revealed to Dr Sigm. Freud' (PFL 4, 199). A note to this effect is placed by the editors of *The Interpretation of Dreams* immediately after these last words of the chapter on Irma: 'When the work of interpretation has been completed, we perceive that a dream is the fulfilment of a wish' (PFL 4, 198–9). Yet, as Lacan (1955) notes, the weight of significance placed upon this dream, and the revolutionary nature of the conclusion dream from it, seem hardly to be linked to the manifest content of the dream interpretation itself, which has removed from it all explicit acknowledgement of its subversiveness and disturbance of sexuality. Lacan asks:

How is it that Freud, who later on will develop the function of
unconscious desire, is here content, for the first step in his demonstration, to present a dream which is entirely explained by the satisfaction of a desire which one cannot but call preconscious, and even
entirely conscious? (1955, 151)

Lacan's own answer to this question concerns the significance of
the dream-analysis's revelations about the structures of ego and
identity, and will be returned to below. But at a simpler level,
Freud seems to be using the dream as a demonstration of his own
mastery – partly as an expression of his identification with the
biblical figure of Joseph (see Frosh, 1994, for an extended discussion of the Joseph–Moses motif), but also, given the content of the
dream itself, as a fantasy of sexual conquest.

Anzieu comments that the analysis of the Irma dream looks
'untidy', but in fact 'is remarkably well structured, and unfolds
like a play, with the characters being introduced in the early acts
and the denouement coming in the last' (1975, 137–8). The play
concerned is a kind of courtroom drama:

The first act begins with a defence speech by Freud . . . and ends
with his feeling afraid. In the second act, Freud stands accused by
overwhelming evidence. In the third, that evidence is demolished by
witnesses and lawyers. The question that lies at the heart of the
tragedy, or the investigation, is now openly posed: who is responsible? (Anzieu 1975, 138)

One answer to this, according to Anzieu's reading, is that the
'injection of trimethylamin' is responsible; that is, 'Irma's complaint has been caused by her frustrated sex life. It is Freud who
is right, despite his detractors, when he advocates the sexual
aetiology of neurosis' (1975, 139). In this part of his analysis,
Anzieu is thus viewing the Irma dream as part of the self-
justifying tendency in *The Interpretation of Dreams*: Freud's over-
turning of his father's curse to discover the secret of mental life.
Irma allows him to demonstrate this discovery with mastery: all
those intractable females and foolish males, who between them
have made a mess of things and yet stand as Freud's accusers, are
despatched and Freud's own achievement is once again asserted.
It is the unclean injection which is at fault, the dirty syringe; any
Freudian could tell that from the material.

Freud himself gives a famous analogy to his defensiveness in the dream, with specific reference to the way the dream is structured as a formal defence plea against accusations of responsibility for Irma's disease:

> The whole plea – for the dream was nothing else – reminded one vividly of the defence put forward by the man who was charged by one of his neighbours with having given him back a borrowed kettle in a damaged condition. The defendant asserted first, that he had given it back undamaged; secondly, that the kettle had a hole in it when he borrowed it; and thirdly, that he had never borrowed a kettle from his neighbour at all. (PFL 4, 197)

Freud as interpreter of his dream can look with irony on the Freud who is the dreamer of it, revealing his foibles in the midst of his desires. But the two Freuds are not so completely divided, the analytic Freud not so much master of his procedures as he would have us believe. Anzieu (1975) comments that 'Freud noted subsequently that thoughts which follow on from dreams are still dream-thoughts. So the thought that dreams are wish-fulfilments is an integral part of the dream content' (140). Analysis of the multiple-plea defence present in the dream itself (Irma herself is to blame for her pains, the pains are organic, they are to do with her widowhood, with the wrong injection, with a dirty needle) produces the generalization that dreams are wish-fulfilments, but this too is a wish-fulfilment, the wish being that Freud should unravel the mystery of dreams. The gender structure of the dream itself magnifies this. The central object of the dream is female: Irma, with her mouth and torso open to inspection by the male subject of the dream (the dreamer) and his associates and competitors. Similarly, the dream itself is laid open for inspection and analysis by the author and psychoanalyst (the dreamer again), dreaming his way to fame on the basis of the body of this dream. The dream is thus associated with the female object, mirror reflecting mirror; analysis of the dream is analysis of the body, peering into Irma's mouth at her genital tubes. Conquering the mystery of dreams and conquering the woman; the mastery is not so mundane, not so simply a contestation of professional disdain.

Freud gives this dream to us as an illustration of his art and, by his careful ordering of the material, edits what happens, allowing the force of the dream to speak more by the centrality granted it – and by the evocativeness of the dream imagery itself – than by the comprehensiveness of the analysis. The superficial analysis given so far, however, already reveals the extent to which sexual mastery and its uncertainty pervade what is expressed in the text. Freud is explicit about suppressing sexual material that is personally revealing, but he also allows the sexuality of the dream imagery to speak clearly in the interpretation, so preserving the energy and disturbance of the dream. Freud recollects 'other medical examinations and . . . little secrets revealed in the course of them – to the satisfaction of neither party' (PFL 4, 185); he thinks of an 'intimate woman friend' of Irma's and recollects that 'I had often played with the idea that she too might ask me to relieve her of her symptoms', but 'she was recalcitrant' (PFL 4, 185); Irma's friend 'would have been wiser' than Irma, 'that is to say she would have yielded sooner. She would then have opened her mouth properly' (PFL 4, 186). Exploring the element in the dream in which an infected area on Irma's shoulder is noticed 'in spite of her dress', Freud comments 'Frankly, I had no desire to penetrate more deeply at this point' (PFL 4, 189). And, finally, there is Freud's reference to Fliess's theory about 'some very remarkable connections between the turbinal bones and the female organs of sex' (PFL 4, 194). Whatever other elements are present in the dream analysis, Freud allows it to speak in barely coded language of sexuality and domination, mostly from a straightforwardly gendered position as the 'penetrating' master, but with sufficient anxiety to allow his own feminine identification some space.

It is with the question of identification that Lacan's (1955) remarkable reading of the Irma dream and its interpretation deals most clearly, and it is this that enables him to show how much more radical the 'specimen' chapter is than it would have been if restricted only to the (nevertheless radical) assertion of the ubiquity of sexual desire. In this context, it is worth recalling Anzieu's comment that the dream of Irma's injection encapsulated the way 'The system of identifications that had governed [Freud] up to then crumbled away' (1975, 132). For Lacan as well, the dream reveals this crumbling, but not so that Freud can be reborn free of previous identifications and able to go his own way. Rather, the dream reveals the *necessary* deconstruction of the identifications which constitute the ego. It certainly deals with the shedding of identifications, with fragmentation and discursive ambiguity; but it deals with these things in order to demonstrate their centrality to the human condition.

Lacan analyses the dream in its two parts, the first being Freud's examination of Irma and the second the discussion among his medical colleagues – his 'congress'. Lacan's view of the ego is succinctly expressed in this seminar:

> the ego is the sum of the identifications of the subject, with all that that implies as to its radical contingency. If you allow me to give an image of it, the ego is like the superimposition of various coats borrowed from what I will call the bric-à-brac of its props department. (1955, p. 155)

This is the familiar Lacanian notion of the speciousness of the ego as a unified entity: what in ordinary life we take as the core component of selfhood is revealed under analysis to be 'bric-à-brac', bits and pieces placed together or on top of one another more or less by chance, covering up an emptiness beneath. In Lacan's reading, the first section of the Irma dream, which has Freud looking deeply into Irma's mouth, brings the dreamer and the analyst face to face with the horror that lies behind this egoic surface.

Lacan states that 'The object is always more or less structured as the image of the body of the subject' (1955, 167), suggesting that as Freud looks into Irma's insides so he sees his own psychic inside – a psychological rendering of the 'premonitory' sense noted by Resnick and Anzieu. What he sees there is 'something of the real, something at its most unfathomable' (1955, 167). In fact, Lacan expresses himself exceptionally lyrically here, in a language full of the imagery of horror and dissolution. He locates the death theme in the dream through reference to the 'three women' in the first section: Irma, the ideal patient and Freud's wife. Freud's own analysis of the three-women theme in his paper on the 'three caskets' (PFL 14, 235–47) is, as Lacan notes, both clear and mystic: 'The last term is death, as simple as that' (1955, 157). Meditating on this at several points in his seminar, Lacan produces the following encounter with what he terms 'the foundation of things, the other side of the head' (154) – an encounter largely contained in one enormous sentence. The first part of the dream,

> leads to the apparition of the terrifying anxiety-provoking image, to this real Medusa's head, to the revelation of this something which properly speaking is unnameable, the back of this throat, the complex, unlocatable form, which also makes it into the primitive subject *par excellence*, the abyss of the feminine organ from which all life emerges, this gulf of the mouth, in which everything is swallowed up, and no less the image of death in which everything comes to its end, since in relation to the illness of his daughter, which could have been fatal, there's the death of the patient whom he had lost at a time adjacent to that of the illness of his daughter, which he considered to be some mysterious sort of divine retribution for his professional negligence – *this Mathilde for that Mathilde*, he writes. (1955, 164)

The extraordinary energy and tumultuous piling-on of clauses in this passage, its hovering around loss as well as death ('*this Mathilde for that Mathilde*'), its imagery of horror, which permeates the seminar – this is a reading resonant of the traditional but by no means trivial cultural association of feminine sexuality and death. Death comes hand in hand with sex, but along with this there is a parallel theme of the return to nothingness symbolized by the desire for the womb, both these elements being present in the three caskets analogy and, more formally, in Freud's (later) conceptualization of the death drive. Reading Lacan on Freud's dream, one has the sense of the dreamer face to face with his own desire as his egoic self is discarded. Looking into the mouth of the other, into the abyss of subjectivity, what is revealed is the impossibility of the position of the conscious, integrated subject. Identifications that hold this ego in place cannot be sustained when faced with the irruption of the real. 'So this dream teaches us the following,' says Lacan (1955, 159). 'What is at stake in the function of the dream is beyond the *ego*, what in the subject is of the subject and not of the subject, that is the unconscious'.

At the moment of this encounter with the real, a second cast of characters enters the dream, this time a trio of men (Dr M, Otto, Leopold). Lacan glosses this as follows:

> The relations of the subject change completely. He becomes some-
> thing completely different, there's no Freud any longer, there is no
> longer anyone who can say *I*. This is the moment I've called the entry
> of the fool, since that is more or less the role of the subjects on whom
> Freud calls. (1955, p. 164)

But these subjects are not external to Freud: being in his dream,
they are aspects of himself, they are the identifications out of
which his ego is constituted. And these identifications are indeed
falling apart, decomposing; the dream reveals the actual state of
psychic affairs – the normal, not the pathological state. As the
dream produces anxiety by revealing the fragility of the self, so
'we find ourselves present at an imaginary decomposition which
is only the revelation of the normal component parts of perception' (Lacan 1955, 166) – that is, so the different and unrelated
elements of the supposedly integrated ego are dramatized. Freud
is present in all these elements, in every member of this cast of
fools hunting around for a way out of the responsibility for the
horror of Irma's insides. For Lacan, it is not the content of the
discourse thus produced which matters, but the presence of these
imaginary elements of the ego and the way they disappear to
reveal behind them something more powerful and insidious, a
name that, despite being completely inscrutable, fixes the whole
symbolic pattern into place.

Freud's report of his dream culminates in his vision of the
formula for trimethylamin ($N - CH_3 / CH_3 / CH_3$) and his comment
about the syringe not being clean. Lacan takes this formula and
addresses it as an inscription of 'another voice', something which
just appears written in the air, without an agency behind it – what
he refers to, again with biblical allusiveness, as its '*Mene, Mene,
Tekel, Upharsin* aspect' (1955, p. 158). This formula, of no significance in what it says, is of ultimate significance because of its act
of speaking; it is thus that it reveals to the dreamer what is at the
heart of the dream. Here is Lacan's exposition of this point:

> In the dream there's the recognition of the fundamentally acephalic
> character of the subject, beyond a given point. The point is desig-
> nated by the N of the trimethylamin formula. That's where the *I* of
> the subject is at that moment . . . Just when the hydra has lost its
> heads, a voice which is nothing more than *the voice of no one* causes
> the trimethylamin formula to emerge, as the last word on the matter,

the word for everything. And this word means nothing except that it
is a word. (1955, 170)

Whether this version of the Irma dream is produced to be in line
with Lacan's already existing theory, or whether the theory follows from the analysis, is an interesting point but not one that is
crucial here. Certainly, Lacan's reading is different from Freud's,
and not just because Freud suppresses material that reveals too
much about his person. Nevertheless, Lacan's meditation on
Freud's meditation on Freud's dream of Irma expresses a dream
of its own, a vision of what it means to be a dreamer and a creator.
'It is not me', is what Lacan understands Freud to be saying. 'It is
my unconscious, it is this voice which speaks in me, beyond me'
(1955, 171). As the ego dissolves, there is a symmetrical relationship between the three women of the first part of the dream and
the three men of the second part. Freud, the dreamer, stands
outside them all, but by the very nature of things he embodies
them all – they are all aspects of his own imagination, creatures of
his dream. Typically, he looks into the throat of the woman to find
horror and dissolution; he looks to the babble of the men for
consolation and connivance at a relinquishment of responsibility
for the destruction he has wrought. But as the ego dissolves and
the identifications out of which it is built are revealed to be no
more than superficial allegiances, so a more truthful formula is
revealed, something which is sexual but not in itself sexed.
Freud's dream encompasses death and otherness, making them
available to the consciousness of the dreamer and analyst. They
are also available to the dreamers and analysts who follow, who
can see Freud's unconscious at work. The dream thus demonstrates Freud's art and some of the truth of his theory, but
not through his mastery, rather through the activity of his
unconscious.

In this reading, sexual difference becomes less fixed that ever.
At first sight, the dream of Irma's injection is a paradigmatically
masculine account of penetration and domination. Repelled by
the woman's intransigence, the man forces himself upon her,
causing her nothing but suffering and at the same time fantasiz-
ing about the perfect woman who is just out of reach. Then a cast
of portentous fools, other men, is called in to play a game of

shifting the blame around, exculpating the dreamer from responsibility for the woman's distress. It is all right; it was broken in
the first place; it is someone else's fault. What could be more
gendered than this? However, reading the dream and its interpretation more fully, there are a series of identifications at work
which conventionally would be associated with both femininity
and masculinity: Freud can take both subject positions, he is the
nodal point (the 'N'), with female and male caskets branching out
from him, but he is not completely expressed by either. The bisexuality of this is also quite conventional, though an advance on
the stereotypy of the previous account. Now Freud, male dreamer
though he is, reveals a capacity for both masculine and feminine
attributes; he can put himself in the shoes of either, and understand what each has to say.

Lacan's reading goes even further than this 'bisexuality',
however. There is still a representational dynamic around sexual
difference: the unconscious speaks of horror and death through
immersion in the woman, the other side of the skin. This losing of
self and identity, this castration, is a conventional element in
Lacanian imagery and it is always expressed through the medium
of the feminine 'Other', that which is excluded from the discourse of the Symbolic. But in the analysis of the dream of Irma's
injection, Lacan shows how rich an understanding of desire
and loss can be built up from this apparently traditional and
perhaps sterile or even misogynistic sexual differentiation, and
how this can disrupt any fixed position on difference itself. As
the identifications which constitute the ego dissolve, the subject is
left referring to something other than what it experiences itself to
be, something that writes the formula for it. This something is
not in itself gendered; it is too impersonal for that. Speaking
for the subject, it muddles up 'subject' positions, mixing what
is one with what is other, subject and object. This does not dis-
pense with sexual difference, but it interrogates it impersonally,
without formal allegiance. There is this 'masculine' and this
'feminine', but the subject is other than these categories; inserted
into them, for sure, but nevertheless outside what they have to
say. The social categories of gender are germane to the identifications of the ego; but behind the ego is something else,
visible when one can look without blinking or turning aside. In

this reading, Freud's 'self analysis' is genuinely heroic: the analytic gaze that challenges all of us to see more than we usually can see.

Disruption and the dream

The Interpretation of Dreams is a text marked by Freud's presence at numerous levels and in different positions: as author, analyst, dreamer and object of analysis. It is a text dedicated to mastery, in which Freud displays a virtuoso command of the principles of dream-interpretation, thus banishing the secrets of the night as well as the doubts of his adversaries. Freud as master is competing against others: the body of knowledge lies there to be uncovered, it is an aspect of nature, something which has eluded Freud's predecessors because of its uncanniness and obscurity – its relationship to the 'dark continent' – but something which is nevertheless a material entity, available to the activities of reason. Indeed, as psychoanalysis is in general concerned with the colonization of the irrational and its subjugation by the forces of reason and science, in this specific instance it is also dedicated to reducing the area of recalcitrance in nature, making the world more predictable and secure.

The traditional sexuality of this description is quite transparent. The obscure is the feminine – nature, the night, the dark continent, the dream. Masculinity is identified with rationality, with mastery of this obscurity, with light in the darkness, with the triumph of science over nature. It is characterized by self-aggrandizement, an economy of competition: Freud explicitly builds his dream book on rivalry with others which in turn derives from his need to overcome his father's disparagement of him. Nature is therefore being attacked for the sake of a strengthened position in the world of men, in just the same way as adolescent male sexuality has more to do with establishing one's masculine status than with desire for the other (Seidler 1985). But nature is also being attacked for its own sake, as an ambivalent object of desire. The boy's 'epistemologic impulse' is conventionally ascribed by psychoanalysts to curiosity about the mother's body: a wish to know it and understand its secrets, but also to act upon it, to take revenge on it for the terrifying dependence characteristic of early infancy, as well as for the abandonment experienced as the mother pushes the child away. The subtleties and unpredictability of the maternal body, the reminiscence of its smell and feel, provide an underpinning for the desire to know and conquer nature, linking with all those mind/body, reason/nature, sanity/insanity dichotomies so familiar in all parts of the social world.

Faced with an actual woman, the ambiguity of Freudian bisexuality becomes more pronounced and violent. Hertz (1983) points to the oral themes in 'Dora', and to some extent this can be seen as a model of psychoanalytic seduction as well as the actual or intended one of Dora's experience. Sprengnether (1985), however, identifies a more potent set of concerns, in which Freud attempts to distance himself from the homosexual strands in Dora's narrative (represented not only by her relationship with Frau K but also by the figure of the nurse which is embodied by many of the women in the text). For Sprengnether, this is no simple squeamishness over lesbianism on Freud's part, but a way of annihilating the femininity which might be found in his own associative network:

> Standing in the way of Freud's inability to identify with Dora . . . are two sets of associations: one that equates femininity with castration . . . and another that equates female sexuality in its clitoral manifestations with rejection of heterosexual intercourse. (1985, 269)

Freud's struggle for control over Dora and his failed attempt to achieve narrative coherence in the writing of 'Dora' itself, are part of the struggle within him for mastery over what he feels to be feminine insufficiency. The great challenges of femininity and the possibilities of transgressing gender categories are too terrible to encounter because they link the male author and analyst with the incomplete object – with that which might make his authority as nought.

That this brings the text back to the issue of castration anxiety should not be taken solely as unequivocal evidence of the absorption of Freud's thought in phallocentric discourse. Clearly, Freud takes up the masculine stance throughout all his writings, the two texts under consideration here included. He is explicit about, and conscious of, this. But the subversion of this masculinist position is also there in the texts: in his own dreams in *The Interpretation of Dreams*; in the unsettled rhythms and gaping lacunae, as well as the occasional forceful voice of the woman, in 'Dora'. Freud's struggle for mastery over these disruptive elements is one major source of the energy of the texts, and possibly of psychoanalysis itself: in trying to tame the unconscious by bringing it into the light, it allows expression of voices which are in reality everywhere, but are usually so hard to hear. Freud flees from this realization; 'Dora' makes it obvious that he can neither allow the woman her space nor acknowledge his own feminine identifications – he repulses them, seeking in that way to triumph. Reflecting this dynamic back into *The Interpretation of Dreams*, where Freud is not so much at odds with his analysand as he is in 'Dora', what comes into focus is just how much of the energy which Freud brings to forcing his view of dreams on to the scientific world can be attributed to his anxiety when faced with his own emotions, and more generally with the irrationality of the unconscious itself. Face to face with the beast which he has dreamed into existence, he can see the way it threatens his potency and self-control; he brings this to light, so that we can all appreciate it, then never afterwards can quite manage to keep it in its chains.

In the scheme of things as they are represented in *The Interpretation of Dreams*, the dream is the object of psychoanalytic enquiry, hence feminine in tone. Mysterious and obscure, a creature of the night, the dream is laid open on the table, dissected and inspected, penetrated with the rational zeal of the Freudian discoverer. Understanding dreams gives power in the world of men; however, it also makes the night less fearsome – it is a way of articulating and dealing with inner horror, repudiated but deeply felt. Interpreting dreams is thus in truth an act of mastery, but it betrays its own dynamic uncertainty. Throughout this chapter, it has been stressed that Freud's own articulation of dream analysis in *The Interpretation of Dreams* is shot through with ambivalence and with the voice of unconscious desire. This voice speaks in his place, showing how his personal identifications slip between those which might be characterized as masculine and those which might be feminine, always searching. The act of writing up the dreams and presenting their analysis to the world, a triumphant act of mastery, is also one in which the irrational is allowed its say, and Freud's own conflict-filled personality is offered up for inspection. Subject and object then shift again: Freud on the table, being examined, the feminine object of masculine desire.

Note

With the exception of the material relating to the 'Dora' case, this chapter is based on Chapter 3 of S. Frosh, *Sexual Difference: Masculinity and Psychoanalysis* (London: Routledge, 1994).

Works cited

Anzieu, D., *Freud's Self-Analysis*, trans. Peter Graham, (London: The Hogarth Press and the Institute of Psychoanalysis [1975] 1986).

Frosh, S., *Sexual Difference: Masculinity and Psychoanalysis* (London: Routledge 1994).

Hertz, N., 'Dora's secrets, Freud's techniques', in C. Bernheimer and C. Kahane (eds), *In Dora's Case* (London: Virago, 1985).

Jones, E., *Sigmund Freud: Life and Work* (London: The Hogarth Press, 1955).

Lacan, J., 'Intervention on transference', in C. Bernheimer and C. Kahane (eds), *In Dora's Case* (London: Virago, [1952] 1985).

Lacan, J., *The Seminars of Jacques Lacan, Book 2* (Cambridge: Cambridge University Press, 1955).

Marcus, S., 'Freud and Dora: story, history, case history', in C. Bernheimer and C. Kahane (eds), *In Dora's Case* (London: Virago, [1974] 1985).

Resnick, S., *The Theatre of the Dream* (London: Tavistock, 1987).

Seidler, V., 'Fear and intimacy', in A. Metcalfe and M. Humphries (eds), *The Sexuality of Men* (London: Pluto Press, 1985).

Sprengnether, M., 'Enforcing Oedipus: Freud and Dora', in C. Bernheimer and C. Kahane (eds), *In Dora's Case* (London: Virago, 1985).

7

Freud's secret:
The Interpretation of Dreams
was a Gothic novel

ROBERT J. C. YOUNG

I thus drew steadily nearer to that truth, by whose partial discovery I have been doomed to such a dreadful shipwreck: that man is not truly one, but truly two. I say two, because the state of my own knowledge does not pass beyond that point. Others will follow, others will outstrip me on the same lines; and I hazard the guess that man will be ultimately known for a mere polity of multifarious, incongruous and independent denizens.[1]

It was to be fourteen years before a little-known novelist fulfilled the prediction of Dr Jekyll's final confession by publishing what was to become the most famous case history in Gothic fiction: the autobiography of a man whose psyche was made up of nothing more than 'a mere polity of multifarious, incongruous and independent denizens'. The close of the nineteenth century witnessed a resurgence of Gothic novels and stories which particularly emphasized forms of psychological terror – examples include Stevenson's *Dr Jekyll and Mr Hyde*, James's *The Turn of the Screw* and Bram Stoker's *Dracula*. It has now become commonplace to provide 'Freudian' interpretations of Gothic fantasy novels, but few have recognized that this exercise is essentially tautological. This is because Freud's *The Interpretation of Dreams* (1900) was in fact itself a Gothic novel. Freud took the increasing psychological preoccupation of the Gothic novel to its logical conclusion: instead of portraying the psychological through a fictional narrative, he wrote a novel that pretended to be a real work of scientific psychology. In choosing to focus on dreams, however, he assumed that even without the apparent trappings of fiction the novel would be recognized for what it was.

But what differentiates *The Interpretation of Dreams* from all other Gothic novels is that its elaborate self-presentation as a scientific case-history was so successful that few readers ever realized that they were being taken in; few got as far as asking themselves the question posed by the narrator of Rider Haggard's *She* (1887): 'was I merely the victim of a gigantic and most elaborate hoax?'[2] The scientific realism of Freud's case-study is so thorough and appears to be so authentic that few have ever penetrated the secret of a book ostensibly dedicated to dream analysis. Freud himself in his prefaces already suggests its evident autobiographical content – that its self-analysis formed a reaction to his father's death and that he had thus very fittingly placed Sophocles' *Oedipus Rex* at its centre. This fictional confession is, of course, deliberately designed to lurk behind the analysis so as to provide a deliberate decoy for the suspicious reader. Within the text Freud himself hints at this pitfall: just because you have a coherent interpretation, he says, do not assume that you have wrapped up the whole thing – there may be another:

> It is only with the greatest difficulty that the beginner in the business of interpreting dreams can be persuaded that his task is not at an end when he has a complete interpretation in his hands – an interpretation which makes sense, is coherent and throws light upon every element of the dream's content. For the same dream may perhaps have another interpretation as well, an 'over-interpretation', which has escaped him. (PFL 4, 669)

Reader beware.

Most famous Gothic novels, such as *Frankenstein* or *Dracula*, have measured their success by the degree to which their central characters have been incorporated into the popular mythology of Western culture. Though it could be argued that 'Dr Freud' has become as pervasive a mythological figure, and has certainly become a legend of sorts in popular culture, *The Interpretation of Dreams* has succeeded in going one stage further: the reality-effect that it generated has been so powerful that, rather in the manner in which distraught viewers send flowers to the funerals of characters in TV soap operas, all over the Western world plausible followers of Freud have ever since been taking money off gullible neurotics by offering them the opportunity to have their own dreams analysed in the manner of the book. Freud himself encouraged this amusing effect by claiming to practise a therapy which he called 'psychoanalysis', and followed *The Interpretation of Dreams* with further apparently theoretical texts on the subject. During his lifetime, Freud was always particularly tickled by attacks from psychiatrists and philosophers who sought to 'disprove' the claims of psychoanalysis – who little realized how much they had already been taken in by seeking to disprove it. He loved to taunt his critics with comments such as 'this is merely due to our being obliged to operate with the scientific terms, that is to say, with the figurative language, peculiar to psychology' (PFL 11, 333–4).[3] Since his psychoanalysis never in fact claimed a scientific method, being rather a practice of literary interpretation, it was of course disprovable, but could never be disproved beyond the observation that its method was not scientific – and could therefore never be proved. Freud's humorous spoof has only been bettered in recent years by the French writer and 'psychoanalyst', Jacques Lacan, who began by working within the orthodox psychoanalytic institution and gradually discovered that the more impenetrable he made his language, the more obscure his writings, and the more he insulted his audience, the greater the reverence in which he was held. When the International Psychoanalytic Association finally came to realize that they had a jester in their ranks, they expelled him. But Lacan's response was to found a new school, the Ecole freudienne, which immediately became even more influential and continues to prosper.

Who was this Freud, who pulled off such a fictional coup, unparalleled in literary history? Some have argued that not only was *The Interpretation of Dreams* a hoax, but that 'Sigmund Freud' was itself a pseudonym. Several of the works now ascribed to him, such as *The Moses of Michelangelo* (1914) were originally published anonymously. This, however, is typical of the genre: anonymity or publication under a pseudonym forms the rule rather than the exception for Gothic fiction as a whole. Freud seems to be suggesting the possibility that he was not writing his own works by his constant allusions to the Shakespeare–Bacon controversy, and by his emphatically stated conversion after reading a book by the implausibly named J. Thomas Looney to the idea that in fact Edward de Vere, Earl of Oxford, was the author of Shakespeare's plays. Here Freud tested his readers' gullibility to the limit by adding the following footnote at the end of his biographical interpretation of *Hamlet* in *The Interpretation of Dreams*: 'Incidentally, I have in the meantime ceased to believe that the author of Shakespeare's works was the man from Stratford'.[4] Similarly, Freud's claim that his professional calling came after reading Goethe's essay on Nature, which was in fact by Tobler and was included only by 'paramnesia' in Goethe's works, seems to hint in a subtler way at the same inauthenticity. In 1921, the fraudian hoax of 'Freud' seemed about to be revealed in the scandal that followed the publication of *A Young Girl's Diary* (1921), a volume which had been edited by Dr Hermine Hug-Hellmuth, the first child psychoanalyst. The book is prefaced with a letter by Freud who describes it as:

> a gem. Never before, I believe, has anything been written enabling us to see so clearly into the soul of a young girl, belonging to our social and cultural stratum, during the years of puberal development. . . . Above all, we are shown how the mystery of the sexual life first presses itself vaguely on the attention, and then takes entire possession of the growing intelligence, so that the child suffers under the load of secret knowledge but gradually becomes enabled to shoulder the burden.[5]

However, doubts were soon voiced about the authenticity of this volume, and some suggested that the diary was in fact written by Dr Hug-Hellmuth herself, or even Freud. For his part, Freud refers to Hug-Hellmuth in *The Interpretation of Dreams* only once, after the following sentence: 'The stricter the censorship, the more far-reaching will be the disguise and the more ingenious too may be the means employed for putting the reader on the scent of the true meaning' (PFL 4, 224). Her scandalous murder in 1924 by her own nephew, whom she had been psychoanalysing, only increased speculation about her relation with the founder of psychoanalysis (to say nothing of the use of psychoanalysis as a form of therapy).

When *The Interpretation of Dreams* was first published some conjectured that it might have been written by the well-known

French psychologist Michel Foucault. But the publication in 1906 of Foucault's own volume, *Le Rêve: études et observations* discounted this theory. (Freud then cheekily cited this text in the 1941 edition of *The Interpretation of Dreams*.) The most likely candidate appears to have been Arthur Schnitzler, best known for his collection of short stories *Vienna 1900: Games with Love and Death*. Schnitzler, whose father was a prominent throat specialist, and whose brother was a distinguished Viennese surgeon, himself qualified as a doctor in 1885. He was deeply interested in psychiatry, and is known to have experimented with hypnosis. From the first, scholars have pointed to the curious way that Schnitzler's writings appear to have anticipated many of Freud's ideas – without considering that he may in fact have been Freud himself. Some have speculated that while he published his fictional work, famous for challenging contemporary bourgeois morality, under his own name, he published his 'psychological' literary texts under the name of his contemporary – Sigmund Freud – a practice in which Dr Freud was allegedly happy to collude in. It is even possible that Schnitzler and Freud collaborated together in the writing of the books. Schnitzler is known to have reviewed Freud's 1893 translation of Charcot's *Leçons du Mardi*, and more significantly, intervened on his behalf in a review of the third edition of *Über Morphiumsucht* (*On Morphia Addiction*, 1887), in which Erlenmeyer attacked Freud's notorious enthusiasm for cocaine.[6] In the end, however, the problem with the pseudonym theory comes down to the fact that there is no absolutely conclusive evidence to substantiate it. Scholars continue to ask, however, how a small-time, apparently pedestrian doctor could have conjured up the extraordinary range of literary and imaginative resources to write a work such as *The Interpretation of Dreams* and to have won the Goethe Prize for literature.[7]

For there certainly was a 'Sigmund Freud' living at that time and practising as a Viennese physician. His medical career was more or less discredited when his widely publicized infatuation with, and addiction to, cocaine led to the protracted death of his friend Fleischl. In the absence of substantive evidence to the contrary, it seems that it was this same Freud who thereafter, while continuing to practise as a general practitioner as far as he could, devoted most of his energies to his fictional works. It is clear that increasingly Freud began to regard the two selves as having completely separate personalities. In the course of a discussion of the forgetting of names, for example, Freud openly alludes to the other 'Sigmund Freud', suggesting that his identity as a writer may differ from that of the academically minded doctor who narrates the books in the first person:

> One cannot help having a slightly disagreeable feeling when one comes across one's own name in a stranger. Recently I was very sharply aware of it when a *Herr S. Freud* presented himself to me in my consulting hour. (PFL 5, 64)[8]

A few years later, Freud could not resist adding: 'However, I must record the assurance of one of my critics that in this respect his feelings are the opposite of mine' (PFL 5, 64). Administering to his patients everyday with complete respectability, by night Freud's *alter ego* led the literary life of a famous psychiatrist dabbling in the fantasmatics of metapsychology, revelling, as *The Interpretation of Dreams* shows, in Gothic horror and stories of sexual perversion, indulging in megalomaniac delusions of grandeur, and obsessed by megalomanic identification fantasies with three of the greatest soldiers-cum-dictators in European history before Hitler: Hannibal, Cromwell and Napoleon. 'Dreams', he claimed, 'are often most profound when they seem most crazy' (PFL 4, 575).

Freud and the Gothic

Freud himself, as is to be expected, devotes much attention to Gothic fiction in his writings. His general literary provenance can be detected in a number of ways. In the first place, most of the apparently analytic concepts developed by Freud are derived from literature – the Oedipus complex, sadism, masochism, narcissism – and Freud frequently reveals his literary identity by 'proving' his arguments by reference to literary examples. This, of course, immediately distinguishes the 'science' of psychoanalysis from all other sciences, human or physical. Apart from the daring autobiographical essay 'Creative writers and day-dreaming', Freud's later writings were increasingly more overtly concerned with literary text (Jensen's *Gradiva*, Goethe's *Dichtung und*

Wahrheit, Dostoevsky's *The Brothers Karamazov*, Schreber's *Memoirs*, Rabelais), with fairy-tales or with cultural and anthropological issues (for example, *Moses and Monotheism*, *Totem and Taboo*, *Beyond the Pleasure Principle*). Freud's literary provenance is most explicitly apparent in his other major Gothic work, 'The uncanny', an essay which, like *The Interpretation of Dreams*, also lures the reader in by claiming at the beginning to be a scientific, psychoanalytic investigation of a paranormal effect (though here Freud jokes: 'I should not be surprised to hear that psychoanalysis, which is concerned with laying bare these hidden forces, has itself become uncanny to many people for that very reason' (PFL 14, 366)). The essay quickly moves into an analysis of Hoffmann's 'fantastic narratives', by means of which it starts to produce uncanny effects of its own. Freud ends by confessing that the uncanny is predominantly produced by fiction rather than actual experience, and continues with a critical examination of how the writer achieves this deceitful trick: a technique at which he is only too adept himself (PFL 14, 370–4).

In some of his so-called 'case-histories', in a typical realist gesture, Freud cunningly anticipates the reader's reaction to their clearly fictitious, novelistic nature by emphasizing his own scientific priorities:

> I am aware that – in this city at least – there are many physicians who (revolting though it may seem) choose to read a case history of this kind not as a contribution to the psychopathology of the neuroses, but as a *roman à clef* designed for their private delectation. I can assure readers of this species that every case history which I have occasion to publish in the future will be secured against their perspicacity by similar guarantees of secrecy.... (PFL 8, 37)[9]

This kind of disavowal of any literary dimension or pretension is wholly typical of the Gothic narrator, and thus immediately betrays its literary provenance. The literary critic Steven Marcus came closest to locating the secret of Freud when he analysed the 'Dora' case-history as a piece of fiction. Marcus argued persuasively that its distinctiveness lay in the fact that Freud's text contained not only a novel, but also simultaneously its own interpretation. However, the technique of including a self-interpretation contained within a literary text was already well developed by the Romantic period, and is characteristic in particular of the method of De Quincey in his dream books:

> I the child had the feelings, I the man decipher them. In the child lay the handwriting mysterious to *him*; in me the interpretation and the comment.[10]

It is striking that in *The Interpretation of Dreams*, Freud represses all reference to his greatest literary precursor, the Romantic Gothic writer Thomas De Quincey, or to the remarkable *Confessions of an English Opium Eater* and *Suspiria de Profundis*, which together constitute the first example of the genre of autobiography through dream analyses. It was De Quincey who invented the term 'sub-conscious', which even today people often employ when thinking that they are making a 'Freudian' analysis. While Freud cites R. L. Stevenson's chapter on dreams in *Across the Plain* (1892) in his extensive bibliography, De Quincey's work is nowhere mentioned, despite the dreams of hellish torture machines, deep shafts (for Freud, lined in leather) and such like that are so closely associated with De Quincey's writings. Freud does not even refer to him in his short essay 'A note upon the mystic writing-pad' which is so clearly indebted to De Quincey's famous chapter on 'The palimpsest' in *Suspiria de Profundis*. This extraordinary omission marks what, after Macherey, we could call a symptomatic absence, signalled by a footnote in *The Interpretation of Dreams* in which Freud prints, *in spaced type*, a quotation from James Sully's essay 'The dream as revelation': 'like some palimpsest, the dream discloses beneath its worthless surface-characters traces of an old and precious communication' (PFL 4, 215–16, n. 2). In the essay which Freud cites, Sully himself had cited De Quincey on the action of memory in dreaming only a few pages earlier.[11] Reference to De Quincey surfaces only once in the entire corpus of Freud's writings – in the safety of *Jokes and their Relation to the Unconscious*, where he cites De Quincey's witty portmanteau word 'anecdotage'. Doubtless Freud repressed all other explicit reference to his major literary forbear not because of the anxiety of influence but rather because in his other life, which he led with all semblance of normality, he had once almost exposed the Mr Hyde within him through his notorious predilection for cocaine, the ramifications of which are alluded to in the dream of Irma's injection, the model dream in *The Interpretation of Dreams*. The association with the opium-eater was too close for comfort.

Techniques of the Gothic novel

Despite its camouflaging self-presentation as a work of psychiatry, *The Interpretation of Dreams* nevertheless fulfils many of the typical formal criteria of Gothic novels, which are for the most part designed to place the reader in a position of intellectual uncertainty. These characteristically involve 'scientific' investigations of paranormal phenomena, which incorporate autobiographical journals or diaries. Other standard Gothic features of Freud's text include the narrator's almost obsessive involvement in the quest to reveal the hidden meaning of dreams, the appearance of forms of pastiche and self-mocking humour, and the shifting narrative voices that make up the fabric of Freud's narrative. In the manner of Beckford's *Vathek*, *The Interpretation of Dreams* was first published in German before it was translated into English, the version by which it is now best known. It was subsequently encrusted and elaborated with a typically Gothic, parodic scholarly apparatus of ever increasing footnotes, revisions and citations of discussions of itself. Freud commented himself that his interpolations and footnotes to the text 'threaten at times to burst the whole framework of the book' (PFL 4, 49) – though, of course, such devices are the very means through which it is held together.

The formal characteristics of its Gothic provenance are indeed striking. Although the Victorian Gothic novel tended to abandon the machinery of castles, locked rooms, staircases, ghosts and disguises, all these elements occur in Freud's novel. The presentation of the analysis as part of a scientific discourse represents a characteristic move in the Gothic tradition which began with the first work of science fiction, Mary Shelley's *Frankenstein* (1818). Whereas the eighteenth-century Gothic writer relied on the evocation of the medieval past or the exotic orient as a means of projecting the reality of the impossible world of the supernatural, the fantastic and the uncanny, nineteenth-century writers typically sought the reader's acceptance by developing a form of hyperrealism that enclosed the fantastic within a plausible scientific framework, using realism as a means of projecting fantasy and the unreal. In the manner of Dr Watson, the narrator of *Sherlock Holmes*, Freud chooses to relate his story through the voice of a medical doctor. There are in fact clear links between Victorian Gothic fiction and the Victorian detective novel: the latter initially presents the phenomenon of the ineffable in the form of the marvellous or inexplicable only to reveal its explanation through the power of scientific rationality, whereas the Gothic uses the mode of scientific rationality as a way of establishing credibility for its story of the ineffable. What is unique about *The Interpretation of Dreams* is that it succeeds in belonging to both genres: it begins by setting itself up in the detective story mode by promising to reveal the scientific secret behind the irrationality of dreams. But while its narrative employs the dry method of a conceptual analysis of the ideological structure of dreams, this is deployed only to reconnect the reader to the mystery of the dream, 'its point of contact with the unknown', and to reinstate the ineffable in the form of nightmarish horror.

Gothic writers sought to make the implausible plausible not only by setting it within the context of scientific realism, but also by developing the narrative technique of using multiple narrators, found manuscripts (a procedure most notably employed by Freud in his short story, 'A seventeenth-century demonological neurosis'), diverse kinds of documents, and the like. All these devices are used by Freud in his quest to make the implausible narrative of the discovery of the secret of dreams acceptable to the sceptical reader. Although the mode of scientific discourse which he utilizes clearly prevents him from using the range of narrators or different forms of writing employed by, say, Stoker in *Dracula*, Freud establishes an equivalent form of multiple authorship not only through the varied voices of his patient's reported dreams, but also through the habitual interpolations of extracts from fictional scientific papers allegedly authored by other specialists in the field (Ferenczi, Rank, Robitsek, Rosegger, Sachs, Silberer and Tausk). In a dream reported from Rank, the dreamer, in a self-referential twist typical of this anachronistically postmodern novel, reads *The Interpretation of Dreams*. In the editions from 1914 to 1922, two complete chapters that were supposed to be written by Rank, one of which was devoted to 'Dreams and creative writing', were included at the end of Chapter VI ('The dream-work'). However, Freud subsequently considered this too obvious a give-away and therefore removed them. Even without them, however, the palimpsest of different narratives which makes up *The Interpretation of Dreams* clearly has the function of augmenting the plausibility and authority of the central narrative voice.

The topic of the book, dreams and their interpretation, is, of course, an impeccable one for the genre. In the manner of many Gothic novels, such as *Frankenstein* and *Wuthering Heights* (1847), a dream is staged early on that offers an interpretation of the book itself – in this case, the dream of Irma's injection. It was during the original attempt to analyse this dream that, as Freud puts it, 'the "meaning" of the dream was borne in' (PFL 4, 195) upon him. 'Insight such as this', he comments elsewhere, 'falls to one's lot but once in a lifetime' (PFL 4, 56).[12] In this inspirational moment, the secret of *all* dreams is revealed as 'the fulfilment of a wish'. The dream itself, on the other hand, leaves out the metafictional overriding preoccupation that will be articulated later in the dream of the self-dissection of Freud's own pelvis, namely Freud's own desire to reveal the secret of dreams. In Irma's injection, such desire is alluded to only covertly in the imagery of secrets, of penetration, of Irma's recalcitrance and her reluctance to open 'her mouth properly', or submit to Freud's 'solution'. The main focus of the analysis is taken up with the revelation of a secret, namely the universal meaning of dreams: in a Gothic device typically used when the material becomes too far-fetched for credibility, the reader is immediately invited to share in an ironic distancing from such an implausible claim. After the great moment of revelation, Freud points out that rather than accept the disturbing implication that his solution for Irma's complaint was a misdiagnosis, in the dream he provides a whole series of different, incompatible explanations for it. As Freud notes, while all these interpretations of Irma's illness consistently exculpate him, they:

> were not entirely consistent with one another, and indeed . . . were mutually exclusive. The whole plea – for the dream was nothing else – reminded one vividly of the defence put forward by the man who

> was charged by one of his neighbours with having given him back a
> borrowed kettle in a damaged condition. The defendant asserted
> first, that he had given it back undamaged; secondly, that the kettle
> had a hole in it when he borrowed it; and thirdly, that he had never
> borrowed a kettle from his neighbour at all. So much the better: if
> only a single one of these three lines of defence were to be accepted
> as valid, the man would have to be acquitted. (PFL 4, 197)

If the reader misses the joke here, Freud was later to make its
ridiculousness explicit in *Jokes and their Relation to the Unconscious*:
'Each one of these defences is valid in itself, but taken together
they exclude one another' (PFL 6, 100).[13] If so, then the dream
cancels out its own wish. Such ironic deflations subtly undermine
the seriousness of the careful achievement of the scientific realism
of the book's case-study, its multiple narrators, found manuscripts, profusion of footnotes, editor's comments, etc. A further
example of this self-ironising technique comes in *The Interpretation of Dreams*, when Freud draws attention to the ways in which
the tragedy of Oedipal drama is offset in dreams by the humour
of its unconscious representations: 'Some of these representations,' he notes dryly, 'might almost be described as jokes...'
(PFL 4, 533). Six years later, of course, he was to develop this
idea more comprehensively in *Jokes and their Relation to the
Unconscious* (1905) – but if the unconscious was allowed to be a
joke, Freud's secret, that *The Interpretation of Dreams* was also a
joke book, though obliquely hinted at, was never overtly
revealed.[14]

The *Interpretation of Dreams* conforms to the tenets of the
Gothic genre in a number of other ways. In the first place, its
mode is performative: while ostensibly offering the reader knowledge, in the manner of realist fiction, its real project is to produce
theatrical effects during the reading process. Unlike the realist
novel, which offers the reader apparently truthful information
about its subject matter, the project of the Gothic novel is rather to
make the reader undergo an experience – typically, a frisson of
horror or of sexual excitement (or preferably both). Freud himself
calls attention to this dramatic quality of dreams which always
create a 'situation' out of their images. They:

> represent an event which is actually happening . . . they 'dramatize'
> an idea. But this feature of dream-life can only be fully understood if

we further recognize that in dreams . . . we appear not to *think* but to *experience*. (PFL 4, 114–5)

The dramatic effects that *The Interpretation of Dreams* seeks to produce are reinforced by the wealth of theatrical references to Sophocles and Shakespeare. As Horace Walpole explained in his preface to the first Gothic novel, the *Castle of Otranto* (1765), the Gothic style, with its restless mixed mode of tragedy and horror combined with absurdity and ironic, self-deflating humour, was consciously inspired by the mixed-genre style of Shakespeare's drama. Freud follows this form conscientiously, blending the horror in his text with the wry humour of his commentaries.

The link with Shakespeare is repeated in many Gothic novels through a struggle of power between the generations, between children and their parents, and, particularly, between father and son. By placing *Oedipus Rex* and *Hamlet* at the centre of his dream-interpretation, Freud sets up the typical familial power structure of Gothic fiction, developing it into a whole series of conflictual relationships imaged through the characteristic device of the *Doppelganger*. Freud's nephew John, bizarrely a year older than Freud himself, is produced as the formative double of this kind. They are simultaneously both psychic opposites and images of each other: 'My nephew [John] reappeared in my boyhood, and at that time we acted the parts of Caesar and Brutus together. My emotional life has always insisted that I should have an intimate friend and a hated enemy' (PFL 4, 622). Freud remarks how easily his friendships, like dreams themselves, reverse things into their opposites – in doing so making them, we may note, impossible to interpret. The typical male bonding structure is reinforced in subsequent relationships with Josef, Professor Fleischl, Otto the family doctor and Fliess, Freud's more than confidant. Typically, this brotherly bonding develops through the projection of stereo-typed women through whom the men express their homoerotic relationships. A good example of this can be found in *Dracula*, where the circuit of men who exchange their blood through Lucy Weston also enables her in a manner of speaking, as Van Helsing observes, to marry them all – something that earlier in the novel she had already said she would like to do. Van Helsing, like Freud, combines ancient wisdom with modern science; however his risqué comment about Lucy Weston is nothing to Freud's constant harping upon incestuous desires, repressed homosexuality and extravagant forms of perversion. At the same time, the theme of the New Woman, whom the Gothic novel typically desires to repress, is dealt with in Freud's novel by a dream in which he projects monstrosity onto two characters from Ibsen's *A Doll's House* and *The Wild Duck*. We shall see how Freud returns to this topic in a later, highly significant dream about a 'monstrously passionate woman'.[15]

Anxiety about gender relations in Gothic fiction is usually accompanied by apprehension about class relations (as, for example, in *The Monk*, or *Caleb Williams*), a feature clearly in evidence at the margins of this text. The comfortable references to servants (for example, in the examination in a sanatorium dream) show Freud feeling no cause for scruple. As a good bourgeois man, he shows himself quite content to describe the dream-process itself according to the model of the capitalist and entrepreneur – while the dream-worker remains characteristically absent. Elsewhere, however, the text evinces greater anxiety – no doubt the invention of the term 'dream-work', displacing labour into the realm of dreams, is symptomatic. Freud recounts a form of class war taking place on a staircase in a Viennese house which he habitually climbed when visiting a patient:

> When I paid my morning visits to this house I used as a rule to be seized with a desire to clear my throat as I went up the stairs and the product of my expectoration would fall on the staircase. For on neither of these floors was there a spittoon; and the view I took was that the cleanliness of the stairs should not be maintained at my expense but should be made possible by the provision of a spittoon. The concierge, an equally elderly and surly woman (but of cleanly instincts, as I was prepared to admit), looked at the matter in a different light. She would lie in wait for me to see whether I should again make free of the stairs, and if she found that I did, I used to hear her grumbling audibly; and for several days afterwards she would omit the usual greeting when we met. (PFL 4, 337)

The smoker's cavalier attitude, buttressed by his own class position, finds itself more menaced in a dream, when the dreamer flees for protection to a mother figure, who turns round to reveal herself, horror of horrors, as a member of the working classes. Freud recounts how the dreamer:

> *fled for protection to a woman, who was standing by a wooden fence, as though she was his mother. She was a woman of the working classes and her back was turned to the dreamer. At last she turned round and gave him a terrible look so that he ran off in terror. The red flesh of the lower lids of her eyes could be seen standing out. (PFL 4, 291)*

Such terror in the face of working-class hostility is reiterated throughout the book by Freud's repeated citation of Maury's dreams of the French Revolution, of the Terror and the guillotine, of anarchist bombs, as well as his own dream of the revolutions of 1848. On the other hand, in a typical expression of nineteenth-century bourgeois class hostility in the other direction, Freud represents himself as one of the 'bourgeois plebs' pitted against the aristocracy, whom he dreams up in the flattering form of sea-slugs. In tune with the nationalist and colonial anxieties of late nineteenth-century Gothic fiction, he includes dreams involving German nationalists in Austria, and his father fantasized as a Hungarian Garibaldi. And while Freud, like many writers of his time, reproduces typical contemporary racist ideological notions regarding primitivism and savagery (presuppositions which determined the unlikely concept of the unconscious operating outside of time and of history), he also includes a dark projection of anxiety about increasing anti-Semitism, a social fantasy that psychoanalysis, alas, found itself powerless to cure or even to understand (PFL 4, 572).[16]

Shock horror

The Gothic novel was the first kind of novel to construct its narrative around the revelation of secrets; the detective novel then turned the revelation of a central secret into its guiding narrative form. At first sight, *The Interpretation of Dreams* appears to abandon this characteristic model, for the 'secret' of the book is unexpectedly revealed by the end of Chapter II: the meaning of the dream is that '*its content was the fulfilment of a wish and its motive was a wish*' (PFL 4, 196). The shrewd reader, however, can surmise that the claim that dreams are the fulfilment of a wish is something of a tautological joke in the context of a book whose overriding wish is to discover the secret of dreams. Freud's technique is to lure the reader into the illusion that the ineffable mystery of dreams has finally fallen to the big guns of scientific probing. The analyses that then follow to 'prove' this thesis are, however, really a device to compel the reader to experience more and more terror through forcing him or her to endure dreadful dreams. Freud's demonstration, through a seemingly endless succession of dreams and their analyses, of what he unhappily calls the 'final solution' to the enigma of the meaning of dreams, in fact submits the reader to a repetition effect of horrific dreams of compounding grotesqueness alternated with disorientating absurdity. Meanwhile the elaborate 'interpretations' of the dreams return the reader to apparent normality and rationality – and yet as they become more and more complicated and far-fetched, it seems more and more as though their function is to turn even the most banal dream text into the realm of the absurd and the fantastic. The reader is increasingly impressed by the author's extraordinary skill in transforming the most recalci-trant material of apparently banal dream-text into an ingeniously elaborated interpretation: in this sense, *The Interpretation of Dreams* operates as a manual of practical criticism in looking-glass land. Normal literary values are reversed, so that the dream 'text' is a brief, mundane piece of writing, whereas the interpretation develops against all odds into a richly imaginative and fantastic literature. Where the dream itself is not horrific, dull or even pleasant, dreams are transmuted through a gloomy Gothic inter-pretation, as in the charming castle by the sea dream where the analysis ends with the demonstration of how it conceals 'gloomi-est thoughts of an unknown and uncanny future' (PFL 4, 603).

The first dreams to which we are introduced seem relatively harmless, domesticated and benign. The book opens beguilingly with a dream of being Napoleon's wine merchant, followed by alarm-clock dreams, children's simple dreams, the smoked salmon dream, the entrancing dream of the botanical monograph, of buying vegetables, tuning the piano and visiting Rome. The dreams rush past without the reader noticing that gradually Freud begins to slip in dreams whose effect is to generate a cumulative horror through the events they describe, a horror often focused on the family, and representations of the death of loved relatives – for example, the aunt who sees her sister's only remaining son in a coffin:

> Last night, then, I dreamt that *I saw Karl lying before me dead. He was lying in his little coffin with his hands folded and with candles all round – in fact just like little Otto, whose death was such a blow to me.* (PFL 4, 235)

Yet even here, initially, the reader is quickly reassured. According to Freud, this is typical of the sort of dreams that 'have some meaning other than their apparent one', and he duly interprets the dream as a desire for a visit from an estranged former friend, a Professor of Literature, no less, with whom the dreamer is still in love. A similar dream is then repeated towards the end of the book; but significantly it is there described as being a dream of the very opposite type, namely a dream which needs no interpretation. This most sinister, most uncanny dream of all comes at the beginning of Chapter VII. Freud begins by masking its origins so as to ensure that it will remain uninterpretable and uncontainable in its effects. He claims for it a circular origin: that it was told to him by a woman patient, who had herself heard it in a lecture on dreams. Freud adds, 'its actual source is still unknown to me' (PFL 4, 652): it is the navel of dreams, the point of contact with the unknown. Within Freud's narrative, the patient from whom he heard it did not merely recount it to him, but obligingly redreamt it, thus internalizing it and making it her own, and a legitimate object of his analysis. Freud deliberately avoids the *mise-en-abyme* of how you interpret a dream in which the dreamer has redreamt someone else's dream by stating that it requires no interpretation. Instead, he teasingly gives it a status which is accorded only once elsewhere in the book (the dream of Irma's injection), namely of being a 'model' dream. The dream itself, which is remarkably brief, moves into the imaginative realm of childhood by reworking the nursery rhyme 'Ladybird, ladybird' ('... fly away home; Your house is on fire, your children will burn ...'):

> After a few hours sleep the father had a dream that *his child was standing beside his bed, caught him by the arm and whispered to him reproachfully:'Father, don't you see I'm burning?'* (PFL 4, 652)

Despite the claimed obscurity of its origins, Freud argues that the dead child was indeed actually burning, a candle having fallen upon him. What is it about this dream that makes it, as Freud observes, so moving – so moving that his patient in fact redreamt it, and commentators have subsequently returned to it again and again, trying to tease out its enigmatic secret? This despite the fact that it is presented as a transparent dream, one that needs no interpretation? The return to life of the dead child, the reproachful complaint and the father's grieving guilt, make it the most powerful, inexplicable Gothic moment in the book. But if it operates as an 'open' text, it is also the dream which closes the narrative of dream-interpretations: in the first dream, of the aunt who sees her sister's son dead in a coffin, Freud denies its content and argues that it is precisely not about wishing for the death of loved one. However, this is then followed by a section on 'typical dreams' whose longest, most comprehensive section concerns 'Dreams of the death of persons of whom the dreamer is fond'. It is here that Freud introduces the theme of the Oedipus complex by citing both *Oedipus Rex* and *Hamlet*, arguing that such dreams, in fact, after all involve an unconscious wish for the death of the loved one. But finally, in the dream of the burning child, Freud reverts to his first suggestion, namely that, despite its content, such a dream is not about wishing for the death of the loved one at all. He achieves this recuperation by reversing *Oedipus* and *Hamlet* – so that the dead son returns to reproach the guilty father. Once again, dreams – or the dream interpreter – can always obligingly reverse things into their opposites.

The book is thus framed by these two disturbing dreams of the death of loved children – a preoccupation that Freud's *The Interpretation of Dreams* repeats from De Quincey's *Suspiria*. The horror generated in between is not confined to *Oedipus Rex* and *Hamlet*: instead, while ostensibly analysing the formal structures of dreams (the 'dream-work', the 'psychology of dream processes', etc.) Freud quietly presents us with a procession of Gothic horrors whose cumulative effect is increased by our attention being ostensibly focused on the concomitant technical descriptions of how dreams operate: the dream of a mother seeing her only daughter of fifteen lying dead in a coffin, of a mother witnessing her daughter being run over by a train, a child seeing his father carry his head on a plate; of a mother cutting her son's head off; of giving birth to a child with a deformed skull; of

Fliess's sister dying in three-quarters of an hour; of a father being in a train accident (followed by a whole succession of dreams about the death of fathers); of Freud handing over his sons to a stranger; of a twenty-month-old baby's distress when his father was leaving for the front.

Even after the dream of the burning child, the horror continues to accumulate: late in the book comes the dream of his mother's death, remembered from his seventh or eighth year:

> I saw *my beloved mother, with a peculiarly peaceful, sleeping expression on her features, being carried into the room by two (or three) people with birds' beaks and laid upon the bed.* (PFL 4, 740)

Here the tall figures with birds' beaks are Egyptian gods whom Freud contrives to associate with copulation; the expression on his mother's face is copied from a memory of his grandfather lying in a coma a few days before his death. With these family horrors come other forms of ghastly violence, in both the dreams and the analyses, which only lead one to wonder about Freud's bizarre and sometimes sick imagination: of peering at the white scabs inside Irma's mouth; of the constant illness of his friend Otto; of a raging mother carrying out infanticide; of seeing the signs of syphilis on the hand; dreams of being naked; of the crushing of the may beetle in the casement; of running after a little girl in order to punish her and then copulating with her on the stairs; of hats turning into genitals; of being tied up with silk cloths while two university professors carry out an operation on the dreamer's penis; a whole gamut of castration dreams; of a seal-like creature coming up through a trap door; of an amorous chimpanzee and a gorilla-cat being hurled at a woman; of a man dreaming he was a pregnant woman; of women who grow beards; of a man dying without knowing it; of butchers' boys eating the flesh of burning dead bodies; of Freud giving a now-deceased friend a piercing look so that he melts away; of asking a question which makes the governor of a garrisoned castle drop dead; of a young man mutilating his own genitals; of a woman dying in childbirth; of a Museum of Human Excrement, in which the Gulliver-like Freud micturates; of monsters and devils on the tower of Notre Dame; of his own son wounded with bandages on his face; of Crassus having molten gold poured down his throat;

of death wishes, hysteria, paranoia, regression, vomiting, convulsions, revulsion, disgust, sadism, masochism, punishments, executions, murders, torture instruments, revenge, brutality, torment ...

Freud's imperial romance

What is all this intense psychic violence about? Within its milieu of psychic gore, another dark dream is concealed which contains the metafictional centre of the novel, a dream, Freud tells us, concerned with writing his Gothic novel: the double castration dream of Freud dissecting his own pelvis and going in quest of female power. The representation of the process of self-analysis of *The Interpretation of Dreams* as self-*dissection* also suggests that Freud is identifying with the famous dissector and mortician of Gothic literature – Count Frankenstein, himself another transgressive searcher, in his workshop of filthy creation, for secrets of life and death which should have remained hidden, knowledge of which eventually rebounds upon him. In the Preface to the first edition of *The Interpretation of Dreams*, Freud claims that his subject matter does not 'trespass beyond the sphere of interest covered by neuropathology' (PFL 4, 44). This academic stance is quickly transformed into a developing obsession, comparable in scope only with Frankenstein's 'fervent longing to penetrate the secrets of nature', to strive for 'immortality and power' and 'the deepest mysteries of creation'.[17] Freud's novel too is concerned with the pursuit of forbidden transgressive knowledge beyond the limits of the human – knowledge which then rebounds with a vengeance upon the perpetrator: 'he who would tamper with the vast and secret forces of the world may well fall a victim to them'.[18] In the manner of his forebear, Freud's search for the secret of dreams combines the cutting edge of the science of modernity with the deepest mysteries of hermetic secret lore, and ancient Egyptian wisdom. This hunt for prohibited knowledge, which inevitably merges with illicit forms of sexual desire, shows that Freud's book, like *Frankenstein*, is a romantic quest novel, its central subject his yearning to discover the secret of dreams, a longing that turns out to be closely allied to dreams that 'satisfy their craving for an answer to the riddles of sex' (PFL 4, 679). For the dream of self-dissection begins with castration only to move on to sex, specifically, feminine sexuality. Its subject turns out to be nothing less than a fantasy based on Rider Haggard's *She*. So while the ostensible topic of the dream book is announced as the revelation of the secret of dreams, namely that they have a meaning that is the fulfilment of a wish, Freud here goes on to reveal that the secret desire of his book about the meaning of dreams is to find the solution to the enigma of woman herself.

In the nineteenth century, it has been suggested, the Gothic moved away from romance into the realm of science fiction. However, as Patrick Brantlinger has argued, the earlier romance form was not obliterated but simply displaced – into the 'imperial Gothic' of colonial fiction.[19] It is in this dream that Freud himself moves into such a mode. He has already hinted at this in structuring the whole book as an imaginary walk, and of dreaming of psychoanalysis itself as a journey, tropes which allude to the genre of travel writing and adventure story – in Chapter IV, Mungo Park himself makes an appearance. The links between the imperial fiction and psychoanalytic narration are clear: in Anne McClintock's words, 'true to the trope of anachronistic space, the journey into the interior is, like almost all colonial journeys, figured as a journey forward in space but backward in time'.[20] In the dream of dissecting his own pelvis, Freud invokes the romantic form of the imperial Gothic not merely by the metafictional device of dreaming about writing about *The Interpretation of Dreams* – but overtly by deploying the imagery of Henry Rider Haggard's *She* (1887) and *Heart of the World* (1896) as the central imaginative material of the dream.

Gilbert and Gubar argue that 'the very topography as well as the motion and direction of Haggard's quest-plots helped Freud conceptualize the psychic geography' to be found at the end of the 'royal road to the unconscious' (PFL 4, 769).[21] At the same time, the dream reveals that Freud identified his own sexuality with that projected in Haggard's popular escapist romances which were designed explicitly for male readers. Haggard gamely dedicates *King's Solomon's Mines* to 'all the big and little boys who read it'.[22] Freud recounts how he defends himself from the hostile challenge of Louise N who refuses his gift of *She* along with the claims of psychoanalysis, with the following more prudish comment about the self-revelation of writing *The Interpretation of Dreams*:

> I reflected on the amount of self-discipline it was costing me to offer the public even my book upon dream – I should have to give away so much of my own private character in it.
>
> After all, the best of what you know
> May not be told to boys. (PFL 4, 587)

Freud reveals that he easily identified with Haggard's gruff, self-confessedly misogynistic narrators, who preface their romances with authenticating details of found manuscripts and ancient sources much as Freud himself leads us through the textual history of dream interpretation in the interminable first chapter of *The Interpretation of Dreams*. In Haggard, close male friendships transcend male–female relationships ('one who was dear to me with a love passing the love of woman').[23] Rather more casual love and sex between white men and black women is an habitual preoccupation; typically, the black woman is then required to die so as to leave the white man free. In *She*, the male Amahagger worship their women – and then slaughter them. 'As for women, flee from them, for they are evil, and in the end will destroy thee,' warns the wise old man Billali in the novel:[24] women in general are distrusted by Haggard as evil, even – especially – the ideal-ized, exotically beautiful women, Maya and Ayesha, who act as guides to the male heroes of the two books. It is these two phallic, castrating women that Freud dreams about in his dream about self-castration, about dissecting his own pelvis, about writing *The Interpretation of Dreams*. Both *She* and *Heart of the World* are novels about seeking out the secrets of nature by exploring the unknown, dark continents of Africa and Central America. In *King Solomon's Mines*, Africa is itself imaged as a female body that has to be surmounted at the point of 'Sheba's breasts' and then penetrated in its dark, unknown interior.[25] As Maria Torgovnick suggests, psychoanalysis and colonial fiction share this 'axiomatic identifi-cation of "primitive" landscape with the female body'.[26] *She* was to return once again not just in Haggard's *Ayesha – The Return of She* (1905) but also in Freud's texts when, a few years later, he compared the enigma of female sexuality with the dark continent of Africa. Like Holly, Freud identifies himself as the explorer of darkest Africa; like Strickland and Don Ignatio in *Heart of the World*, he is the searcher for El-Dora-do, the 'City of the Heart', for the enigmatic secret here revealed to be not so much the meaning of dreams as the riddle of the 'eternal feminine' of female sexuality.

In his commentary on the dream, Freud gives the following explanation of the Haggard material, which hinges on the comment that 'STRANGELY ENOUGH' he was assigned the task of dissecting his own pelvis, assisted by Louise N:

> The following was the occasion of the dream. Louise N., the lady who was assisting me in my job in the dream, had been calling on me. 'Lend me something to read', she had said. I offered her Rider Haggard's *She*. 'A *strange* book, but full of hidden meaning', I began to explain to her; 'the eternal feminine, the immortality of our emotions ...' Here she interrupted me: 'I know it already. Have you nothing of your own?' – 'No, my own immortal works have not yet been written.' – 'Well, when are we to expect these so-called ultimate explanations of yours which you've promised even *we* shall find readable?' she asked, with a touch of sarcasm. (PFL 4, 586–7)

Louise N, epitome of the New Woman, clearly has no desire to read the fantasies, sexual or otherwise, of boys' adventure books, or *The Interpretation of Dreams* for that matter. In the dream, Freud identifies the search for ultimate explanations in *The Interpretation of Dreams* with Haggard's heroes' quest for the secrets of life and truth in Africa and unlimited wealth in America. His claim that the book is 'full of hidden meaning' simply repeats the narrator's own comment about *She* ('this history of a woman ... was some gigantic allegory, of which I could not catch the meaning').[27] The book seals up its own meaning, like dreams themselves.

But what is the significance of Freud's interpretation of *She* as a book about 'the eternal feminine' and 'the immortality of our emotions' (PFL 4, 586–7)? Ayesha herself is of course 'almost eternal', represented as a woman who has killed her lover Kallikrates, but who then waits two thousand years for him to be reborn and to return to her. When he returns, as the beautiful, dumb blond Leo Vincey, he does so according to the injunction: '*seek out the woman, and learn the secret of Life, and if thou mayest find a way slay her*'.[28] The eternal feminine must be destroyed. Freud's comment alludes to the chapter entitled 'Ayesha unveils'. Holly, the narrator, a sceptical, possibly Jewish, Cambridge academic with an interest in antiquarian subjects, Egyptology, lost civilizations and stoical, platitudinous, homespun philosophizing about the human lot, is undergoing an audience with the veiled She-who-must-be-obeyed and daringly asks to see her face. By way of warning, she reminds him of the myth of Actaeon, who 'perished miserably' (PFL 4, 154) because he looked on too much beauty. If he saw her face, she predicts, he would eat out his heart in 'impotent desire' (PFL 4, 154). When he sees what he describes as the dark erotic sublimity of Ayesha's face, Holly duly declares himself blinded and smitten forever by this 'Venus Victrix'. At this point of Holly's absolute erotic devotion, however, Ayesha catches sight of his ring which contains the scarab of her long-lost lover; at first she goes into a terrorizing fury, but then continues more calmly:

> 'It is very strange,' she said, with a sudden access of womanlike trembling and agitation which seemed out of place in this awful woman – 'but once I knew a scarab like that. It – hung round the neck – of one I loved,' and she gave a little sob, and I saw that after all she was only a woman, although she might be a very old one. (PFL 4, 157)

Ayesha thus reveals that powerful *femme fatale*, matriarch with 'an intellect so powerful', or Mother Goddess as she may be, she is 'after all . . . only a woman'. The word 'strange', which Freud emphasizes by capitalising the phrase 'STRANGELY ENOUGH' in the dream, and which he connects with his comment 'a *strange book*', here links with Ayesha's comment in which she exposes both 'the eternal feminine' and the vulnerability of the immortality of her emotions. It is on the revelations of such profound material that Freud bases his understanding of women and the mystery of female sexuality – here betraying, as he himself admits, so much of his own private character. The dream about writing *The Interpretation of Dreams* discloses that the quest for the secret of feminine sexuality is what really lies at its heart. On the one hand, the dream reassuringly recalls the discovery that the all-powerful Ayesha is a vulnerable woman after all; on the other hand, structurally it opens with a self-castration assisted by the formidable Louise N, and closes with Freud's terror at the prospect of being engulfed by the abyssal chasm, a terror so extreme that he awakes from the dream in 'mental fright'. This ending recalls the sheer mental fright that causes Job, the man-servant in the novel, to expire before he can recross the chasm. Though doubtless Freud is saved by being master rather than servant, the finale of his dream suggests a sympathetic identifica-tion with Job, who is so extreme a misogynist (and racist) that he is the only man in the book who shows himself proof against She herself.

But the real horror of Freud's Gothic novel came in its performative after-effect: transforming Haggard's male fantasies from the realm of popular culture into the normative basis for the psychoanalytic understanding of feminine sexuality.

Notes

1 'Henry Jekyll's Full Statement of the Case' in Robert Louis Stevenson, *The Strange Case of Dr Jekyll and Mr Hyde*, ed. Jenni Calder (Harmondsworth: Penguin, [1886] 1979), p. 82.

2 A. Rider Haggard, *She*, ed. Daniel Karlin (Oxfoxd: World's Classics, 1991).

3 Freud, Beyond the Pleasure Principle.

4 See Nicholas Royle, *After Derrida* (Manchester: Manchester University Press, 1995), pp. 85–90, 93–6.

5 Anon, *A Young Girl's Diary*, prefaced with a letter by Sigmund Freud, trans. Eden and Cedar Paul (London: George Allen and Unwin, 1921), p. 5.

6 See Ernest Jones, *The Life and Work of Sigmund Freud*, ed. Lionel Trilling and Steven Marcus (Harmondsworth: Penguin, 1964), pp. 103–4, 543.

7 In *Frend as a Writer* (New Haven, CT: Yale University Press, 1987), p. 1, Patrick Manoney points out that this was the only prize that Freud ever received from Germany in his lifetime.

8 Freud, *Psychopathology of Everyday Life*.

9 Freud, 'Dora'.

10 Thomas de Quincey, 'Suspiria de Profundi', in *The Confessions of an Opium Eater and Other Writings*, ed. Grevel Lindop (Oxford: World's Classics, 1985), p. 113.

11 James Sully, 'The Dream as Revelation', *Fortnightly Review* 53 (n.s.) (1893), 360.

12 Haggard continued: 'As though a man's brain could harbour a host of "Shes"! Such literary polygamy is not possible. Only one love of this kind is given to him'. Introduction to *She* p. xii.

13 Cf. my 'Psychoanalytic criticism: has it got beyond a joke?', *Paragraph* 4 (1984), 87–114.

14 Cf. the discussion in the footnote to *The Interpretation of Dreams*, PFL 4, 405.

15 Sandra M. Gilbert and Susan Gubar, *No Man's Land: The Place of the Woman Writer in the Twentieth Century* (New Haven, CT: Yale University Press, 1988), p. 6.

16 An earlier dream involved picturing Dreyfus on the Ile du Diable (250).

17 Mary Shelley, *Frankenstein*, in *Three Gothic Novels*, ed. Peter Fairclough (Harmondsworth: Penguin, 1968), pp. 296, 306, 308.

18 Haggard, *She*, p. 29.

19 Patrick Brantlinger, *Rule of Darkness: British Literature and Imperialism, 1830–1914* (Ithaca, NY: Cornell University Press, 1988).

20 Anne McClintock, *Imperial Leather: Race, Gender and Sexuality in the Colonial Contest* (New York: Routledge, 1995), p. 242. Cf. Gilbert and Gubar, *No Man's Land*, p. 43.

21 Gilbert and Gubar, *No Man's Land*, p. 43.

22 H. Rider Haggard, *King Solomon's Mines*, ed. Daniel Butts (Oxford: World's Classics, 1989), p. 1. See Gilbert and Gubar's comment on this aspect of the book, *No Man's Land*, p. 7; their point is corroborated by John Sutherland, *Longman Companion to Victorian Fiction* (Harlow: Longman), p. 270.

23 H. Rider Haggard, *Heart of the World* (London: Longman, Green and Co., [1896] 1898), p. 6.

24 Haggard , *She*, p. 110.

25 Among many commentators who make the obvious inference about this topography, see R. Stott, 'The dark continent: Africa as female body in Haggard's adventure fiction', *Feminist Review* 32 (1989), 69–89.

26 Maria Torgovnick, *Gone Primitive: Savage Intellects, Modern Lives* (Chicago: University of Chicago Press, 1990), pp. 156, 275.

27 Haggard, *She*.

28 *Ibid.*

Notes on contributors

RACHEL BOWLBY, Professor of English at the University of York from 1998, is completing *The Last Shopper* for Faber. Her previous books include *Still Crazy after all these Years: Women, Writing and Psychoanalysis* (1992), *Shopping with Freud* (1993) and *Feminist Destinations and Further Essays on Virginia Woolf* (1997).

JOHN FORRESTER is Reader in the Department of History and Philosophy of Science at Cambridge University. His publications include *Language and the Origins of Psychoanalysis* (1980), *The Seductions of Psychoanalysis* (1990), *Dispatches from the Freud Wars* (1997) and, with Lisa Appiganesi, *Freud's Women* (1992).

STEPHEN FROSH is Professor of Psychology at Birkbeck College, University of London and Consultant Clinical Psychologist and Vice-Dean at the Tavistock Clinic. He has written numerous academic papers and his books include *The Politics of Psychoanalysis* (1987), *Sexual Difference, Masculinity and Psychoanalysis* (1994), and *For and Against Psychoanalysis* (1997). He is currently, with Ann Phoenix, involved in a research project on young masculinities.

JAMES HOPKINS is Reader in Philosophy at King's College, University of London and an editor of *Mind*. He has written numerous articles on philosophy and psychoanalysis and has edited *Philosophical Essays on Freud* (with Richard Wollheim) (1982) and, with Anthony Savile, *Psychoanalysis, Mind and Art: Perspectives on Richard Wollheim* (1992).

LAURA MARCUS is Reader in English at the University of Sussex. She is author of *Auto/biographical Discourses: Criticism, Theory, Practice* (1994) and *Virginia Woolf* (1997), and is co-editor of *Close Up 1927–33: Cinema and Modernism* (1998) and *Culture, Modernity and 'the Jew'* (1998). She is currently working on *'The Tenth Muse': Cinema and Modernism*.

TREVOR PATEMAN is Reader in Education at the University of Sussex. His publications include *Language, Truth and Politics* (1987), *What is Philosophy?* (1987), *Key Concepts: A Guide to Aesthetics, Criticism and the Arts in Education* (1991) and *Language in Mind and Language in Society: Studies in Linguistic Reproduction* (1997). He is currently working on *Space for the Imagination*.

ROBERT J. C. YOUNG is a Fellow of Wadham College, Oxford and Reader in English Language and Literature, Oxford University. He is the author of *White Mythologies: Writing, History and the West* (1990), *Colonial Desire: Hybridity in Theory, Culture and Race* (1995) and *Torn Halves: Political Conflict in Literary and Cultural Theory* (1996). A new book, *Postcolonialism: An Historical Introduction* is forthcoming. Robert Young is also so General Editor of a new journal, *Interventions: The International Journal of Postcolonial Studies*.

Select bibliography

Works by Freud dealing substantially with dreams

Date in square brackets is date of first publication unless otherwise stated.

'Project for a scientific psychology' [1895], SE I.

The Interpretation of Dreams [1900], SE IV, V.

On Dreams [1900], SE V.

'Fragment of an analysis of a case of hysteria' ['Dora'] (original title: 'Dreams and hysteria') [1905], SE VII.

Delusions and Dreams in Jensen's 'Gradiva' [1907], SE IX.

'The handling of dream-interpretation in psycho-analysis' [1911], SE XII.

'An evidential dream' [1913], SE XII.

'The occurrence in dreams of material from fairy tales' [1913], SE XII.

Introductory Lectures of Psychoanalysis Part II [1916–17], SE XV, XVI.

'A metapsychological supplement to the theory of dreams' [1917], SE XIV.

'From the history of an infantile neurosis' [1918], SE XVII.

'Supplements to the theory of dreams' [1920], SE XIII.

'Dreams and telepathy' [1922], SE XIII.

'Remarks upon the theory and practice of dream-interpretation' [1923], SE IXX.

'Some additional notes on dream-interpretation as a whole' [1925], SE IXX.

New Introductory Lectures on Psycho-Analysis (Lectures 19 and 30) [1933], SE XXII.

The Complete Letters of Sigmund Freud to Wilhelm Fliess 1887–1904, ed. and trans. Jeffrey Moussaieff Masson (Cambridge, Mass., Harvard University Press, 1985).

Studies of *The Interpretation of Dreams* and Freudian dream theories

Adams, Leslie, 'A new look at Freud's dream "The breakfast ship"', *American Journal* of *Psychiatry* 110 (1953) 381–4.

Anzieu, Didier, *Freud's Self-Analysis* [1975] trans. Peter Graham (London: The Hogarth Press and the Institute of Psychoanalysis, 1986).

Bloom, Harold (ed.), *Sigmund Freud's The Interpretation of Dreams* (New York: Chelsea House, 1987).

Buxbaum, Edith, 'Freud's dream interpretation in the light of his letters of Fleiss', *Bulletin of the Menninger Clinic* 15 (1951) 197–212.

Decker, Hannah S., 'The Interpretation of Dreams: early reception by the educated German public', *Journal of the History of Behavioural Sciences* 11 (1975) 129–41.

Elms, Alan C., 'Freud, Irma, Martha: sex and marriage in the "Dream of Irma's injection"', *Psychoanalytic Review* 67 (1980) 83–109.

Erikson, Erik H., 'The dream specimen of psychoanalysis', *Journal of the American Psychoanalytic Association* 2 (1954) 5–56.

Felman, Shoshana, 'The dream from which psychoanalysis proceeds', in *What Does a Woman Want?* (Baltimore, MD: Johns Hopkins University Press, 1993), pp. 68–120.

Ferguson, Harvie, *The Lure of Dreams: Sigmund Freud and the Construction of Modernity* (London: Routledge, 1996).

Flanders, Sara (ed.), *The Dream Discourse Today* (New York and London: Routledge, 1993).

Fliess, Robert, *The Revival of Interest in the Dream* (New York: International Universities Press, 1953).

French, T. M. and Fromm, E., *Dream Interpretation* (New York: Basic Books, 1964).

Frieden, K., *Freud's Dream of Interpretation* (Albany, NY: State University of New York Press, 1990).

Grigg, Kenneth A., '"All roads lead to Rome": the role of the nursemaid in Freud's dreams', *Journal of the American Psychoanalytic Association* 21 (1973) 108–26.

Grinstein, Alexander, *Sigmund Freud's Dreams* (New York: International Universities Press, 1980).

—, *Freud's Rules of Dream Interpretation* (New York: International Universities Press, 1983).

Hartmann, Frank R., 'A reappraisal of the Emma episode and the specimen dream', *Journal of the American Psychoanalytic Association* 31 (1983) 555–85.

Hirschmuller, Albrecht, 'Freud's "Mathilde": ein weiterer Tagesrest zum Irma Traum', *Jahrbuch der Psychoanalyse* 24 (1989) 128–59.

Jaffe, Samuel, 'Freud as rhetorician: elocutio and the dream-work', *Rhetorik* 1 (1980) 42–69.

Kitcher, Patricia, *Freud's Dream: A Complete Interdisciplinary Science of Mind* (Cambridge, Mass.: MIT Press, 1992).

Keiper, A. and Stone, A. A. 'The dream of Irma's injection: a structural analysis', *American Journal of Psychiatry* 139 (1982) 1225–34.

Langs, Robert, 'Freud's Irma dream and the origins of psychoanalysis', *Psychoanalytic Review* 71 (1984) 591–617.

Lansky, Melvin R. (ed.), *Essential Papers on Dreams* (New York: New York University Press, 1992).

Lehmann, Herbert, 'A dream of Freud in the year 1910', *International Journal of Psychoanalysis* 59 (1978) 181–7.

Loewenberg, Peter, 'A hidden Zionist theme in Freud's "My son, the Myops ..." dream', *Journal of the History of Ideas* 31 (1970) 129–32.

Lyotard, Jean-François, 'The dream-work does not think', *Oxford Literary Review* 6:1 (1983) 3–34.

McCaffrey, Phillip, *Freud and Dora: The Artful Dream* (New Brunswick, NJ: Rutgers University Press, 1984).

Mehlman, Jeffrey, 'Trimethylamin: notes on Freud's specimen dream', in Robert Young (ed.), *Untying the Text: A Post-Structuralist Reader* (London: Routledge and Kegan Paul, 1981), pp. 177–88.

Rand, Nicholas, and Torok, Maria, 'Questions to Freudian psychoanalysis: dream interpretation, reality, fantasy', *Critical Inquiry* 19 (1993) 567–94.

Resnik, Salomon, *The Theatre of the Dream*, trans. Alan Sheridan (London: Tavistock, 1987).

Rosenfeld, Eva M., 'Dream and vision: some remarks on Freud's Egyptian bird dream', *International Journal of Psychoanalysis* 37 (1956) 97–105.

Schorske, Carl E., 'Politics and patricide in Freud's Interpretation of Dreams', in *Fin-de-siècle Vienna: Politics and Culture* (Cambridge: Cambridge University Press, 1981).

Schott, Heinz, 'Traum und Geschicte. Zur Freudschen Geschichtsauffassung im Kontext der Traumdeutung', *Sudhoffs Archiv* 64 (1980) 298–312.

Schur, Max, 'Some Additional "Day Residues" of "The Specimen Dream of Psychoanalysis"', in Mark Kanzer and Jules Glenn (eds), *Freud and his Self-Analysis*, (New York: Jason Aronson, 1979), 87–116.

Sharpe, Ella Freeman, *Dream Analysis: A Practical Handbook in Psychoanalysis* (London: The Hogarth Press, 1949).

Welsh, Alexander, *Freud's Wishful Dream Book* (Princeton, NJ: Princeton University Press, 1994).

General studies on Freud

Appignanesi, Lisa and Forrester, John, *Freud's Women* (London: Weidenfeld and Nicolson, 1992).

Borch-Jacobsen, Mikkel, *The Freudian Subject* (Basingstoke: Macmillan, 1989).

Bowie, Malcolm, *Freud, Proust and Lacan* (Cambridge: Cambridge University Press, 1987).

Brennan, Teresa, *The Interpetation of the Flesh: Freud's Theory of Femininity* (London: Routledge, 1992).

Brome, Vincent, *Freud and his Disciples* (London: Caliban, 1984).

Clark, Ronald W., *Freud: The Man and the Cause* (London: Weidenfeld and Nicolson, 1980).

Decker, Hannah S., *Freud in Germany: Revolution and Reaction in Science, 1893–1907* (New York: International Universities Press, 1977).

Ellenberger, Henri F., *The Discovery of the Unconscious: The History and Evolution of Dynamic Psychiatry* (New York: Basic Books, 1970).

Forrester, John, *Language and the Origins of Psychoanalysis* (Basingstoke: Macmillan, 1980).

—, *The Seductions of Psychoanalysis: Freud, Lacan and Derrida* (Cambridge: Cambridge University Press, 1990).

—, *Dispatches from the Freud Wars: Psychoanalysis and its Passions* (Cambridge, Mass.: Harvard University Press, 1997).

Frosh, Stephen, *The Politics of Psychoanalysis: An Introduction to Freudian and Post-Freudian Theory* (London: Macmillan, 1987).

—, *Identity Crisis: Modernity, Psychoanalysis and the Self* (Basingstoke: Macmillan, 1991).

Gay, Peter, *A Godless Jew: Freud, Atheism, and the Making of Psychoanalysis* (New Haven: CT, Yale University Press, 1987).

—, *Freud: A Life for Our Time* (London: Dent, 1988).

—, *Reading Freud: Explorations and Entertainments* (New Haven, CT.: Yale University Press, 1990).

Gardner, Sebastian, *Irrationality and the Philosophy of Psychoanalysis* (Cambridge: Cambridge University Press, 1993).

Gilman, Sander, *The Case of Sigmund Freud: Medicine and Identity at the Fin de Siècle* (Baltimore MD: Johns Hopkins University Press, 1993).

Grosskurth, Phyllis, *The Secret Ring: Freud's Inner Circle and the Politics of Psychoanalysis* (London: Jonathan Cape, 1991).

Jacobus, Mary, Reading Woman: *Essays in Feminist Criticism* (London: Methuen, 1986).

—, *First Things: The Maternal Imaginary in Literature, Art and Psychoanalysis* (New York and London: Routledge, 1995).

Jones, Ernest, *The Life and Work of Sigmund Freud* (New York: Basic Books, 1953), 3 vols.

Kofman, Sarah, *The Enigma of Woman: Woman in Freud's Writings* (Ithaca, NY: Cornell University Press, 1985).

Lacan, Jacques, *The Four Fundamental Concepts of Psychoanalysis*, trans. Alan Sheridan (Harmondsworth: Penguin, 1977).

—, *Ecrits: A Selection* (London: Tavistock, 1977).

Laplanche, Jean, *Life and Death in Psychoanalysis*, trans. J. Mehlman (Baltimore, MD: Johns Hopkins University Press, 1976).

—, *New Foundations for Psychoanalysis*, trans. David Macey (Oxford: Basil Blackwell, 1989).

Laplanche, Jean and Pontalis, J.-B, *The Language of Psycho-Analysis*, trans. Donald Nicholson-Smith (London: The Hogarth Press, 1983).

McGrath, William J., *Freud's Discovery of Psychoanalysis: The Politics of Hysteria* (Ithaca, NY: Cornell University Press, 1986).

Mahoney, Patrick J., *Freud as a Writer* (New Haven, CT.: Yale University Press, 1987).

Marcus, Stephen, *Freud and the Culture of Psychoanalysis* (New York: W. W. Norton, 1984).

Meisel, Perry (ed.), *Freud: A Collection of Critical Essays* (Englewood Cliffs, NJ: Prentice Hall, 1981).

Mitchell, Juliet, *Psychoanalysis and Feminism* (London: Allen Lane, 1974).

Neu, Jerome (ed.), *The Cambridge Companion to Freud* (Cambridge: Cambridge University Press, 1991).

Ricoeur, Paul, *Freud and Philosophy* (London: Yale University Press, 1970).

Le Rider, Jacques, *Modernity and Crises of Identity*, trans. Rosemary Morris (New York: Continuum, 1993).

Rieff, Phillip, *Freud: The Mind of the Moralist*, 3rd edn (Chicago, IL: University of Chicago Press, 1979).

Roazen, Paul, *Freud: Political and Social Thought* (London: The Hogarth Press, 1969).

—, *Freud and his Followers* (London: Allen Lane, 1976).

Robert, Marthe, *The Psychoanalytic Revolution: Sigmund Freud's Life and Achievement*, trans. Kenneth Morgan (London: George Allen and Unwin, 1966).

Sprengnether, Madelon, *The Spectral Mother: Freud, Feminism and Psychoanalysis* (Ithaca, NY: Cornell University Press, 1990).

Sulloway, Frank J., *Freud, Biologist of the Mind: Beyond the Psychoanalytic Legend* (London: Fontana, 1980).

Timpanaro, Sebastiano, *The Freudian Slip*, trans. Kate Soper (London: New Left Books, 1976).

Whyte, L., *The Unconscious Before Freud* (London: Julian Friedmann, 1978).

Wollheim, Richard (ed.), *Freud: A Collection of Critical Essays* (New York: Doubleday Anchor, 1974).

—, *Freud*, 2nd edn (London: Fontana, 1991).

Yerushalmi, Yosef Hayim, *Freud's Moses: Judaism Terminable and Interminable* (New Haven, CT: Yale University Press, 1991).

Index

Note: 'n.' after a page reference indicates the number of a note on that page.

Abraham, Karl, 63n.68, 110
absurdity in dreams, 77
actions, 136–9, 142–3, 155–6
Adler, Alfred, 61n.39
ambition dreams, 91, 112–13
    day-dreams, 171, 173, 176, 180, 181
anti-Semitism, 53–4, 220
anxiety dreams, 57n.7, 78
Anzieu, Didier, 40–1, 42, 85, 188–9,
    191
    Irma dream, 48–9, 186–7, 190, 194,
    195, 196
Artaud, Antonin, 34
Austin, J. L., 31
authorship of *The Interpretation of
    Dreams*, 208–10
Autobiographical Study, An, 44, 102,
    109
autobiographics in *The Interpretation of
    Dreams*, 18, 43–56, 84–5, 102–3

Baudelaire, Charles, 33
Baudry, Jean-Louis, 35–6
Bauer, Ida, *see* Dora
Beckford, William, 214
belief-like representations, 142, 145
Benjamin, Walter, 32
Bernays, Martha, 3
Beyond the Pleasure Principle, 7, 32,
    57n.7
bird-beaked figures dream, 188–9, 224
bisexuality, 58n.21, 190, 201, 203
Bonaparte, Marie, 185
Borch-Jacobsen, Mikkel, 42–3
Brantlinger, Patrick, 226
Breton, André, 91
Breuer, Josef, 4, 10, 33, 90
Brontë, Emily, 216
Burckhard, Max, 106–7
burning child dream, 8–9, 20, 222–3

'Case of female homosexuality, A',
    178
causal coherence, 129–30
causalist approaches to interpretation,
    130–1
censorship
    of dreams, 22, 67, 95
    of *The Interpretation of Dreams*, 98;
    see also Fliess, censorship
character, 8
Charcot, Jean Martin, 175, 176, 210
children, 10, 78–80
Chomsky, Noam, 76–7, 123
cinema and dreams, relationship
    between, 34–7
'Claims of psychoanalysis to scientific
    interest, The', 30
class relations, 219–20
competence, 76–7
composite photography, 54–5, 60n.32
condensation, 17, 28, 71, 75, 152
counter-transference, 192–3
counter-wish dreams, 99–100,
    106
Count Thun dream, 188
creating writing, 29, 174–82
'Creative writers and day-dreaming',
    29, 171–2, 211

Daudet, Alphonse, 162, 174–5, 176,
    178, 179–81
day-dreams, 141, 161, 164–74
    in fiction, 29, 174–82
day's residues, 3, 161–4
death, 52, 223–4
    of Freud's father, 10–11, 50, 52, 187–
    8
    of Freud's mother, 224
Delage, Yves, 13, 14–15
De Quincey, Thomas, 213, 223

Derrida, Jacques, 39, 43, 84
Descartes, René, 17, 18, 125
desire, working of, 131–2, 140–3, 145, 148
Dilthey, Wilhelm, 29
displacement in dreams, 23, 28, 73–4, 75, 152
disruption and the dream, 202–5
dissimulation, 91, 98
distortion in dreams, 22–3
Dora, 4–5, 184, 185–6, 192–3, 203, 204
Doyle, Sir Arthur Conan, 215
dream day, 3
dream screens, 37–40
dream-thoughts, 79–80
dream-work, 27, 77
Dreckology, 87–8
dynamic energy, 13

Eckstein, Emma, 49, 58n.21
ego, 40–1, 197, 198, 199, 200, 201
'ego and the id, The', 40
Empson, Jacob, 159n.9
Empson, William, 27
Erikson, Erik, 32, 109–10
Erlenmeyer, Albrecht, 210
exhibitionism, 91

fallen women, rescue of, 177, 178
'false memory syndrome', 59n.22
Farrow, Pickworth, 115–16
Felman, Shoshana, 43, 50
femininity, 50–1, 183–4, 189, 190–1, 202, 204–5
    Dora dream, 185–6, 192, 193, 203
    Irma dream, 187, 201
Ferenczi, Sándor, 108–9
fiction, 29, 174–82
figuration, 77
films and dreams, relationship between, 34–7
first-person authority, 124–5, 135–6, 138–9, 155–6
Flanders, Sara, 42
Fliess, Wilhelm, 185
    analysis of Freud's dreams, 86, 87–8

censorship of The Interpretation of Dreams, 47–8, 88–9, 90, 95, 96, 101
correspondence with Freud, 10–12, 44, 45, 49–50, 86, 87–8
illness, 111
Irma dream, 196
resolution of friendship with Freud, 187
followers of Freud, 107–12
Foucault, Michel, 122n.62, 210
Foulkes, David, 79
'Fragment of an analysis of a case of hysteria', 5
    see also Dora
free associations, 21, 69, 81–2, 140
    Irma dream, 144, 145, 146–7, 150–1, 152
Freud, Anna, 50, 185
Freud, Martha, 118n.6
functional phenomena, 108

Galton, Francis, 17, 54–5
gender issues
    Gothic elements, 218–19
    Irma dream, 193, 195, 200–1
    origins of psychoanalysis, 183–5
    see also femininity; masculinity
Genette, Gérard, 76
Gilbert, Sandra M., 226
Gilman, Sander, 53–5
Gomperz, Heinrich, 102
Gothic elements of The Interpretation of Dreams, 20, 206–7, 211–14
    Freud's imperial romance, 225–30
    shock horror, 220–5
    techniques, 214–20
Grinstein, Alexander, 85
Grosz, Elizabeth, 40
Gubar, Susan, 226

Haggard, Henry Rider, 207, 226–30
hallucinatory dreams, 8–9
hallucinatory wish-fulfilment, 7
Hammerschlag-Lichtheim, Anna, 49
    see also Irma
hermeneutic approaches to interpretation, 130–1
hermeneutic connections, 129

Hertz, N., 192–3, 203
Hervey de Saint-Denis, Marie-Jean-
   Léon, 13
Hildebrandt, F. W., 14, 16, 17
histories in *The Interpretation of
   Dreams*, 1–20
Hoffmann, Ernst Theodor Amadeus,
   212
Hofmannsthal, Hugo von, 53
horror, 221–5
Hug-Hellmuth, Hermine, 209
hypnosis, 4
hysteria, 183, 191
'Hysterical phantasies and their
   relation to bisexuality', 166, 167,
   177

Ibsen, Henrik, 219
identity and identification, 28, 43, 46,
   52–6
importance of *The Interpretation of
   Dreams*, 2
inability to dream 'properly', 78
indiscretions, 91, 93
infantile mentation, 6, 8–9
inscriptions, 30–3
insomnia, 78
intellectual ramifications of *The
   Interpretation of Dreams*, 1–2
international psychoanalytic
   movement, 83–4
Introductory Lectures on Psychoanalysis,
   4, 21, 24
   day-dreams, 165, 166, 168, 172, 173
Irma, 5, 48–50, 143–54, 186–7, 193–
   202
   Gothic elements, 214, 216–17
   premonitory element, 189–90

Jakobson, Roman, 75
James, Henry, 206
Jewish identity, 53–5
*Jokes and their Relation to the
   Unconscious*, 213, 217
Jones, Ernest, 44–5, 104, 107, 108, 109,
   115, 185
   on Freud's self-analysis, 85, 184
Jung, Carl Gustav, 24, 45, 110–12

Khan, Masud, 78
Klein, Melanie, 80
Kohut, Heinz, 110

Lacan, Jacques, 28, 30, 31, 75, 80, 88,
   122n.56, 191, 192
   Irma dream, 186, 193–4, 196–200,
      201
   spoof, 208
language
   of dreams, 26–9, 30–1
   theories, 9
   understanding of, 124–39, 154–6
Laplanche, Jean, 30–1
Lassalle, Ferdinand, 60n.35
latent dream, 3, 21, 22, 23, 97–8
le Rider, Jacques, 53
Lewin, Bertram, 37–40, 42
linguistic coherence, 129–30
linguistic competence, 76–7
Looney, J. Thomas, 209
'lost dream', 47–8, 101
love, 171, 173, 180, 181

manifest dream, 3, 21, 22, 23, 97
Marcus, Steven, 192, 212
Marin, Louis, 64–5n.111
masculinity, 183–4, 189, 201, 202, 203–
   5
Masson, André, 118n.6
maternal body, 50–1
Maury, Alfred, 13, 220
McClintock, Anne, 226
memory, 10
memory-traces, 6, 8
men, rescue of, 177–8
mental apparatus model, 6–8, 32–3,
   35–6
metaphors, 70, 75
'metapsychology of dreams, The', 40
metonymy, 73–4, 75
Metz, Christian, 35
modernity, 31–2
Montaigne, Michel Eyquem de, 52,
   64–5n.111
Moses of Michelangelo, The, 208
motivational causal connections, 129,
   130

Musil, Robert, 53
'My son the Myops' dream, 191

narrative stucture of dreams, 75–6
narrative theory, 66–7
Neumann, Eric, 63n.68
neurones, 6–7
neuroses, 4, 10, 11, 81
New Introductory Lectures on Psychoanalysis, 9, 57n.7
Neyraut, Michel, 44
Nietzsche, Friedrich, 59n.31
nightmares, 78
non vixit dream, 112–13
'note upon the mystic writing-pad, A', 7, 32–3, 35, 213

occultism, 20
Oedipus complex, 6, 11–12, 154, 189
    Gothic elements, 217, 223
    negative, 190
On Dreams, 3–4, 94–5
On Morphia Addiction, 210
optative tense, 28–9
optical unconscious, 17, 33–43, 55–6

pacification of desire, 131–2, 141–3, 148
Pearson, Karl, 54
Penley, Constance, 35–6
performance, 76–7
phobias, 81
Pontalis, J.-B., 34, 42
positivism, 12–13
pre-linguistic infants, 79–80
present tense, 29
primary processes, 5, 7
primitive mentation, 9–10, 23
'Project for a scientific psychology', 5, 6–8, 10, 36
Propp, Vladimir, 76
pseudonym theory, 208–10
psychoanalysis
    origins, 183–6
    role of dreams in, 1–5
'Psychoanalysis and telepathy', 4
psychopathology, 4

Psychopathology of Everyday Life, The, 175, 179
psychosis, 78
publication of *The Interpretation of Dreams*, 1, 90
punishment dreams, 57n.7
Purkinje, Johannes, 41–2

Quetelet, Adolphe, 55

Rank, Otto, 108, 215–16
reactions to *The Interpretation of Dreams*, 90–1, 102, 104
    see also reviews of *The Interpretation of Dreams*
readers of *The Interpretation of Dreams*, 88, 92–106, 113–14
regression, 8–9, 36
representations in *The Interpretation of Dreams*, 20–43
repression, 80, 82
rescue fantasies, 177–8, 179–80
residues of the day, 3, 161–4
resistance to interpretation, 22
Resnick, S., 189–90
reviews of *The Interpretation of Dreams*, 56n.1, 106–7
'Revision of dream-theory', 9, 57n.7
Ricoeur, Paul, 98
Rie, Oscar, 90
Robert, W., 13
Robert, Marthe, 44
romanticism, 12
Rome dreams, 188
Rousseau, Jean-Jacques, 46

Sachs, Hanns, 102, 108
scepticism towards Freud's ideology, 96, 97, 98–9
Scherner, Karl Albert, 13, 49
Schnitzler, Arthur, 53, 210
Schorske, Carl, 52–3
Schwab-Paneth, Sophie, 91, 113
secondary revision, 5, 6, 7, 77, 167, 169
secrecy in *The Interpretation of Dreams*, 97–8, 216, 220–1
seduction theory, 59n.22

self-analysis, 10–12, 43–7, 85–7, 115–
    16, 184
  readers' perspectives, 91–2
  self-dissection dream, 51, 52
self-dissection dream, 51, 52, 55, 225–
    6, 227–30
self-knowledge, 124–5
Seltzer, Mark, 55
'seventeenth-century demonological
    neurosis, A', 215
Shakespeare, William, 208–9, 218
Sharpe, Ella Freeman, 27–8, 36–7
Shelley, Mary, 214, 216, 225
Silberer, Herbert, 24, 108
Simmel, Georg, 32
sleep, omnipresence in dreams of
    wish to, 6
somatic stimuli, 15
'special type of object-choice made by
    men, A', 177
speech, 128, 136–40, 154–6
Sprengnether, M., 203
statistical thinking, 103
Stekel, Wilhelm, 24, 25, 26, 107–8
Stevenson, Robert Louis, 206, 213
Stoker, Bram, 206, 215, 218–19
structural linguistics, 27–8
Strümpell, Adolf, 16
Sully, James, 13, 213
surrealism, 34
Swoboda, Hermann, 58n.21
symbolism, 9–10, 24–6, 28, 49, 67–8,
    107–8

tense in dreams, 28–9
Torgovnick, Maria, 227
training of psychoanalysts, 84, 116,
    184
transference, 190
transitional space, 42

'uncanny, The', 212
unconscious
    optical, 17, 33–43, 55–6
    royal road to the, 17–20, 81, 165

value of dreams, 15–16

Walpole, Horace, 218
Weininger, Otto, 58n.21
Welsh, Alexander, 94, 110, 121n.55
Winnicott, Donald, 42
wish-fulfilment, 2–3, 10, 11, 67
    challenges to theory, 106–7
    day-dreams, 166–7, 168, 169,
        173
    Gothic elements, 220–1
    hallucinatory, 7
    Irma dream, 49, 50, 143–9, 151–2,
        153–4, 195
    and readership, 96–100, 103
Wittgenstein, Ludwig, 80, 158n.6
'Wolf-man', 37, 39
women, rescue of fallen, See fallen
    women
word play, 74